JUST
DESSERTS

by the same author

REFLECTING MEN at twice their natural size
(with Dale Spender)

SALLY CLINE

JUST DESSERTS

Women and Food

ANDRE DEUTSCH

This book is dedicated to
BA SHEPPARD and WENDY MULFORD.

It is also for CHERYL LEAN who
imaginatively mixed the book's ingredients then waited; and for my daughter
MARMOSET ADLER, with whom I have
shared more meals than with anyone else.

First published 1990 by
André Deutsch Limited
105–106 Great Russell Street
London WC1B 3LJ

British Library Cataloguing in Publication Data

Cline, Sally
  Just desserts: women and food.
  1. Food – Sociological perspectives
  I. Title
  306'.3?

ISBN 0 233 98510 7

Printed and bound in Great Britain by
WBC, Bristol and Maesteg

Contents

Acknowledgements   vii

Introduction   1

One: A NICE JEWISH GIRL   11

Two: THE JAM SANDWICH SYNDROME   39

Three COMPULSORY CATERERS, DISCRETIONARY COOKS   67

Four: STOCKCUPBOARD SYMBOLS, SUPERMARKET
       SERVITUDE, AND SELF-ESTEEM   86

Five: PROPER MEALS, IMPROPER OCCASIONS   104

Six: TABLE MANNERS AND TYRANNY   132

Seven: DISTORT AND DISORDER   164

Eight: THE CALORIE-COUNTING CON   203

Nine: WHO SAYS FAT IS BAD?   216

Notes   243

Bibliography   250

Index   257

Acknowledgements

The major acknowledgement goes to the women who talked to me. Their names have been changed, but it is their voices and feelings which have made this book possible.

I owe a great debt both professional and personal to Sarah Patterson. She has read and revised drafts, offered criticism, companionship and care, with intellectual generosity, exceptional patience and unwavering support. Without her help, particularly through my illness, writing this book would have been harder.

Cheryl Lean's professional contribution to this book is memorable. Her inventive ideas, energy and sense of the ridiculous made working with her a joy. Her theoretical analysis of the book's material made Chapter 2 substantially stronger.

For lengthy interviews and valuable insights I thank Sheila Kitzinger, Prudence Jones, Troy Cooper, Joy Magezis, Dr Reuben Andres, Anne Murcott, Christine Donald, Toni Laidlaw, Fay Weldon, Susie Orbach, the Spare Tyre Theatre Company of Clare Chapman, Katina Noble, and Harriet Powell, Judy Chicago (whose magnificent exhibition and book *The Dinner Party* and whose views on women's power and creativity excited and enlarged my own), and most of all Dale Spender, who gave me days of her time and helped keep the author in good literary order. Dale and Candida Lacey helped me with the initial shaping and design of this project. Their special comforts in my convalescence and commitment to the book's spirit helped me through some bleak hours.

I want to thank the London CBC office especially Herrie Ten Cate and Anne Koch for her warmth and good radio guidance.

In Canada I am indebted to the CBC team: in Toronto to Bernie Lucht; in Halifax to Havoc Franklin for his patience, to Dan Lawson for those jolly times, and to Colin Henderson for his quiet empathy. I thank Heather Laskey for her first reading and aid with the script. For encouragement and hospitality I thank Betty Ann Lloyd, Shelley Finson, Barbara Cottrell, Victor Thiessen, Keith, Laurel and Heather Loudun, Barbara Harris, Carol Millett, Kate McKenna, Jean Hartley, Scarlet Pollock, Martha McGinn. I thank Graham Metson for many magnificent meals, Adele McSorley for a summer's solace, space, wit and wisdom; and Margaret Atwood for the gems inside *The Edible Woman*.

In Sennen Cove, Cornwall, I thank Jean Adams for the writing time and affection offered again at beautiful Sunset Heights, and Jean Beaumont for the justly famous desserts at the Singing Teapot.

Research for this book was excellently carried out by Margaret Owen (on catering and religious food symbolism), by Jane Shackman (on ethnic groups) and by Clare Sambrook, some stunning work on the relationship of food to literature and the attitudes of young women. Clare brightened and shook up many of my notions. I am sorry for reasons of space more could not be included.

I found useful pointers in the work of the BSA Sociology of Food Group, in the discussions of the Cambridge Women and Food Group, and in the unpublished thesis, 'A Call for Our Language: Anorexia from Within' by Takayo Mukai of West Virginia University.

The time-consuming typing and tape transcriptions were painstakingly done by Teresa Hall and Marion Garrett, and a great deal of last-minute extra typing performed by Polly Stokes to whom many thanks. Marion transformed many a rough jigsaw into a first-rate manuscript. I thank Karen Gregory and Mark Farnham at Cambridge Catering Company, Whittlesford, for hours of photocopying. Michele Thomas of Heffers Bookshop offered me resourceful book retrieval and her usual fund of fascinating information.

Tessa Sayle, my literary agent, gave me faith, warmth and scrupulously honest criticism, which meant a lot to me. Esther Whitby who took over the last stages of the book was enthusiastic and supportive throughout.

As for my editor and friend, Sheila McIlwraith (now departed and already missed), who has for several years put up with my alliteration and OTT adjectives, and dealt creatively with my words, I can only say that the book's best bits are due to her sharp eye, diplomatic ways, and unshakeable belief in our project.

This book was considerably delayed by a long illness. For medical help and all kinds of support I want to thank Addenbrooke's nurses Jo, Joanna, Julie, Louise, Lucy and Sally; staff nurses Kate Douglas, Maggie Peters, Mick Parsons; doctors Bernard Reiss, Sarah Stead, Joanna Taylor, Trevor Wheatly; most particularly ward clerk Chris Freeman for her daily humorous attention and innumerable kindnesses. Of my remarkable friends, family and colleagues, I thank Alison West, Bobbie Wells, Celia Kitzinger, Cheryl Lean, Davina Belling (for that magic transatlantic visit), Deb Thom, Diana Mutimer, Elaine Gallagher, Elaine Hobby, Elsie Sheppard, Jan Graves, Jen Kitzinger, Joy Magezis, Julia Ball, Kath Mullen, Kate Pretty, Lesley Annand, Leisa Frost, Lowana Veal (for indexing aid and heavy coal duty), Marge Brash (for making taperecording possible), Martha Hatch, Mavis Driver, Meg Ashworth Jones, Miranda Williamson, Michelle Stanworth, Nicky Mayhew, Pippa Brewster, Rebecca Stewart, Teresa Hall, Viv and Joe Eastwood, Ant Vivis, Dave Richards, my bank manager Eric Dodgson, Martin Graves (for enormous imaginative practical help), and Jim Frost (now sadly deceased who was always available for good deeds even when most seriously ill himself).

I am especially grateful to Sue Benson who took work off my shoulders and was an unfailing resource; to Jane Shackman for cousinly assistance and sisterly support; to Carol Jones and Mary

Wynne who encouraged my first bike ride and listened to innumerable drafts; and to Aunt Het (Harriet) Shackman for her constant concern and sturdy example of how to deal with difficult times. It is my deep regret that my uncle, David Shackman, who gave me years of intellectual support, died before he could comment on this work. I should like to remember him here.

Stella King showed me how to put the structure back into my life. Vic Smith and Kath Bowles helped me to implement it. Vic's sparkling presence for sociology and snacks made Wednesdays a delight; Kath's arrival with history satchel and support made Thursdays a treat.

Several people and organisations especially enabled me to come through a black time and finish this book. I am deeply indebted to the Society of Authors and the Trustees of the Francis Head Bequest for their timely help and financial aid during my period of disablement. Marmoset Adler, my daughter, devotedly took time off acting to be with me in the hospital, and what a difference that made. Her information and skilful ideas for the Jewish and Tyrannical chapters have been appreciatively incorporated. Thank you, Marm. I relied on my friend Anne 'Sister' Christie and my homeopathist Joel Jaffey for their traditional and alternative medical insights to keep up my spirits and keep down the pain. Rosemary Frost (a good neighbour like no other), Ba Sheppard, Wendy Mulford, and Sarah Patterson between them dealt with my domestic, artistic and financial burdens until I recovered, and took a load off my mind.

Ba Sheppard's strength and vision preceded the hours of work she put in on the final draft, and accompanied the years of work she put in as part of the process.

Wendy Mulford who shares the snackerels and the struggle has suffered all of this book with me. Her concern and understanding have sustained me. Love and gratitude.

April 1989

Introduction

Jam doughnuts are forbidden. Grown women steal into bakeries and come out hiding jammy spoils in leaking brown bags.

Our children exhaust us; our lovers forsake us; our jobs bore us; women reach into the fridge for consolation.

We love food. We fear fatness. We serve others. We deny ourselves. We do an efficient job in the workplace but measure our worth by a number on the bathroom scales.

Women who are angry, because they are powerless to change their situations, or powerless to demonstrate their feelings, quell unexpressed rage or resentment with food.

I know. I have done it. I have smoothed down resentment with a jar of peanut butter. I have comforted myself with jam sandwiches.

Women control food because they cannot control their lives.

In our culture women have a complex emotional and symbolic relationship to food. Men do not.

Women have access to food in a way that they do not have access to power.

That these two facts, borne out by numerous research findings, are strongly interrelated, is the substance of this book.

In today's society where Western women's expectations and potential rights and opportunities appear to have increased, but where our hold on any real power has not, food and eating have increasingly become terrain for a struggle between the sexes. Eating and not eating can be seen as an expression of women's contradictory sexual roles. In an era when women's fierce and optimistic spirit is increasingly challenged, when our political

1

and social demands to take up more space are met by a new cultural constraint to eat less, to become increasingly thinner, many women express the conflicts they feel through their behaviour over food and eating.

Food has always been an area of intense pleasure for both sexes. Recently it has also become a battleground. The kitchen, women's traditional domain, the stage of our greatest performances or our worst disasters, has become a realm in which many women stand confused.

For men the picture seems simpler. Food for men is fuel. They eat when they are hungry. When women are hungry we often deny ourselves nourishment, while offering it to others. When women wish to express love, we turn to food. For us food is a great deal more than mere nutrients. It has become a repository of a million meanings.

There is no area of a woman's life quite like her relationship to food. It is an area fraught with fascination and contradiction, with longing and disgust, with resolution and strange capriciousness. For most women, food is a major preoccupation. An obsessive engagement. Complete strangers who would not dream of discussing anything but the most superficial topics together, will willingly begin an intimate conversation on food and body image.

For many women interviewed in this book serving food to others is an expression of their affection, a statement about their vulnerability. Reject-the-meal-I-serve-you, reject-the-woman-I-am, is a notion ingrained in many of these women's unacknowledged responses. For the same women, eating food themselves has become a symbol of self-loathing; an aversion centred on the food they eat, and the shape and size they are, irrespective of what nourishment and goodness the food contains or what that shape and size actually is.

For most of us in the West, food has warm and positive meanings, yet it is curiously also something one group fears.

The problems and delights which women face over eating, and more significantly over body image (to which it is so closely

2

allied); the discrepancies we encounter between what we are supposed to look like and to feel, and what we actually are and what we *do* experience, are not a product of individual deficiency or neurosis, but are a structural part of the society into which we have been socialized. We express our troubled social identity through a tortured, often inexplicable, relationship to food.

Women have been creating dinner parties for centuries. We have been breastfeeding babies and providing family meals for epochs. This study views those meals and their sometimes humorous, sometimes tragic consequences from the viewpoint of those who do the cooking. And the shopping. And the preparing. The major consumers of a vast and lucrative food industry. It is a bitter paradox that while in the Third World food is so short that people starve, here in the West food is available in such abundance and variety that eating is hard-sell big business, with women the prime targets for babyfoods, children's meals, slimming products, convenience and fast foods, and everyday household and gastronomic purchases.

That there is a sexual dynamic within our society, that there is a power relationship between the sexes is undeniable. These electric elements have today found an extraordinary manifestation in and through food. It is the contention of this book that women use food differently from men because we do not have power. By looking at food we can get at the kernel of the political relationship between the sexes. For food is a crucial political area. Women's subordination is locked into food; an issue even feminists have not yet sufficiently investigated.

There have been some very interesting discussions about certain problematic areas such as food disorders. Specific topics like bulimia and anorexia (which, though an integral part of this investigation, are by no means the major part) have been the object of powerful sociological and psychological studies.[1] Female food disorders have sadly become a growth industry and the subject of heated debate in popular magazines as well as in academic journals. What is less often emphasized is that all women, not merely an extreme few, match their passion and

3

devotion to food with an addictive and emotional irrationality. All women have a peculiar investment either in not eating too much, or in compulsive binges followed by heart-rending bouts of regret and guilt. All women, not merely an 'overweight' number (and the standard or normative weight for women is a contested feature of this research) see fatness as a stigma. All women are socially controlled by the new male mythology that fat-is-bad, which has led to what can only be described as fat oppression, by women as well as by men. So far even feminists, interested in uncovering the current male stereotypes of femininity, have not gone far enough in challenging it. An important section of this book therefore asks such uncomfortable questions as who says fat is bad? How are women discriminated against for being overweight? And do we ourselves partake in this harassment of fat women?

For some women comfort arises from breastfeeding. For others security stems from a full larder or is engendered by a wok purchase. The connections between these diverse food areas have been largely overlooked. The compelling relationship between all women's food patterns and patriarchal practices in this culture recurred again and again in collecting the data for this book.

This study seeks to remedy the absence of significant critical debate about the seemingly mundane, apparently less ambiguous topics such as food preparation and consumption; the hidden messages in recipes and cookbooks: images of food in art, literature and popular culture; slimming propaganda highlighted by the health and advertising industries, and above all the joys and anxieties of women who endlessly cook for others but strictly deny themselves. These are spheres which have received less systematic and less serious attention.

Anorexia has been usefully explored, by Susie Orbach and others,[2] as a metaphor for women's condition, but I believe that women's total relationship to food can be viewed as a striking cultural comment. Women's behaviour patterns differ from men's in quite routine matters of food management.

Just as the key features of anorexia are starvation amidst plenty and denial set against desire,[3] and the striving for less space (some would say invisibility) versus the wish to be noticed; so are these common features of all women's eating and consumptive patterns in a society where men control women and where women's control of the central issues in their own lives is minimal.

Food has become a symbol of women's emotional needs, a rhetoric of protest as well as a language of joy and anguish. In order to understand what contemporary Western women are trying to say, we need to look at what these women eat or do not eat, at how we deal with cooking and shopping, at what women learn in childhood and from family meals about their adult place in society.

The overwhelming power of food in women's lives, the role of women as feeders of others, has allowed us to be the quarry of a thriving propaganda machine (run by the health services, the advertising and slimming industries, and the media) which all help to monitor women's food intake and to ensure that women will police each other over food and fatness. Body image has become the crux of this policing process by women and men alike. This is not surprising as we live in a society where we are judged as bodies, where women's bodies sell fast cars, micro-computers and idealized heterosexual sex. So we judge other women by bodies, and each of us is dissatisfied with her own. Among the 150 women I interviewed, only two were content with their own bodies and only a few looked favourably on those of other women. I did not find any woman for whom fatness was not or had not at some time been an issue. It seems women monitor each other and feminists are not immune.

Men control our bodies and our lives with the power of stigma and approval, and we in turn try to control our bodies with our food intake. Food and its denial has become part of this society's masculist and heterosexual imperative. We are socialized to win men's love and approval with our meals and our shape, to reflect male values with what we serve and how we service, and to retain this affection and respect by eating less and behaving differently ourselves.

5

When I began research on this book I recognized that there is a critical association between women's problematic relationship to eating and our struggle for identity. I accepted that women's oppression is bound up in and intimately connected to food, but I planned to carry out my investigation through largely impartial, objective strategies. The theory separated from the self.

I had decided to use three methods. The first method was to interview and tape the experiences and attitudes of women whose contribution to food was practical, women who bought food, prepared it, cooked it, made decisions about it, obsessively thought about it, or frighteningly deprived themselves of it.

I talked to women who saw themselves as full-time home-makers, and women who had a second role as a full- or part-time paid worker or student. We discussed the way *they* perceived their domestic role and the way in which they felt *men* perceived it, and the extent to which these perceptions coloured and moderated their practices in the kitchen.

Some women lived in households which contained at least one adult male, usually their father, brother, husband or lover. Some lived on their own, or with other women, or with children but no men. For some this was accidental, due to widowhood, divorce or desertion. For others it was a positive policy of single parenthood, feminism, lesbianism, or commual child care. All of the women, however, had experienced a domestic structure centred on food in which men took part. Although I interviewed several black women, and have drawn on the work of black women writers, this study starts from the experience of a white woman writer and largely speaks to and reflects the experiences of other white women in this culture.

The second method was to interview and tape a series of women theorists and practitioners who have, in specific ways, made a serious sociological, psychological, literary or gastron-omic contribution to our understanding of food, fatness, female body image and eating disorders.

The third method was to spend several months in Great Britain and Canada with my Canadian Broadcasting Corporation radio partner, Cheryl Lean, analysing, interviewing, editing and scripting material on women's complex relationship to food in order to produce two full-length, hour-long radio documentaries on the subject matter of *Just Desserts*.[4]

I hoped this would be sufficient. For once I felt it would be comfortable to leave myself out. Let other women tell their stories. Let other women's experiences become the data for the theory. The last non-fiction book I wrote, *Reflecting Men*,[5] was so crammed with what some reviewers called overtly candid confessions that, frankly, I had little desire to repeat the experience or reap similar reviews!

I changed my mind one disenchanted evening in Halifax, Nova Scotia. Cheryl Lean and I had spent six weeks daily challenged and thwarted by the competing demands of working as feminists inside a nationally networked male medium. That night we had worked for nine hours flat out on the documentary. Cheryl, a skilled editor and film-maker, could not solve the technical problems. I had a block with the script. Both of us were absolutely frustrated that we did not have the ultimate control of the programme. Only a selection of what we, as women, considered important about the relationship between women and food would actually receive airtime. The final selection would not be in our hands.

This is Cheryl's description of how we attempted to solve our professional problems:

'I was desperately disheartened so I made three batches of popcorn. Then we ate them, but it did not solve anything. You got more and more angry and decided that all we could do was to go out and stuff ourselves with food. We had avocado pear with prawns and a delicious side order of potato skins followed by cheese and spinach crêpes with an exotic savoury sauce of sour cream, mushrooms and brandy. We followed this with chocolate profiteroles and several large gin-and-tonics, then we returned to work. We had still not solved anything and we must have put on several pounds each.'

It was not an atypical evening for us. It was not an uncharac-

7

teristic answer to problems beyond our control. Irrational bingeing was not the behaviour pattern of our tolerant and tolerable male producer, nor of the other men we chose to work with. It *is* a pattern with which many women will identify.

I realized then that it was becoming less and less possible to keep myself out of the social picture. Food has not merely shaped and disordered many areas of my life. I have expressed or suppressed many significant emotions through the medium of food. What is personal for me has political undertones. Sour cream and mushrooms are context-bound. The need for cheese and spinach crêpes is culture-specific. And repressed desires for chocolate profiteroles are part of a rigidly imposed cultural restraint.

That was the evening I first recognized the need to come to terms with what food has meant in my life, and how both consciously and unconsciously I, like most women, have been coerced over food. Later that night I made my first confession about food to my radio partner.

The previous day, at lunchtime, Cheryl had asked me to go to the local sandwich shop and bring her a big coke and a large, three-layer sandwich. I had returned with a diet pop and a very small, filled roll. I told her that the shop had run out of anything else.

I lied.

That evening I told Cheryl (and admitted to myself) the truth.

'This is what really happened,' I said. 'I walked into the sandwich bar and, in front of me in the queue, was a really big woman, fat as well as tall, dressed in outrageous bright scarlet. No attempt to hide her size! She ordered a huge jumbo chicken salad sandwich. The little woman behind the counter raised her eyes in slight surprise but said politely: "You can pick your dressing. Either lettuce or tomato or cukes or dill or onions or sprouts?" The big woman in scarlet nodded appreciatively to everything. "Yes," she said, "yes, yes."

'The slim woman behind the counter apparently did not hear her. "Lettuce perhaps?" she said helpfully, allowing her eyes to stray momentarily over the customer's figure.

8

'But the big woman was still saying yes to lettuce, yes to cukes, yes to tomatoes, yes to dills; in fact, yes to everything. She had them all.

'The assistant wrapped the bulging, exciting-looking sandwich and then said pleasantly: "You'll want a diet Coke?"

'"No!" said the fat woman in scarlet. "No, not a diet Coke!"

'"Diet juice?" said the woman behind the counter. The big woman smiled. "No, thank you. I don't want a diet juice." The slim assistant looked a trifle weary. The sandwich bar was filling up. "Diet pop, then?" she said, controlling her emotions.

'"No, thank you. I don't want diet pop," the customer said patiently.

'The woman behind the counter became exasperated. "YOU DON'T WANT DIET POP? WE DON'T HAVE ANY OTHER DIET DRINKS!"

'The fat woman pulled up her scarlet sleeve, rested a podgy pink hand on the counter, and said assertively: "I don't want a diet drink. I DON'T DIET. I want a coke."

'Everybody in the queue turned and stared at the big woman. Behind me a harassed mother said to her little girl: "Can you believe it, the fat lady didn't want a diet drink!"

'I was next to be served. The shop was full. I didn't have the nerve to order what you wanted, Cheryl, so instead of a jumbo sandwich and a suger-saturated Coke, I'm afraid I settled for a very small roll and a diet pop.'

That incident, of which I am suitably ashamed, demonstrates the extent to which all women are coerced over food, and shows just how complex our relationship is to something we pretend to ourselves is simple.

During the course of interviewing women it became even clearer to me that my experiences and theirs have many significant meeting points. It became impossible for me to leave myself out, and it is with my participation in the process that I shall begin.

ONE
A NICE JEWISH GIRL

The process began early, as it does for all Jewish girls. Nice ones, anyway. Niceness didn't come easily to me and its accomplishment was intricately laced into food. If you were a Nice Jewish Girl growing up in the forties and fifties, there were two things you learnt. The first was: Nice Jewish Girls Don't Do It. The second was: Nice Jewish Girls eat a good deal instead. They act as sous chefs in the kitchen while their mothers cook; abundantly in times of joy, excessively in times of stress. They learn to boil practically everything, and to serve the men of the house first.

Doing It, of course, was s-e-x. I still think of it as a scandalous word with breathtaking hyphens between the letters, whereas I think of food as a joyous noun with its letters rolled scrumptiously, temptingly into one delectable description. Nice Jewish girls grew up knowing that one difficult day they would *have* to do it, but only with a nice Jewish boy (preferably a doctor or an accountant), and only when they had done the decent thing and got married, in white, to the accompaniment of a huge hot and cold buffet served while the dozens of aunties and uncles danced the hora.

There was simply no question of marrying 'out'. Boys who were goys[1] could not be trusted. Their gentile mothers did not keep meat and milk in separate compartments, they fried *bacon*, and encouraged their sons to court danger with prawn cocktails. They even went into hamburger bars! It was, of course, out of the question to do it either before the day of the pure white dress or with a girl. I, who hankered after doing it with everyone of

11

every possible religious and sexual variety, and who was determined to get wed in scarlet, found being nice in the Jewish sense a very hard training. To my excitement-seeking mind the culinary atrocities of non-Jewish boys with their wicked inheritance from their gentile mothers were a constant seduction. While I helped my own mother make squidgy cheese blintzes,[2] and overtly eschewed boys who ate bacon, I secretly dreamt of the day I would sneak into a goyisha kitchen and watch the sausages sizzle!

My father came from a large East End working-class family with about twelve children, in which the men were educated and the women prepared meals. Uncle Martin, the eldest, had broken the sacred taboo and had married OUT . . . This dreadful deed had been apparently highly successfully consummated with my attractive, intelligent Auntie Olive, who was racy, amusing, had a job as a bookmaker and certainly seemed a cut above making chicken and kneidlech[3] soup! The women in our family were horrified, despised and envied her, and secretly speculated about what went on in her kitchen. If I had not been so scared I could have told them, because I went to Yorkshire to stay with them every summer, and it was in Auntie Olive's kitchen that I first tasted egg and bacon! If that wasn't bad enough, the woman had dared to use lard! Although that first night I was terrified of burning in Hell for partaking of alien rubbish, when I found myself alive and well the next day, I knew I was set fair for a life of sin.

However, as the virtues of faithfulness in bed and ritual cleanliness in the kitchen were, for me, culturally entwined, for years my gastronomic indoctrination never allowed me to do more than indulge in sin on the side. I was as rigorously hemmed in by the heterosexual and cultural imperative to wed a good Jewish man as I was by the religious injunction to cook in the correct Jewish manner. I could no more have married out than I could have eaten milk and meat together, or refrained from marrying at all.

Occasionally I would wonder what fate might befall a nice

Jewish girl who disobeyed orders. Dark matters were hinted at. I took no notice. Later on when I went to see *Fiddler on the Roof* I saw the extreme punishment made explicit. Chava, the fiddler's daughter, rebelliously insists on marrying a gentile. Her father, Tevya, wretched but resolute, sits shivah and mourns her as if she has died. Her brokenhearted mother and sisters have no choice but to follow suit.

In those days I was too respectable, too conformist, and frankly too scared to face such a fate. So I married. Not once, but twice. Hardly surprisingly, my first husband, Neville, and my second, Larry, were both Jewish and (though lapsed) had been brought up to obey the dietary laws.

However, before, after, and even during, my marriages, I had a series of secret romances with big blond boyfriends, who indulged in pork chops and ate greasy chips from newspaper. The most memorable of these was burly Brodie, the foreign reporter, who for three years met me at airport restaurants all over the world and offered me prawn cocktails along with his attention.

Of considerable significance in the later years is the fact that my important partnerships with women have all been non-Jewish, and food has played an integral part in them. My recollections of Margrit, in the late sixties and seventies are of a fierce-spirited fair-haired young woman who fried bacon in a casual, somewhat cynical, manner as if the action had no import. That it was scandalous in the sixties for a well-brought-up Jewish girl to enjoy a caring relationship with another woman seemed less critical than the matter of the fat the woman fried their food in.

It took a decade from the seventies through the eighties of the lasting relationship with my friend Ba for me to come to terms, relatively calmly, with the enormity of non-Jewish cooking. I was an amazed spectator as she brazenly served up superbly cooked utterly gentile meals to me, my daughter Marmoset, and her three girls Bec, Cas and Vic. If Margrit's approach to alien pork had been disarmingly detached, Ba's unique contribution

13

was her compelling mixture of high seriousness and lighthearted efficiency. She *knew* that food mattered. She also seemed to know, although at the time we never discussed it, that watching taboo food being cooked is a voyeuristic experience which combines provocation with gravity.

Memories of those years that mingle laughter with pain, return again and again to those deeply satisfying scenes of kitchen life. Ba's competent, unblushing approach to roast pork on Sundays vied outrageously with her winter beef casseroles topped with dumplings of impermissible suet. As for breakfasts, the sizzling-sausage fantasy of a Jewish childhood became a routine reality of a non-conformist 'Sabbath' morning. During weekdays, Ba, an organized ex-schoolteacher, insisted on laying the breakfast table the night before with an array of turquoise and orange melamine bowls and plates, ready to be piled high with toast and Marmite and several different jumbo cereals. In a busy, noisy household of six, this certainly saved time, and lessened the pre-school strain. But on Sundays rules were relaxed and, late and lazily, we all gathered for the big fry-up, the one meal of the week in which squabbles were replaced by content. Indeed the forbidden pleasures of this traditional Christian feast are among my most provocative memories of the last domestic decade. Ba, in faded jeans and a dark blue denim shirt, whirled around the kitchen, waving the huge frying pan, expertly cracking eggs, cutting tomatoes, peeling mushrooms, slicing rind off the bacon, tossing sausages into the pan, sculpting and mixing ingredients like quicksilver; whilst Miffy, the most intelligent of our three cats, waited attentively for her share of the rind. 'Come on everyone, sit down kids. Let's get this show on the road! Who wants baked beans? How many for mushrooms? Now fried eggs for everyone. Vic, what about you?' Vic, the youngest, the one we all spoilt, of course wanted mixed-up egg. A different pan, another complex operation. Her mother, sunny and skilful, remained unhassled, laughing away her craft. 'I've watched the canteen ladies at school, haven't I?' The rest of us accepted what we were offered. Marm and Bec wanted it all. Even Cas, the most finicky about

14

food, had no fads on Sunday mornings. 'Now Sal, what about you? More bacon?' More, more, I muttered, wondering if I'd blushed, gulping back the instantaneous image of Father's displeasure.

That this primordial sense of sin associated with sausages at breakfast has still not left me was shown recently in my literary partnership with my writer friend Wendy. On a writing retreat this year in Cornwall, I awoke one morning to that same glorious embargoed smell. 'I'm in a hurry today, got to get a train, trying to rustle up hot sausage sandwiches,' Wendy said. I leapt out of bed, rushed to the frying pan. 'Let me do it,' I said eagerly. I prodded the sizzling creatures and forked them onto the bread. It is hard to credit the extraordinary excitement which filled me as I whispered to myself, 'Oh I hope they are pork!'

I found an appealing Christian breakfast among Maya Angelou's memories in her autobiographical book. *I Know Why the Caged Bird Sings.*[4]

> On Sunday mornings Momma served a breakfast that was geared to hold us quiet from 9.30 am to 3.00 pm. She fried thick pink slices of home-cured ham and poured the grease over sliced red tomatoes. Eggs over easy, fried potatoes and onions, yellow hominy and crisp perch, fried so hard we would pop them in our mouths and chew bones, fins and all.

Sunday breakfasts, though of a very different species, were important throughout my childhood. It was the one meal my father occasionally cooked. He would make matzoh brei, a mixture of scrambled eggs, fried with small strips of unleavened bread or matzoh. He sang in his strong bass voice as he muddled his way around the kitchen; the end product was delicious, the kitchen in total disorder. It was not only the one repast I recall him making, it was also the only time he was allowed or chose to enter the kitchen. That was Mother's domain. She had a grip on it, as she had a grip on us.

My mother's family was smaller than my father's, and it was

middle-class and anglicised. Her eldest brother, my Uncle Henry, was a judge, her second brother, Uncle Philip, had a top admin. job with an airline (but kept it kosher by working for El Al), little Uncle Dennis (the baby) was an electrician, and my favourite Aunt Het (whose exotic Boxing Day banquets added a festive Christian counterpoint to the rest of our overflowing Jewish blowouts), worked in the House of Commons. Only my mother had not received higher education. On her mother's death, being the eldest and a girl, she had been forced to look after the family and for years energetically produced a piquant production line of family meals. After her marriage, she worked in my father's accountancy office, did his book-keeping and secretarial work and was, and is, a highly efficient, organized woman. In another time and another place she might have been a business executive in her own right. But her life and her keen mental abilities were restricted. She produced meals alongside memos, filed napkins instead of cards, memorized recipes as well as poems (she was an inveterate reader), and though keen for me to have a good education and a professional career, to make of myself what she had not, she instilled in me the fundamental virtues of being a neat housewife and a fine cook. Oddly, I do not ever recall her allowing me to cook independently. The kitchen was her place, not mine. At eighteen I had never been much more than mother's helper, and could hardly boil an egg unsupervised, yet I knew I had to succeed at cooking as at everything else. I was expected to do it all, and to do it all *well*. At some cost to my health, I have always pushed myself to do just that.

I grew up to believe, as many women I have interviewed still believe, that my place in society was intricately tied into food. Whether or not women work full- or part-time, whether or not they have children, the issue is that women should be in the kitchen, and if men are there, that is a bonus. Although there were no children during my first marriage, because, like my husband, I worked full-time as a journalist, I spent a great many unnecessary hours cooking and preparing more elaborate meals than my schedule realistically allowed. Nor did I demand the same work from him. I had to prove to myself as well as to him that I could do it all, well. Be a success at work and, if possible, an even greater success as a wife and housekeeper.

The sixties. Twin worlds of Fleet Street and domesticity. Glitter and gold. No real power in either place (although I would not admit that at the time). Determined to shine in both. Despising women's work (no feminist either in the sixties). Cooking like hell to impress my way into a manmade heaven. Cooking in order to be loved, to take up a little space, to pretend to prestige.

I drove myself relentlessly in a job with which I became increasingly disillusioned. To have given up would have signified failure. Trained by my patriarchal Jewish father, I was bent on male-defined success. I kept myself slim, and I kept my husband well fed. I daily despised myself and my career and attempted like some cordon bleu whirlwind to win some self-respect in the kitchen. If I cordon blew it I hardly noticed.

Hospitality, a matter of great Jewish pride, was an integral part of my socialization. I learnt early that although thou shalt not commit adultery, nor all manner of attractive sins, thou shalt, on every occasion involving food preparation, commit unstinting, bountiful prodigality.

Having enough food for the immediate family was not sufficient. Aunties and uncles might at any point drop in and had to be provided for lavishly. This was patently unnecessary as all the aunties, brought up by the same rules, arrived bearing boxes of freshly baked mandelbrot and plava.

More important, however, than the inevitable descent of relations with known tastes, was the ever imminent arrival of the Unknown Visitor. 'We must always be able to welcome the stranger,' intoned the wise old judge, my Uncle Henry. A constant pronouncement. A casual injunction perhaps, but to a child's ear it took on the force of law.

Who was this Stranger? What did Wanderers eat? Was thick, creamy cheesecake fare for Foreigners? Perhaps the stranger had

a savoury tooth. Was tzimmas⁵ good enough? Tzimmas, said my
father with a laugh, was an excellent choice, for tzimmas is the
Yiddish slang for a fuss, and making a fuss of a stranger is still
how I deal with unexpected, even unwelcome, guests.

The only thing I was sure of during my childhood was that
when the stranger arrived he would be male. No one in my
youth, in kitchens or out, made much of a fuss over females.

The humorous and sometimes disastrous consequences that
can accrue from force-feeding a male traveller (who probably
wasn't hungry anyway) is outlined in a satirical chapter of
*Thinking Like a Woman*⁶ by American writer Leah Fritz, herself a
patently Good Jewish Wife and Mother. Jesus, according to Leah
Fritz, was conceived while Joseph was out of town on business.
Far from it being an immaculate conception it was brought about
by a chance meeting with a boy wonder, a newly arrived stranger
in town whom hospitable Jewish Mary entertains and, of course,
feeds.

> Back in Jerusalem things were pretty quiet. Joseph had
> gone on a trip leaving his young wife and their small
> family alone. Mary had tucked the babies in bed and
> she stepped out to breathe the fine clean night air . . .
> A little lonely, a little dreamy and plenty bored . . .
> Then down the road comes this Golden Stranger.
> She's never seen anyone like him. Maybe he was blond,
> maybe he was black, but he surely was young and
> beautiful and Didn't Look Jewish!

Leah Fritz asks, 'What does a Jewish mother do when she sees a
lonely YOUNG MALE stranger wearily winding his way on a
Night Like This?' Mary, being well brought up, has a few
minutes' conversation with him, discovers he is a divinity student
preaching the Gospel of Love, reminds herself that, in her
husband's absence, she should be suspicious of young men. Then
she hears her husband Joseph's voice nudging her mind: 'Mary,
where's your hospitality? A stranger, a mere boy, tired from

travelling, must be hungry. Will it hurt to share with him a little chicken soup?'

That did it. All Mary's magnanimous instincts were aroused. 'Come,' says Mary to the Young Student. 'The Gospel of Love I don't know about, but in my kitchen is plenty of good food for a half-starved boy.'

Mary sets a plate of chicken soup with noodles and matzoh balls before the young man and before you can recite a blessing the two of them are on the couch, the stranger putting the Gospel of Love into action. Well, we all know the rest of the story!

If you think that is far-fetched, you haven't been brought up the way I was. For me it throbbed with accuracy. So shamingly close is it to one of my own youthful experiences that only the pursuit of absolute veracity impels me to record it!

One bright evening, long ago and far away (the mid-sixties, Brighton, Sussex), I lived as a one-parent family with my small daughter Marmoset. Needing a break from childcare I deposited her on my friend Margrit and wandered down to the local pub for a drink and some company. I got talking to a not-so-young Stranger whom I shall call Norman Bark. (He called himself that and I believed him, and it was only when he was put back into prison, whence he had just emerged prior to our meeting, that I discovered it was only one of several aliases!)

Over a few drinks the stranger spun me a far-flung fancy tale about his life which may not entirely have had the ring of truth; but like Mary I was a little lonely, a little dreamy and plenty bored. He, though bald of head, was witty of phrase, told a series of amusing anecdotes and, to cap it all, revealed that he had not eaten for several days. What could a nice Jewish ex-wife do? I took him home with me, fetching my daughter on the way, put her to bed and fed the stranger on homemade vegetable broth and potato latkas. He praised my cooking and preached a persuasive gospel of halfbaked sex. I can only assume (memory being what it is) that he went on praising my cooking, for it took seven months and several policemen to remove him finally from my home where he had successfully sponged, pawned my few valuables, borrowed and sold my car, and used up all the available credit of myself and most of my unsuspecting friends. He had incidentally turned my small terraced house into a repository for the lucrative antiques he was thieving!

Norman's only positive characteristic was that, unlike my ex-husbands, he was a superb cook and insisted on making treats for my young daughter in non-business hours. Today Marmoset, now a sophisticated twenty-two, looks back on that harassing period with the words: 'Mum, I can't imagine how you could have been so naïve, but I expect it was because Norman made the best scrambled eggs of any man we knew!'

I have always been a slow learner. However, after that I did my best not to bring up my daughter to be a hospitable Jewish girl.

In our family, men were pampered at a table over which great trouble had been taken. There was always a white linen table-cloth and proper linen napkins, two long white candles in heavy ornate silver candlesticks, and flowers in season. To this day the idea of paper napkins and the term serviettes have a dreadful ring of vulgarity. So thorough was my training that recently, in a time of comparative poverty when I worked as a char for a rich family, after I had scrubbed the dining-room floor I voluntarily set the table for my employers' dinner, hunted through their drawers until I discovered cloth napkins, then picked a rose from their garden to complete the table setting! If they noticed they certainly didn't pay me any extra!

My mother and my aunties on my father's side, Auntie Rosie, Auntie Eva, Auntie Lily, Auntie Jess and Auntie Annie were in charge in the kitchen. As disciples of Florence Greenberg,[7] doyenne of Jewish cookery writers, they checked the religious division into milk and meat drawers (which grew lax as I grew older and caused my mother some anxiety), and scrutinized the larder to ensure that no food was put away on the dish on which it was served. On their frequent visits, the aunties gathered noisily in this women-only domain, with its wondrous cooking smells, shooed the uncles breezily away, and unanimously asserted that kitchens were not places for men.

Yet the food was always directed at the men. My father and the uncles were fed first, and their tastes and desires in this matter, as indeed in much else, were of paramount importance.

'Give this to your father,' and 'Is your father seated?' were phrases that rang through my childhood. My mother would serve my father first; secondly she would serve any male visitors such as uncles or boy cousins; thirdly older women, like aunties, even if unmarried, and married female cousins; fourthly, unmarried older cousins and other girl children. Then me, and lastly herself. Even if the table was only laid for three of us, my father would be seated at the head. My mother sat opposite him at the foot. She rarely sat down for long, being perpetually on the move, clearing plates, bringing in courses, dishing up and ensuring we all had more than enough. I sat somewhere else. Anywhere else. Children were not important. Girl children hardly counted at all. 'Sit, sit,' my father would say tetchily, but it patently did not matter where I sat.

My mother saved the best bits of food for my father and had the worst herself. She told me that her mother had always reserved the best for Grandpa Michael and, if necessary, ate only scraps. My own mother, who had a fine line in martyrdom, I am sure would have done the same, but as we were comfortably off a great deal of money was spent on food and scraps were not in evidence.

I noticed with curiosity and confusion that my mother offered my father a respect at mealtimes which was never evidenced in any other area of their marital lives. The rows between them were loud and terrible. But if food was in the offing a truce was declared. Warmth and comfort became the two most pervasive emotions that accompanied my earliest food memories. As in most middle-class Jewish households, there was an abundance of food. I never saw an empty fruit bowl. Our stock cupboard was always full. This gave me a tenuous feeling of security which I did not get from anything else in our row-riven family. My parents were often at each other's throats, yet at mealtimes there was a semblance of order and a genuine desire for harmony. No matter how dreadful the conflict had been, for the interim of the meal an attempt at affectionate reconciliation would be made, reasonable relations would be restored. All hell may have been let loose in our household; however, a good meal was on the table. I learnt that food was integral to a decent way of life, and that meals were a place of safety, an outpost of civilization.

It was the forties when I first understood that food was a passport to protection. That it became a lesson for life was made apparent to me in the late eighties when, during a difficult emotional relationship, I realized that some of the problems might have been soluble had not the major quarrels taken place during meals. Within a few months I recognized that this conflict of gastronomic values struck at the foundations of my emotional existence. When my father taught me that mealtimes were sacred, when my strong-willed mother concurred, I doubt if they bargained for such a long-term effect on their daughter.

Most of the time my mother dominated my father and terrorized me, as she overacted the part of the sacrificial Jewish wife and good Jewish mother like a cartoon character. East End Jewish writer, Bernard Kops, in his autobiographical book *The World is a Wedding*,[8] says: 'It is hard to assess the meaning and power of a Jewish Mother. She is practically always a matriarch, holding the family together, bending it to her will, making a living bit of sense out of the senselessness of the Universe.'

A Jewish mother lives for and through her children (sometimes, as in my case, to the point of suffocation), tries to provide for them, and to prepare them perpetually for flight. This love and provision is based on offering food along with offering herself, and preparation for flight, be it across Egypt or down the road to a friend's for tea, must include food parcels for journeys that might never be undertaken, or dreadful casualties that might never befall.

The combination of my eager assimilation into the Guides and Brownies with their Be Prepared motto, my first career as a journalist, where reporters had to be equipped for any eventuality from plunging down a coalmine to attending the royal garden party, and my orthodox Jewish upbringing, means that I rarely leave the house for a journey without a change of clothes and a large packet of sandwiches.

American writer and poet Adrienne Rich, in an essay called 'Split at the Root',[9] points out that a Jewish mother's primary job is to provide nourishment for her children, and that nourishment is rarely expected to be intellectual or spiritual. It is prescribed as emotional nourishment through the physical comfort of food.

Inheriting this notion that mother-love is illustrated by a warm home and a welcoming mountain of intricately prepared meals, meant that I focused it in turn on the seven children I gathered up at different points in my life. Carol, Peter and Wendy, my step-children by my second husband, Larry, and Bec, Cas and Vic, Ba's daughters, along with my own daughter Marmoset, *all* received the same treatment. If they lived out, I made very special meals when they visited. If they lived in, they received trays of hot food, garnished with the statutory flowers, when they were ill. Massive cauldrons of soup or stew when they came in cold and hungry from school. Chocolate cakes as treats and iced birthday cakes for festivities.

Step-parenting and co-parenting had one thing in common: a predictable assortment of difficulties, which on occasions in both cases, instead of confronting I chose to placate and impress with my lunches and suppers. How often, in the early years, I attempted to beguile Cas and win her affection with homemade cakes and jam tarts, or packets of chocolate digestives that were bad for her teeth, because I felt she was the hardest to win approval from. How often did Cas refuse to eat the hearty vegetable casseroles I cooked so caringly? 'Small please, Sal', she would say politely, knowing I minded, then push most of it about on her plate until supper was over. Another memory from my hellish, joyous, exasperating, irreplaceable domestic past, is of Ba cooking up buttered noodles or cauliflower cheese when we were short of cash or time, and Marm stalking through the dining room saying she was not hungry, then later silently sneaking a tray of food to eat alone upstairs. Did she think we did not notice? Did she think we did not mind?

Why do women, perhaps mothers most of all, seek approval with our cooking? Why do women, young and old, offer rebellion through the medium of food? Why is offering food so often an act of love, a statement of vulnerability?

In the years spent with Bec, Cas, Marm and Vic, much of our lives was structured around food. About 3,276 family suppers alone, not counting breakfasts, lunches, picnics or snackerels. I would frequently interrupt my work to cook and bake for them, even when they were of an age to cook for themselves. Subconsciously I may have resented this, but it never once occurred to me not to do it. All seven children were somehow expected to know that this meant I loved them, and they were all expected to offer me affection and approval in return. If they misunderstood the code, I would smoulder silently and gulp back my pique with a large jam sandwich.

When the four girls were very young, Friday night was the household outing to Sainsbury's. (You can't, of course, do without Sainsbury's if you have brought up all those children. And you cannot write about food without recording the hell and splendour of supermarkets.) I have an affectionate memory of Cassie, the amazing organizer, competently packing the goods into the trolley, and quiet Bec tidily taking the correct items off the shelves, while Marm and Vic danced about pulling down overpriced, exotic-looking things which we desired but could not afford; all of us laughing and joking, remembering to put the chocolate digestives in last so that they would be on top for a treat in the car on the way home.

Quirky that I should remember those carefree early years and have overlooked the later supermarket spectaculars when Ba and I and four mopey teenagers would skulk down the aisles, hot and hungry, quarrelsome and difficult, slamming baked beans into the trolley, angry that there was not the right cat food for Miffy,

24

Ziggy and Bod, all of us tired and fractious at the end of a hard week.

As was habitual, I did not express my anger at the time, but on arriving home would retreat to my study with a jar of peanut butter. It was always a large jar, but even when I wasn't hungry I managed to consume most of it.

Now I recall the words of Toni Laidlaw, a therapist I interviewed in Canada. 'Every time a woman eats when she is not hungry she is trying to help herself.'

Toni is a feminist psychologist at Dalhousie University, Halifax, who works in her spare time with ordinary women who have eating problems. I was an ordinary woman, but like most women I was reluctant to believe I ever had an eating problem.

I remember the words of Australian theorist, Dale Spender, whom I interviewed in London: 'If I ask a woman what her worries are about food, and she says she has no worries, my assumption is that she is lying.'

I know she is right, but those words too make me angry. I pull down from the bookshelf Brigid Herridge's *The Food Value Counter: The Essential Dieter's Guide*.[10] 'Peanut butter: 13.1 carbohydrate, 22.6 protein, 53.7 fat, 7.6 fibre.' There was a yellow, buttery smudge next to the key statistic – 623 calories per 100 grams! Every time I went through a 12-oz jar, by any woman's reckoning I had consumed 340 grams, not much under 2,180 calories!

Today I tell myself it does not matter. I am not on a diet. I am no longer worried about calorie intake. I know that the fat-is-bad ideology is a male myth, a patriarchal trap. I do *not* care if I get fat.

All women are socially controlled by fear of fatness. This has led to widespread fat oppression which even feminists have not gone far enough in challenging. This is because understanding how a system works does not prevent women from being controlled by an ideological hold on our consciousness.

I think back over my life and I know that I *do* care. I have always had a deep-seated fear of becoming fat. It is a fear that led me from trivial encounters with diet pills into the abyss of amphetamine addiction. If I did not still care, then I, a highly politicized social scientist, would not own such a thing as a diet book. I certainly would not let it share the shelf with Marx's *Das Kapital*, Roget's *Thesauras* (Susan M. Lloyd's non-sexist edition), and the mammoth *Collins English Dictionary*, a Christmas present from the four girls.

I recognize that when I am angry with my situation, or angry with myself for being out of control, again and again I express that anger through food.

Women who are angry because they are powerless to change their situation, or to demonstrate their feelings, quell unexpressed anger with food. The relief, however, is only temporary. Inevitably the anger returns after the act of eating is over. The social significance of women's anger is that it is deflected against ourselves.

My anger during my days of mothering was as much exemplified by my compulsive eating as the mothering itself was illustrated by compulsive cooking, and both have their roots in my Jewish upbringing. My belief that a mother's goodness is a physical attribute demonstrated through her cooking is shared by many Jewish women writers whom I have read or talked to.

'I had three sons before I was thirty,' explains Adrienne Rich, 'and during the years I often felt that to be a Jewish woman, a Jewish mother, was perceived in the Jewish family as being an entirely physical being, a producer and a nourisher of children.'[11]

Adrienne Rich's children, like myself, were taken irregularly to Passover services, Bar Mitzvahs and other special services where food was of the utmost importance. She and her children stood modestly by while her husband read the blessing in Hebrew.

These are my memories exactly. But alongside learning the institution of motherhood in a Jewish version whose language was food, we learnt the cultural expectations of a Christian patriarchal tradition, similarly steeped in culinary customs. Hers was American, mine British, but both were in the fifties and remarkably similar.

Like Rich and her children, my mother and I stood by whilst my father and uncles performed blessings, gave instructions, and were part of what counted in the fabric of a Jewish household. That my father was weak and my mother strong; that my mother held the hidden power strings and tormented herself and others with her frustrated ambitions; that she felt intellectually superior to my father and his family, did nothing to alter the overt structures of our traditional lifestyle which was lived through and around food.

The most symbolic meal of the Jewish year is Seder Night, held during Passover to commemorate the flight to Egypt. Recollection leads me to believe that all the best ingredients of a vivid Jewish culture came together over this meal. There was loud lyrical music, joyous singing in unison, fun and comradeship, speculative family gossip, and course after course of irresistible dishes. The Seder is conducted through a series of awesome rituals, which even today – years after I rejected them for their rigid patriarchal rules, their claustrophobic religiosity, their overt sexism – still retain a meaningful sense of stability and order, and an evocative reminder of shared good humour.

For the children gathered around our family's Seder table, the most significant ritual was the reading of the Four Questions. The youngest child present over the age of twelve had the frightening task of learning, practising, then reading aloud from the Haggadah[12] the four questions which all begin with the rhythmic phrase: '*Ma Nishtonah Halaila Hah Zay*: Wherein is this night different from all other nights?'

Every year I had enviously watched the older children feverishly prepare, rehearse, and finally perform the four questions. I knew I could learn them faster, read them more fluently, perform with greater poise. I was poor at Hebrew, generally skipped off classes, but had a memory like a computer. Soon, soon, I would say to myself, soon it will be my turn. Finally I was the youngest child in the family over twelve. For weeks I held in my hands the familiar yet alien Haggadah, which opened backwards to reveal the Passover service. For weeks I struggled to learn every Hebraic word and match it to every strange shape on the paper. '*Ma Nishtonah Halaila Hah Zay*: Wherein is this night different from all other nights?' I repeated over and over. I knew why. It was the night when I should stand up before my mother, aunties, cousins and all the men and say the Words.

'Go and help your mother prepare the meal,' said my father. 'I can't, I can't, I'm busy learning the four questions,' I breathed.

My uncles smiled indulgently and one said to my father: 'Your Sally, she's always studying, she should have been a boy. Look at her now learning the four questions. So what next you think?'

'Learning, schmirning, it doesn't do her any harm,' said another.

My father smiled at me: 'No, it does not do her any harm. She is clever, my daughter is a scholar.' Then he pointed towards the kitchen: 'So now, help your mother prepare. Soon everyone will be here.'

I walked away, tossing my hair, Haggadah in hand. I knew the words, I could go on repeating them in my head whilst I mixed dough. As I went, I heard one of the uncles say: 'Your Sally, she should be a lawyer!' and there was a general laugh. I perked up. Nodded furiously. I should, I should. And not any old lawyer. I intended to be a judge, just like my wise old uncle on my mother's side. My father joined in the laugh, and said: 'A girl of mine could be a lawyer, so why not, we move with the times', but his placating tone got drowned by one of the aunties bursting in with: 'All that book learning. She should only grow up lucky enough to marry a lawyer!'

Marching rebelliously into the kitchen to prop up my book in front of the mixing bowl, I flung back my straight, clipped black hair (my mother was for neatness at any price), and put on what the family called my chutzpah look.

(At the time I was not sure what chutzpah was, except I knew it had some relation to nerve or cheek. Years later my second husband explained: 'If a boy who has murdered both his mother and his father seeks mercy from the court on the grounds that he is an orphan, that is *chutzpah*!')

That evening I dressed carefully and decorated my hair with a bright red ribbon. The service started. After what seemed aeons, we reached the moment before the reading of the four questions. I sat up, adrenalin flooding through me. I waited attentively for Uncle Henry at the head of the table to nod towards me. Without even noticing my concentrated gaze, he turned towards my boy cousin J and said: 'Now, my son, it is your turn.'

I shall never forget breaking the sacred silence by screaming: 'It is not his turn, it is not his turn. I am the youngest child of the right age. It is *me*. It is *me*. It is my turn!'

It was like throwing a bomb into a silent Wimbledon finals match. Play had been interrupted. The spectators were appalled. Totally bewildered. SOMETHING HAD GONE WRONG. I looked pleadingly at Uncle Henry, my wise, intelligent uncle, for clarification, the uncle I most respected, the uncle I wished to emulate. There was a terrible silence. Then my uncle said in a kind but unrelenting voice: 'The Book says it is the youngest boy who shall ask the four questions. You, my dear Sally, are a girl. Now, if you will go and see if the soup is at the right temperature, the youngest boy, our dear J, will read aloud the questions.'

Seder Night: the meal of a million memories. Seder Night; the night where a girl of twelve first learnt what her role was in society.

Yes, twelve was a bad year for me. It was the year I learnt that young Jewish women make soup and know their place. Much the same thing, says the Torah!

My mother and aunties taught me the rules governing soup. Chicken soup was incorrect unless it spilled out kneidlech, if you belonged to the old soup school, or kreplech if you had joined the New. My mother, who thought of herself as modern, inculcated me into the ways of kreplech, squares of noodle exactly two inches in diameter filled with mince seasoned with ginger.

29

I learnt that a simple bean and barley soup was not simple at all, as it had to be overflowing with kasha, a speciality buckwheat which itself had to be cooked in one particular way: you fried an onion, put in the kasha, cooked it slightly, added an egg, then when the kasha opened you poured on the water, covered and let it cook like rice.

As for the inimitable borscht, archetypal beetroot soup, the backbone of every Jewish kitchen, there were so many rules about how to get borscht right that a nice Jewish girl could be driven to despair . . . or even to bacon. One auntie assured me that four beetroots must be sliced, simmered and strained. Another auntie swore that one breakfastcupful of grated, cooked beetroot was correct. The auntie who sliced, added beaten eggs, while the auntie who grated omitted the eggs but insisted on shredded white cabbage. What was a girl to do? Fortunately there was consensus about the importance of sour apple and lemon juice, which is, I think, what gives borscht its unique taste.

The laws governing soup implicitly offered me laws to govern my life. In the kitchen I learnt the concept of GETTING IT RIGHT. Not cutting corners. Not using substitutes. As food was a matter of the highest priority in our household, all food laws took on the flavour of moral imperatives. So it was inevitable that that particular injunction spilt over into the rest of my life and turned me into an exhausted (and doubtless exhausting) persistent perfectionist, dedicated to ensuring that everything I achieved professionally was unsurpassed and everything I took on domestically was flawless.

It did however also breed in me a spirit of tenacious optimism. No matter how depressed I became in later years, I went on believing that if I could still put a meal right, I could one day put the world right.

Some foods last a lifetime as memories, and primordial borscht, and bitter sweet chraine, a horseradish pre-eminent amongst sauces, are for me the most pervasive.

My father, whom I remember as a large, untidy, unpunctual

man with a healthy appetite that matched his size, exquisite copperplate handwriting, and an incurable sense of humour, loved gefillte fish[13] which he would spread liberally with this finely grated horseradish sauce. His sense of optimism, of something better being round the corner, meant he dismissed family or work upsets with the words: 'So it's not a tragedy. Come eat the gefillte fish. Put chraine on it.'

It was the same with borscht. Served on every celebratory occasion, it contained a panacea for life. There would be death and disorder in our family, worse in the world at large. My father would listen to my grave, technicoloured accounts, would ladle out large helpings from the tureen (carefully placed in front of him), then twinkle and laugh as he said: 'So, it's not a tragedy. Come eat. Try the borscht!'

And chraine and borscht, redolent with hope and humour, reduced much of the tragedy in both my marriages. Good Jewish food allowed us sometimes to see the funny side.

The most pleasurable memories of my marriage to Neville, like me a Fleet Street journalist, are those of the hasty snacks, always large, always Jewish, snatched between stories. We both worked shifts. He was night editor of a national tabloid, I a feature writer on a rival newspaper. At the close of my workday and the start of his, we would dash to a small café in London's Windmill Street where, over steaming bowls of borscht, or large platters of gefillte fish served with chraine, with feverish intensity we would catch up on the day's news stories whilst neglecting our own.

We paid impeccable attention to our successful public roles and rather less to our declining private lives. If last night's main news story had been catchy, if I had a front page by-line, and the beetroot soup contained the correct amount of raw potato and sour apple, we deluded ourselves we were fulfilled. We shared our professional interests, we shared our gastronomic inheritance. We were very fond of each other. The marriage was never quite right, but then what is? We put chraine on our gefillte fish, we tried the borscht and pronounced it fine, and like my father said, it was not a tragedy. When the time came to split, we halved the cooking utensils, we hugged and grinned, and continued to meet for meals.

I have a shrewd feeling that a Jewish background, a sense of humour and a shared love of borscht and smoked salmon, kept my second marriage going when many more seemingly cogent factors signalled that it should have fallen apart. The relationship even started with a Jewish soup joke.

In my role as a journalist for the now defunct but formerly glossy *Queen* magazine, I went to Edinburgh to interview Larry Adler, the classical harmonica player who had just started to divert his artistry into a one-man cabaret show. I had been told he was extraordinarily gifted. He was. I had been told he was extraordinarily egotistic. He was. I was determined to remain unimpressed. Nobody, however, had told me he was extremely funny, or how he liked food.

I sat down quietly at the back of the unimposing fringe theatre where he was performing, and remained cynically unmoved until, between ostentatious virtuoso pieces on the mouth organ, he told a story:

'A customer at a Jewish restaurant in New York is so well known as a borscht lover that whenever he comes in they immediately serve him borscht, without bothering to take his order. One day, after being served, he beckons the waiter over.

'"Waiter," he says, "taste the borscht."

'"You don't like it?"

'"Taste it."

'"Look, you don't like it, so I'll change it."

'"Taste it," says the customer patiently.

'"Why do I have to taste? You don't like? So, I'll give you a menu, you'll select something else, I'll bring already. And no extra charge. We only want to please you."

'The customer grows angry.

'"*Taste the borscht!*"

'"Look, I got fifty-seven other customers here. I'm gonna taste everybody's borscht? I won't get any work done."

'The customer stands up and leans over the waiter.

'"Will you sit *down* and *taste the borscht*."

'The waiter sits down. He looks around the table. Then he says: "So, where's the spoon?"

'The customer, satisfied, says, "Ah, *hah*!"'[14]

I laughed till my eyes streamed. Then I went backstage and interviewed him. It was not love at first sight, it was laughter at first hearing. It was a complete identification with the best and worst of my upbringing, my own preoccupation with food as a medium for humour. We went out that night and shared the first of many meals, some hilarious, some bitter, some painfully sad. 'So, where's the spoon?' became a key to the code between us. A code that at some entrenched level has not been broken despite a divorce and the passing decades.

Ironically, our shared background created our main problem also. Larry was as firmly locked into Jewish patriarchy as my father and uncles. He loved to eat well, but he had never cooked anything beyond scrambled eggs, and refused to learn. That was my job. In addition to all my other jobs, both independently as a writer, and jointly with him as his stage director and concert manager.

It never occurred to me then to insist he did half the cooking. Or any of the cleaning. Or much of the childcare. He was a well-known musician. He had 'TALENT'. And my pre-feminist subconscious bought easily into the male artist's version of that word. That I had talent and skills too was never a priority. That I felt proud to be in the kitchen, to delight the man I lived with by producing delicacies, *was*. If I was tired, or did not wish to cook, he would willingly take me out for meals. That was never a problem. But it was another way of avoiding the central issue that women should be in the kitchen. Significantly, and with some astonishment, I must record that I have never felt so appropriate, or so feminine, as I did during those years of singlehanded cooking. Such is the power of male ideology. Such is the power of good Jewish food!

Despair, depression, crises and confessionals are magnificent moments for food in a Jewish family. When sadness or emptiness floods over a household, the members, led by the women, encourage each other to eat.

'So, you're miserable, so eat' was my family's favourite maxim, applied equally to me as a schoolgirl, frozen and grumpy after too long on a hated hockey field, and to each aunt in turn bereaved by her husband's death. Food was the primary comforter – but not any old food; food for consolation was invariably cake. Cake in a crisis. Cake when there was conflict. Cake during and after difficult disclosures. Cake that came in white cardboard boxes, tied up with flecked string, and labelled 'Grodzinki's'. Cake that leaves crumbs on one's life.

When my father died and the family spent a week on low chairs in traditional mourning, I was nineteen, unhardened to death. What I recall most clearly are the piercing wails of my aunties at the tombside, as the uncles shovelled earth onto the coffin, followed half an hour later by their eager devouring of the apple strudel, poppy-seed cake, lemon cheeses, and plate after plate of the pinwheel pastry made of dough, cinnamon, nuts and brown sugar that we called ruggalach, which had been tipped from their boxes before we set off for the funeral. For seven days and seven nights, the fur-coated visitors streamed in bearing boxes, leaving my mother only to cut up the challah and spread it with cream cheese. Chief mourners must do no cooking.

It is hard even now to feast upon these delicacies without tasting the sadness. Strangely, a few years ago my oldest friend, Jenni, died (a tragedy of a young epileptic woman having a fit whilst cleaning a bath and drowning over it) and I went with my friend Ba to North London for the funeral. We were an hour early. Was it by coincidence that we drifted into Grodzinski's bakery shop in Golders Green and comforted ourselves with coffee and apple strudel? I think not. Jenni was not Jewish, but funerals are funerals and food was the only balm I knew.

Perhaps that visit to the cake shop was a slip of the subconscious. But a year later Fay, the Jewish mother of my first college boyfriend, died of cancer. Again the funeral was in North

London. This time I went alone, unsupported and isolated. The
years had separated our paths. No one I knew would be there.
This time I got there early on purpose, went to Grodzinski's and
ordered the largest portion of cheesecake in the shop. Only when
I had stuffed it all did I feel strong enough and sufficiently
spiritual to face the crematorium.

For me, the backdrop to death is a good buffet. I have always
had this bizarre idea that the only person capable of giving me an
appropriate send-off gastronomically is me. As my ashes are
about to be flung over my publisher's offices, I imagine myself
worrying and wondering: 'Such a lot of visitors! Is there enough
to eat? Did my royalties raise enough money for smoked salmon?'
This does not, of course, take into account the unpalatable
possibility that I may die friendless and alone with not a pastry
in sight!

Jewish women bake cakes in a crisis, offer them for comfort.
Most ordinary women (not just Jewish ones) use the food they
cook to show love, to seek approval, to win respect, in ways that
men do not.

Do all women do this? Surely not clever women who possess
a strong self-identity, who have careers, who know what they
are about. I think of the women in history I most admire. I
switch on the television. A delightful play about the poet Emily
Dickinson, called *The Belle of Amherst*.[15] Claire Bloom is playing
Emily, dressed all in white; in her later years Emily always wore
white. It is halfway through the nineteenth century.[16] The place
is the distinguished Amherst house in Massachusetts where,
except for brief excursions, Emily lived for the fifty-three years
of her life in seclusion, initially as part of her family, but after
her parents' death alone with her sister Lavinia, cared for by a
servant.

As the play opens, Emily, thirty-one years old, not yet
published, has bravely sent off a batch of poems to Thomas
Wentworth Higginson, a professional man of letters, to enquire

timidly whether her verses 'breathed'.[17] She took this risk embol-
dened by Higginson's article in *Atlantic Monthly* called 'Letter to
a Young Contributor', which aimed to be practical advice for
those who wished to break into print. Emily had heard that
Higginson was a liberal thinker, interested in the status of women
in general and women writers in particular. What better man to
seek criticism from. Or to invite to tea!

To the astonishment and delight of the shy poet, the man of
letters writes back asking for more verses. He enquires about her
age, reading and companionships and decides that he will call
upon her.

Emily is ecstatic. She bakes rhubarb cupcakes. Emily's mother
has always assured her that she bakes beautifully and that any
man she marries will find that out. Emily tells the viewers with
some confidence that she is a highly skilled cook. She seems less
sure that she is a highly skilled poet.

Mr Higginson, illustrious and pompous man of letters, comes
to Amherst. Emily is a nervous wreck. Before the visitor arrives
she tells us:

> Success is counted sweetest
> By those who ne're succeed.[18]

Success so far has not come Emily's way. Is she now about to
become famous? To improve her literary confidence in these
frightening minutes, she reminds herself of her mother's praise
about her cooking.

Mr Higginson arrives and introverted Emily, dressed in a
white gown – like a lily herself – presents him with two exquisite
lilies. She holds them upright like giant, sweet-smelling candles.

> I had a Terror since September . . . I could tell to none
> And so I sing as the Boy does by the Burying Ground
> because I am afraid.[19]

Mr Higginson accepts the lilies graciously and eats his tea. It
is true, he says, that young Emily has 'an incomparable lyrical
gift, an audacity of ideological association and verbal assurance',[20]

but her poems lack structure. Higginson recognized that the young woman had remarkable talent, but what embarrassed him was his inability to classify the poems. Her verses are elusive of (male-defined) criticism. As he wrote later to a friend, he was of the opinion they were 'remarkable, though odd . . . too delicate . . . not strong enough to publish'.[21]

Emily learns that her poems will not do. Her words are womens' words. Women have emotional, exciting ideas, but they lack form. In his view it is not worth Emily's trouble to attempt to get her poems published. Women are good at making cakes. Emily should learn her place.

'Have you tasted the rhubarb cupcakes?' she says with style, holding back her tears. Fame, she knows, now, is not going to be hers. Stoutly she reminds us that 'Paradise is within'.[22]

After he has departed, she admits sadly that this is the day 'the great hope fell'. It seems she already knows that 'perhaps no one will ever read my poems'.[23]

Watching the play I became enraged that talented, despairing, unsung Emily should be baking cakes and offering flowers, afraid of the judgements of a pompous bore whom the world would doubtless never have heard of had he not been immortalized by turning down a great poet's words.

Indeed, Emily's prognosis is not mistaken. The slowly developing lyrical sphinx, dressed in milk-white, chooses to shut herself away in the family tomb. She wrote 1,775 poems in her lifetime, but only ten were published before her death in 1886.

How many rhubarb cupcakes did she bake in that lifetime? How many men whom she believed superior, and from whom she received scant recognition did she cook for?

Whenever Emily found a word she really loved, a word that made the truth 'dazzle gradually', she would say excitedly: 'Now there's a word to lift your hat to!'[24] But in the bitter moments after Mr Higginson's departure, words do not come easily to her. She goes into the hall, stands miserably in front of the large mirror and looks at her tear-marked face. '*Plain*! You're plain!' she says to the reflection. 'Plain. Now there's a word not to lift

37

your hat to!'[25] And she flings furiously away. Then, like the strong and persistent woman she undoubtedly was, she says vehemently:

> How dreary – to be – Somebody!
> How public – like a Frog –
> To tell one's name – the livelong June
> To an admiring Bog![26]

Holding her tattered self-respect together, she says stoutly: 'I would rather undress in public than have my poems published.'[27]

Good for you, Emily, I find myself shouting. You kept on writing as well as baking those damn cupcakes. Poems and cupcakes – now there are words to lift your hat to! Your poems have gone down in literary history, Emily, and your rhubarb cupcakes show me that, at heart, you are a Nice Jewish Girl!

TWO
THE JAM SANDWICH
SYNDROME

Like most of us, I am accustomed to certain regular rhythms in my life. A fixed address. Sleeping on the same side of a double bed no matter who I am sharing it with. The Sunday papers plopping through the letter box. Chilled orange juice and Earl Grey tea as soon as I wake up. Above all I seem to require the 'right' food at the correct time to make me feel my world is in order. I could not countenance pork chops for breakfast, or sugar puffs and hot milk as a pub lunch. I am not alone in this, for in every society, food is part of the social order, meals structure our days even more than the clock. There are specific food rituals and customs, and even mealtime or menu sequences, and when changes are made to these, people feel disrupted, disturbed and sometimes aggressive.

Take the matter of Delia's dreadful dinner party. Delia, not being a fool but an extremely competent cook as well as a skilled social psychologist, knows that we eat the contents of a meal in a particular sequence. Delia, however, did not stick to the rules. In the pub, the day after her extraordinary meal, two women told me what had happened.

'Last night's formal do at Delia's wasn't a meal,' said Anne ferociously. 'It was pure *shit*. Delia needs to have her head examined! I was so angry I wanted to walk out at once and go straight home!'

Anne is a down-to-earth gardener who certainly never calls a spade anything more refined, but she is not easily given to rages. She treats people and social situations as she does plants, with quiet care and attention and not too much pulling up of the roots.

Delia must have done something utterly outrageous to provoke such an outburst.

'She asked us to this formal dinner to celebrate those articles she'd had published with a whole set of people we didn't know at all, and we don't know her well either. Then she proceeded to make fools of us!' shrieked Fiona, looking extremely distressed and quite unlike the soothing, and rational nursery nurse I knew.

All seven of the women guests had been slightly involved in helping Delia during her research. Obviously the dinner was intended to be a sign of her appreciation, but her preparations were not designed to put her guests at ease.

'It was hateful and confusing,' said Fiona. 'It made me dreadfully anxious. I was glad when it ended.' What exactly had Delia done to upset this woman's habitual calm? 'Oh I wasn't the only one to be upset,' asserted Fiona. 'That Marge, the so-called clever one, almost burst into tears and left the room before the pudding, well what should have been the pudding, except we'd had the pudding at the start of the meal. That was the problem.'

Anne took up the story. 'Everyone was very dressed up, and except for us, were strangers to each other. There were candles and flowers on the table, silver cutlery, a real air of graciousness. We all thought we were in for a good time. We stood around with a sherry and olives which made you think you knew where you were. Then Delia asked us to be seated, and she brought in the first course which was a huge cheese board with all sorts of sophisticated cheeses with walnuts and peppers. With it she offered grapes, a sweet liqueur, and the coffee perk. I thought it was weird but I decided it might be a Scandinavian meal. After all, Delia is a great traveller and probably has some fancy foreign ideas. Perhaps it was a smorgasbord starter with cheese and ham. Except there wasn't any ham.'

'It wasn't the ham that was missing, it was the sense,' said Fiona bitterly. 'That cheeseboard was followed by icecream and chocolate sauce with rhubarb crumble as an alternative with a good dessert wine. Oh yes, all the trimmings. Then came chicken and pineapple with fresh veg and a small green salad and of course white wine. That was followed by turbot in a mayonnaise sauce garnished with lemon. By this time I suspect everyone was quietly freaking out although they were all trying not to show it and attempting to follow Delia's conversational leads. Except poor Marge, who simply stopped eating and said she was getting over a stomach upset. But when she saw the mushroom soup sprinkled with watercress she looked as if she might cry. Suddenly she left the room before Delia served the final course which was avocado vinaigrette for those of us who were still trying to stick it out.'

I felt enormously sympathetic. No matter how excellent the meal, served back to front it would have put anyone in a panic. How would I have behaved? How would you? Would we have had the coolness to question Delia about her strange behaviour? Probably not. Certainly none of Delia's guests had managed to. I asked Anne and Fiona why they hadn't.

'I'm not really sure,' Anne said slowly. I realized she had been asking herself the same question. 'Maybe it was because I didn't know anyone there except Fiona. Maybe because it was a celebration for Delia and I've always thought of her as a woman who knows what she is doing. The most difficult thing to contend with was that she was acting like everything was quite ordinary. As if having a meal backward is normal. Maybe it *is* in her circle! That made it much harder to speak out. I felt angry but I also felt slightly afraid, as if anything could happen. There was a sort of madness in the air.'

Fiona had a simpler explanation. 'I began to think there must be something the matter with *me* not with her. The more distressed I got, the more I felt I ought to be able to deal with a strange social situation without getting in such a panic. But I couldn't. At first I thought Delia had made a mistake and brought in the last course first, and that she'd realize and put it right. But she didn't. So there I was stuck with food I might have liked but which left me utterly bewildered. I couldn't handle it at all.'

I think few of us would have dealt with it any better, or even differently. For food is so deeply embedded in our social structure that when any of its taken-for-granted features are flouted, we become bewildered.

The anger and distress felt by Anne and Fiona are normal responses to an abnormal situation. In the search for reassurance, another predictable response is to look for patterns, to try to make sense of the strange happenings as Fiona did by thinking Delia had made a mistake, and Anne by telling herself it might be a Scandinavian meal. We look for reassurance, we hang on to ideas of normality, because we expect meals to offer us a place of safety.

When Delia served dessert wine with pudding and white wine with chicken, she was following custom. But because she stuck to some food rules but broke others, this intensified the Alice-in-Wonderland effect. Delia, who supposedly put on a meal in gratitude to her guests, succeeded in making them feel abused and dislocated. My own immediate response to the story was that Delia had 'overdone it'. Delia had flipped! For she had also flouted the unspoken unwritten rules that lie beneath a woman's role as cook and caterer. For in our culture it is women, not men, whom we expect to nurture us with food. It is women whom we expect to make us feel secure. Kitchens are women's domain where they are expected to act wisely and well. When they do not, they challenge and disrupt our basic social conventions.

When many years ago I had a nervous collapse, I broke down and broke the rules in my own kitchen. My symbolic way of letting my husband know I was cracking up over the dual roles of good wife and good worker was to break all the china instead of laying the table. Was Delia's débâcle too an unreasonable reaction to her role as cook and provider, or merely a terrible joke? Whatever the underlying reasons, the presentation and wrong order of the dinner led her guests to feel betrayed.

It is not just the correct sequence of food at a mealtime which buttresses social order and stability; so does correct table behaviour; and even a particular kind of table-talk. 'Keep off religion, politics, and sex!' my father warned. 'Unsuitable topics for meals,' he said sternly. Although as a teenager I thought him old-fashioned, nevertheless certain conversational norms ensure that mealtime interaction is standardized and predictable. When people meet at dinner, there is a surface acceptance of the other guests which involves a pattern of polite, friendly and often neutral talk. When this fiction of acceptance between hosts and guests, and between table companions, is strictly adhered to, it offers us an appearance of order.

When we are invited out, we expect the assembled company to be amiable. No one will ask us embarrassing questions. No one will show us up. No one will put us down. Our host, and more particularly our hostess, will put us at ease. Should the conversation reach troubled waters, it is the hostess on whom we count to smooth it over with her best olive oil.

Would that such proprieties had been observed that never-to-be-forgotten evening at Jeanni and Jerry's! If your nerves can stand another tortured tale, listen to what happened.

Ba and I had just moved with the girls and the cats from a small village into Cambridge. We were perched on ladders, up to our elbows in pots of paint, plastering and decorating, when Jeanni, whom we knew quite well, called round to bid us a friendly welcome to the neighbourhood. 'How lovely that you are living so close by!' she said. 'Come to supper tomorrow night. Jerry and I will make a special welcome meal and invite some people for you to meet.'

After three days of take-away fish and chips with plaster-specks clogging up the batter, it sounded wonderful. The next night we dragged off our decorating clothes and got dressed up. We were tired but excited at the prospect of an entertaining evening, ready to enjoy ourselves.

On our arrival, Jerry, whom we did not know well, remained crosslegged on the floor, talking to his other guests, all strangers to us. He did not pay us much attention, and I recall thinking that he was probably shy. Jeanni was busy in the kitchen. Fortunately dinner was served almost at once. Over the hors d'oeuvres the conversation was general and not untoward. But as soon as Jeanni began to ladle out the soup, Jerry, a lecturer in politics at a technical college, turned to me and began a series of contentious discussions. No one else joined in, and remembering my father's words about avoiding difficult issues at mealtimes, I answered as pleasantly as I could. By the time we had finished the soup, Jerry had decided to pull me apart, tear me down, and mentally batter me with the most alarming display of verbal ferocity I have ever encountered. The other guests looked uncomfortable, but not one of them said anything.

Jeanni collected the plates, removed the soup, and brought in the main course as if she had not noticed. Jerry by now was in his stride. Verbal attack followed verbal attack. He shouted, his hostility that of a man insane. His wife calmly served the vegetables, offered the wine around, and smiled a lot. I began to feel I was a character in Edward Albee's *Who's Afraid of Virginia Woolf* when the host and hostess play a horrible game of Get the Guests! Surely this was not real? Surely this was not happening to me?

At the other end of the table Ba looked frozen with disbelief. She had stopped speaking as had most of the other guests, every one a silent witness to Jerry's extraordinary display of temper. I was nearly in tears, as much from rage as from distress. Minute after minute I waited for Jeanni to take action: to evict this lunatic, to administer arsenic, to restore order or at the very least to change the conversation! She did none of those things. She did not once rise to my support. She did not once admonish or deflect her husband. She behaved throughout the meal as if nothing out of the ordinary was occurring, as if it was a routine mealtime event for her husband to attack, to pillory, to attempt to reduce to tears a specially invited guest, who was one of her friends.

I have no idea what the other guests thought or felt. I only know that like Delia's dinner guests, they did not speak out, they did not comment on the strange social situation in which we were all trapped.

Every rule of good table behaviour was being trampled upon and there seemed nothing I could do. I felt bewildered, outraged, the victim of a mealtime madness I had not predicted, I could not understand, I could not control.

I do not know how Ba and I managed to sit through four courses and coffee; but some vestige of what we saw as correct and sane behaviour kept us in our seats, kept us silent. Some twisted notion of survival on our own civilized terms would not let us leave until the meal was over.

I have never been more glad to shut a door behind me.

We were too shocked to converse on the way home. But later I asked Ba why she had not spoken up during dinner. 'Vic would have said it was "well out of order",' she said, laughing at the phrase. 'And it really was. I was just as stunned as you were; the shock seemed to take my powers of speech away. I kept waiting for Jeanni to shut him up, to hustle him off to the kitchen, to lecture him on manners, or to suggest we adjourned for coffee. But when Jeanni acted as if it was normal, I began to lose hold on what was going on. It was Jeanni I was angry with.'

Like myself, Ba was more outraged at Jeanni's behaviour than at Jerry's, because we expect women to do it right. This was the same at Delia's party. If a man had served up that meal, the guests would have thought it eccentric but they might have tried to laugh it off. The women at Delia's, like Ba and I at Jeanni's felt a sense of betrayal by another woman. Not only were our social expectations thwarted, but our trust had been abused. When someone says come for a meal, the power lies with her (or him). It becomes a highly symbolic event. In effect the hostess says: Trust me to feed and nurture you.

The guest who accepts in effect says: I trust that your kitchen is clean, your food nutritious. I trust that my table companions will not be my enemies or behave like my enemies. I trust all will be in order. Like a babe who has to take in whatever is put in its mouth, we put ourselves into the care of someone else. Food is part of the power relations in society.

A meal is a step up from a mere drink. Whether with a

colleague, a lover or a neighbour, a meal takes us further into a relationship. Traditionally we 'break bread' with those we are comfortable with. As Ramona Koval says in *Eating Your Heart Out*:

> 'Eating together is frequently a public statement of a committed relationship, and in many places a family is defined as a household of related people whose food is cooked together. In some New Guinea cultures, so strong are the links between mothering, food and love, that the words for mother, breast, breastmilk, sweet potato, nurture and sustenance are all from the same origin.'[1]

Food is so strong a symbol of solidarity that some of us, especially children, find it hard to eat in unfamiliar surroundings or with strangers. Cas and Bec, when they were teenagers, disliked eating meals away from home. If Bec's boyfriend asked her to supper with his mum, she felt she was on trial and could barely swallow a mouthful. Cas disliked eating tea at her schoolfriends' because, she said, 'They don't serve the right kind of meals, it feels uncomfortable.'

The meals that contravene this comforting food tradition are the formidable business lunches or the terrible ordeal of the staff christmas outing. At such times we may have to eat with people we actively dislike, or with whom we feel in direct competition. Meals become events at which we are expected to sell or restrain ourselves rather than places to relax. Is it because staff dinners, business lunches, funerals and weddings are such stressful situations that they are habitually laced with a great deal of alcohol? Certainly some of us need it to get through them! I have two friends who take tranquillizers before a meal with their employers.

Food is part of the nurturing process throughout the world, but in different places it takes on special meanings. Each culture marks its own society with special foods and food rituals. What is a permitted and enjoyable food in one society is looked on as taboo or revolting in another. In every society some of us choose to eat what others avoid. Anthropologists point out that people never indiscriminately eat all the edible material available. From childhood we learn to make selections and classify material into food and non-food.

Sometimes these categories operate throughout whole nations. The Chinese, we are told, eat dogs and monkey brains; the French eat horse. Few people in Britain can tolerate the thought – these animals are our friends, or too like us. Some African tribes eat roasted insects. Most Westerners, brought up to recoil at creepy crawlies, shudder at the idea of this crunchy protein-rich dish. But the food/non-food classification differs within nations also – compare the consumption of offal in Scotland and the north to that in the south of England – and even from household to household. Children who nibble olives at their parents' knees won't find them disgusting later on unless, like Judith, a computer programmer with a cool, bold manner, they accumulate unfortunate associations.

'My mother-in-law used to perch them on top of tiny salted biscuits covered with squiggly anchovies. She domineered me dreadfully. "Speak up, Judith," she said as she handed me a silly salted cracker. I trembled and the olives fell off every time! Even today when someone at a party hands me a bowl of olives I can't touch them.'

Food taboos can make a group feel separate and special, but sometimes a food prohibition can bring problems. Listen to Sihra, a young Muslim woman, brought up in a tradition where fasting is considered spiritually and physically beneficial, and pork is taboo. Educated at a British comprehensive she discovered her schoolfriends linked fasting to a fear of fat.

'At school my girlfriends would go on horrendous short-term diets, because of their figures. I understood that, but they never understood why I fasted between dawn and sunset during the month of Ramadan. They laughed and called me a freak. Even

47

the teachers were unsympathetic when I said fasting made me tired by the last lesson. They thought I was copping out. School dinners were the hardest. I could only eat meat if it was Halal,[2] never pork because that would taste of sin.'

Sihra felt that her English friends' abstinence from food held a very different meaning from her own. 'They thought overeating was unfeminine, and being fat was the pits, but they did not exercise our control or feel our purity. The English girls in my class were always *upset* about the food they did not eat, I was always *glad*. Even if I felt faint I knew it would be deeply wrong to break my fast. Some of the English girls binged in the middle of their diet. For me to do that would be to do evil.'

Ahni, a Hindu believer, is similarly subject to cultural taboos which change the meaning of food for her. 'When you are allowed only fruit then the fruit tastes holy. Our community will not eat beef because the cow has the gentle loving qualities of the good mother.'

To Sihra, pork would taste of sin because from childhood it has been a forbidden food. For Ahni eating beef would be as outrageous as eating one's mother. It is because food has emotional meanings beyond its basic nutritional benefit that Ahni and Sihra can accept food taboos as part of a set of spiritually influenced rules designed to create a disciplined life. Their cultures lead them to put a moral and spiritual meaning into consuming or denying themselves food.

Food is part of the way the world works. The joy or displeasure it evokes has little to do with its nutrient value, and much to do with good or bad memories, or with our cultural heritage. Food is one of the ways we construct our social worlds. It has meanings far beyond its chemical or physical function, which means that for most women every mundane meal is mixed from ingredients highly charged with emotional impact.

Helena, an Israeli woman, spoke for many when she said, 'I don't see food as nourishment, I see it as hate and love. I want it but I know I must not have it, so it is not positive in my life. My favourite food is thick creamy icecream with chocolate but I can never enjoy it because I know what it does to me. I never stop watching my weight and food intake. I measure every food in my head, even if I'm not going to eat it. I love food, really *love* it, but it never leaves me feeling good. Food is not the meals I eat, but my whole world. Food can make my world good, food can turn my world bitter. Food is my enemy and my friend. I never know which it will be when I wake up, but I know that food will be the first thing I think about.'

For women like Helena, food is the fear of a fat future. For other women food is the memory of good times past. Often these are childhood memories of family kitchens where the comforting smell of baking wafts through their minds. 'I've only got to smell apple pie baking and hear the bubbling of apples on the stove to get taken back to Mum's kitchen, with her standing at the Aga, and us kids hanging around. They were good times for me and my brothers.' Sheena was talking to me in a café near her office in Truro, where just such a smell was drifting in from the kitchen. She laughed. 'Even in this café with you, a stranger, and with that tape machine, the smell of apples makes me feel comfortable, so talking to you isn't so bad.'

Food that recalls warm memories of home cooking can evoke this sense of security, even if home is many miles away. In Liverpool Colleen an exile from Northern Ireland, told me: 'Soda bread is still home to me. It's hard to get over here, because you can't easily find the buttermilk and soda flour. But when I make it, even with plain flour, and let the ordinary milk go sour in a hot place, the smell of it just on the curdle puts all the Irish back in me. I'm wrapped up warm and safe.'

For some women, when food is tied to ideas of home and family it means affection and stability. For others, it means misery and rebellion. Food is about anger, joy, rejection or comfort. It is never about carbohydrates, fats, proteins or energy! Food is Helena's heaven and hell. Food is Sheena's security, a cradle for Colleen. Across classes and cultures, emotional ingredients colour women's perceptions of food.

What is constant across cultures is that food gives us a feeling of regularity. Meals acts as 'hinges of the day'.[3] We build them into our routine. For nearly ten years my friend Kathy and I have tried to have a drink and where possible a meal out once a week on the same night. Other women I know achieve this regularity by having a set menu for different days of the week. Kathy's own family in which there were nine children was typical:

'Dinner was always at one: Sundays was roast; Mondays leftover cold meat; Tuesday mincemeat, gravy and mash; Wednesday stew with dumplings; Thursday cottage pie, and Friday fish of course. Saturday didn't seem to count. Tea at night was always beans on toast or bread and butter dipped in the sugar bowl. Even on the beach there was routine: sugar sandwiches when we were poor, then when more of us were earning Mum made paste or pilchard. You remembered the poor days by the gritty taste of sand in the sugar,' Kathy laughed.

Even confectionery had its regular place. 'You knew it was paynight Fridays cos Dad would bring home the sweets. For the children, quarter pound of Merry Maids, quarter pound of rum-and-butter, and one small Mars Bar to be shared by the nine of us. We'd have to slice it into nine pieces. Mum got a small bar of Dairy Milk for herself, which made us envious. It was always the same, the rituals never altered. As I was the eldest, as soon as I started work I had to follow the routine. I got paid Fridays so I used to buy Mum her half pound Cadbury's Dairy Milk chocs.'

Kathy's story also shows us that routine food habits often mirror class differences. As Cait, an Irish woman, explained: 'As a child in our road, if you went out to tea you always knew how much their dad earned by what was on the table. If it was a milk bottle and brown sauce, their dad was like ours. If it was a jug of milk and salad cream they were toffee-nosed. The only time you saw a jug in our house was the jug of flowers on the kitchen windowsill. Some of *them* had flowers on the table!'

Most of us do not relish changes to food customs, particularly at festivals. Christmas and Thanksgiving are characteristic in decreeing not only the menu but also the conditions of family behaviour. 'You had to have pumpkin pie with icecream at Thanksgiving,' Cheryl Lean told me. 'Grandmother insisted the turkey was decorated with acorn squash which you mustn't have the rest of the year. The dressing had to be spices and sweetbreads with scallop potatoes. Mother had to make almond shortbread cookies like boomerangs and none of it appeared at any other time. You couldn't break any of those food rules.'

Festivals are traditional times for families to gather, for children to be spoilt. As one woman said: 'For a member of the family not to turn up, or not to bring their children, would definitely need a decent excuse. It was practically obligatory.'

The problem with the compulsory aspect of family festivities is that if you choose *not* to eat the regulation menu, or not to join your family, or indeed anyone else's, it is difficult not to feel excluded, stigmatized, lonely or at least as if your alien conduct requires explanation.

When I first gave up eating meat, I always felt I had to justify myself apologetically for not eating turkey at Christmas. One year I decided to confront the situation and order myself smoked salmon, which as one of our culture's prestige foods carries its own kudos, rituals and in our household quite a lot of envy! The identification of Christmas with turkey and children is, however, so powerful (even for a lapsed nice Jewish girl) that last Christmas spent with Ba and her mum Elsie but, for the first time in a decade *without* any of the girls, initially felt so strange that I was actually *glad* to see the monster bird on the table. At least some of the trappings felt right!

Despite the smallness of our group none of us wanted to change the traditional fare or predictable procedure. There were the obligatory walks, the statutory pickles and red cabbage, and inevitably Elsie's Amazing Games and Creative Christmas Quiz.

(One had had one's hopes that the quiz might have vanished with the children . . .) 'No changes on that front,' Elsie said firmly. 'We've got quite sloppy enough swapping fruit salad for Christmas pud, and this year, without Catharine, we shan't have our Christmas cake. She was the only one who really liked it,' Elsie said wistfully. 'She won't get a cake like mine in the army!' I often think Elsie herself would be an asset to an army Christmas, feeding a regiment, spotting stray tinsel on uniforms, marshalling shirkers into an unflagging series of Army party games. And of course the Army, like all regulated institutions, offers as much stability and familiarity with its food rituals as Christmas does.

The Second World War affected the whole nation's eating habits, yet it brought with it new food routines, even a strange sense of stability.

Aggie, now a sixty-year-old grandmother, remembers it clearly:

'Before the war our dinner was at one, our tea at six, then cheese and biscuits before bed at ten. Mother never allowed us snacks. But once the air raids came everything changed. It was a cold or a toastie, before the big darkness, when we knew they'd be coming over. Nothing that would lie too heavy on our stomachs. Mother said you had to settle the stomach before you picked up your candles and ran to the shelter. But once we were down there, we had these forbidden snacks. I remember the bright moonlight nights and us eating rich teas and lincolns. Mother always packed sandwiches in greaseproof paper done up with a rubber band. At first everything was higgledy-piggledy, but Mother soon saw to that. She got her little routine going so we knew where we were. If the air raids had been bad and we needed comforting the sandwiches were tinned sardines, you got them on points, one tin per family, so it was special. Once we got used to our regular new snacks we stopped being frightened.'

Arnold Palmer points out that 'the sudden alterations in our hours of eating which occurred in 1940 are illuminating and exceptional'[4] because variations in nations' eating habits are very rarely as abrupt as this. But even more interesting is the fact that even though the times of meals had to change, women ensured that the contents had a new but routine quality which ensured their families felt secure in times of threat and disorder.

Much less overwhelming events than war, however, affect our eating habits too, for eating is a social activity and whenever we change our social situation, our eating habits and the meanings we attach to food also change.

Take me and the jam sandwiches for instance. Not that I wanted to tell you about them. It was writer Susie Orbach's suggestion. Susie and I were discussing food and its meanings over tea when she suddenly said: 'Tell me about the jam sandwiches.'

We were at her house and it was a very plain tea. Not a pot of jam, not a jaffa cake in sight. Newly decorated spacious white room, freshly watered plants, big comfy clean cushions, no clutter, no little bowls of salted nuts or half-eaten chocolate bars, not a bag of crisps anywhere. Susie is obviously not a nibbler. Of course not. She is the author of that record-breaking food book, *Fat Is a Feminist Issue*[5] and co-founder of London's Women's Therapy Centre which offers feminist psychotherapy and compulsive eating workshops. A woman from whom I should have expected nothing less!

Tell them about the jam sandwiches? Not likely! This was no place to embark on another richly revealing confession!

'Tell them about the jam sandwiches. Make it personal,' Susie repeated. She has a pleasing transatlantic accent but a rather persistent style.

What? Jam sandwiches? How could I waste time discussing such a trivial matter? I had expected an intellectual discussion on the meaning of food which, like the meaning of life, is open to any number of philosophical interpretations and, in the manner of philosophies and religions, carries with it if not gurus at least

53

the odd high priestess. Surely another revelation of my idiosyn-
cratic eating habits was not a worthy topic for this research.

Susie was waiting sympathetically. I decided to think about it.
I had already established that food often holds the key to the
meanings in women's lives. If this is true for other women, it
was probably true for me. In other words the descent into jam
sandwiches, which had occurred a few months before our
meeting, was more significant than I wanted to admit. I felt
uncomfortable. What I wanted was a bag of spring onion crisps.
At home I kept them by the computer. I tried to concentrate on
our discussion. I ought to be like Susie and keep them out of
sight. I daresay she hasn't had a packet since she wrote that damn
book! Susie had brought the tea in on a tray. No hearty mugs.
Delicate china cups. Delicate china tea. No biscuits. No toast.
By now I was postively aching for a spoonful of jam from one of
the nine pots (YES, NINE!) in the storecupboard at home. Of
course there were excellent reasons for having nine different pots
. . . I only purchased the Whittlesford Village honey to support
village life; any woman would have been seduced by the cunning
label on the Village Green lemon curd which said 'Made in the
heart of the English countryside to the traditional recipe'; how
could I resist Sunwheel Pear and Apple spread, patently wholesome with no additives, when the two friendly women who ran
Mistletoe Farm Wholefoods offered to deliver a crate? As for the
Sainsbury's raspberry conserve with extra jam – it was the girls'
favourite so I had to keep it for when they turned up for tea.

I have noticed that if I write freely enough sooner or later what
I had no intention of saying pops up on the paper. The possibility
of the girls turning up for tea was quite different from the
knowledge that the girls would be home for tea and I would
make it.

Had I taken to jam because I had stopped making regular
meals for a child-filled household? It sounded so pathetic,
unfeminist, irrational. Women in the West use food emotionally,
irrationally, symbolically . . .

'We control food because we cannot control our lives,' Susie was saying conversationally. (My sentiments exactly!) 'You need to ask what the jam sandwich syndrome means to you.' I am sure it was Susie who used the word syndrome first. She is a therapist. They use words like syndrome. They use it about women with food disorders. Thank goodness I am not a woman with a food disorder. Just an ordinary woman with an ordinary love of food. Well, love and hate. Well, hate and fear. Well, a sort of obsession . . . nothing serious of course . . .

'Women use food against themselves to give their lives meaning when a particularly significant meaning has gone out of their lives.' That was what Toni Laidlaw had told me. She had pointed out that on the death of a lover or a husband, women will eat more or less and often substantially differently. Sometimes they cannot bear the painful reminder of a particular food they used to share, so they give it up. My favourite widowed aunt found it difficult to have her nightly campari and soda when she got in from work, because my uncle had always poured it for her. A good friend who sat in bed on Sunday morning surrounded by the papers sharing toast and honey when her lover was alive, in the aftermath of bereavement got dressed early on Sunday mornings, read the papers downstairs and never had toast and honey again.

Had a significance gone out of my life? Yes, I supposed it had. It was hard to think about. I hoped Susie might produce jaffa cakes, or perhaps crumpets with melted butter. If there was enough butter I should not actually miss the jam. If there was jam too, I should not have to bother with meanings! I watched the clock surreptitiously. She did not leave the room. Nobody entered bearing biscuits. Some women are obviously in control around food. 'If you can't tell them about the jam and its meaning you may not be able to write the chapter,' Susie said in her helpful manner. There are some pieces of advice a writer can do without! But I gave in. I'm even prepared to admit it wasn't Susie who first used the word 'syndrome'. Sociologists use jargon too! Syndrome, says the dictionary, is any combination of signs or symptoms indicative of a particular disease, disorder, or condition. Syndromes are rife with meanings. So although there were nine different jams, there was only one meaning. The meaning of loss and loneliness.

When I went to interview Susie, I had been conducting a difficult domestic and literary experiment. I had decided to live on my own for a time in a small village, sharing a work-space and a computer called Ethel with my writer friend Wendy and faced with a growing pile of books to write. The girls had grown up, three had left home. Bec now lived with a big dog and a big husband, Cas was abroad in the army, Marm was acting and 'resting' in London; and even though young Vic was only a few miles away, studying A levels at the local technical college, for the first time in years I saw her only intermittently.

It is well established, that because eating is a convivial activity and most people prefer to eat in company, many who live alone, (especially if they are elderly) tend to skip meals, refrain from cooking or substitute boiled eggs, or toast and tea for 'real' meals. It also depends on what people who live alone choose to eat, as to how we respond. Because we invest an eating situation with emotions, we are more likely to feel saddened at the thought of an elderly widow dipping her toast into her tea, than we would if she was tucking into avocado, salmon pâté and roast venison, gulping it back with champagne.

With no cats to feed, no girls to cook for, no compulsory supermarket shopping, I felt adrift. My life was full but it was not filled with cooking. The solid fuel central heating system, run on an ancient eccentric fire, was considerably more trouble than children. Keeping it fed meant walks through woods in search of kindling, sawing logs, heaving buckets of coal, all before I could get to the computer; a major commitment. I should not have wanted anyone to think I was having an easy life! But more and more I found my memories of the girls surfacing, my attention straying away from my writing, to food; my hands reaching into the fridge. I gave up cooking and I took up jam sandwiches. Jam for breakfast, jam for lunch, jam for supper. With an occasional jacket potato. Each day I would obsessively add to the growing number of pots in my cupboard. The future seemed reduced to jam tomorrow.

Of course, I told myself, I was lucky to live alone; the idle dream of many a harassed housewife. Of course I was in perfect control of my life. I was a professional writer. Words had become my daily bread. Food was just an adjunct 'Make crisp Ryvita your daily bread. Only 26 calories,' said the label. Ryvita, said the packet, is the basis of a healthy diet. Wholemeal of course. It sounded safe. But why did I snatch three, and spread them thickly with Extra jam, before starting a new chapter? A writer on food in charge of her life does not eat jammy Ryvita. A mature woman in charge of her life does not eat any Ryvita, not at two-thirty in the afternoon after a jam-sandwich lunch. The Sainsbury's Extra jam reminded me constantly of the girls. But I no longer lived with the girls, or the cats, or the hamster. I did not have to help bury the rabbit or go to the supermarket. I was extremely fortunate. I had only to shop for myself. So how come that one day, the week before I visited Susie Orbach, I found myself cutting a few country corners and purchasing ready-sawn firewood from the shop on the way to Sainsbury's in the city?

Once inside the familiar store I did manage to miss out on the catfood and baked beans; but immersed in the past, I pulled down cans and packets from the accustomed shelves. The trolley was laden. I began to feel more secure. I started to rationalize my purchases. I did after all live in the country. It would be snowing soon. I might get cut off. Best keep the cupboard piled high. I reached the cash till. It came to £68. The amount we used to spend on a household of six. I was in debt before I entered the store. What was the matter with me? I drove home feeling disturbed.

In my head I was writing; tracking down a theory, trying out an argument. Reaching for the crisps, still there on the dashboard. I was established with a workplace. I'd bought a carload of food. I was unsettled on my own. For the first time in twenty-five years I was not a domestic creature. Could I be a Proper Woman if I did not cook Proper Meals? Could I find myself if there was no one else around me? No special adult to care about my sentences, my salads, and my soul? To share the fun of making love, or wallpapering the bathroom. To mow the lawn or fix the hanging baskets while I typed a peaceful piece of prose. To divide the chore of cooking and turn it into pleasure. That special adult who cooked the winter stews; who said how wonderful my quiche was when it took two hours to prepare. I drove on, looking at the pile of food, tracing through the meanings. I'd finished the crisps.

At home, slowly, I put away the food. There was a tube of Smarties I did not remember having picked up. A jar of Marmite I had vowed to keep off. It was far too salty. Marmoset's childhood favourite sweets were Smarties. Vic's teatime special treat was toast and Marmite. What has the line 'Red smarties only Mum,' to do with ecstasy? What have Marmite sandwiches to do with anguish?

My jam-sandwich discovery had been painful but illuminating. The idea that eating should be a shared activity has the strength of compulsion. When women no longer share their regular meals, both their food purchasing habits and their eating routine are thrown into disarray. Certain foods from the shared life become a haunting reminder of the past. A very common phenomenon amongst women whose situation has been transformed by death, desertion, or a move away from the family home, is to continue to buy food for those who no longer live with them. Just as I did.

Peggy, a widow I met in Scarborough, whose children Kenny and Margaret had left home, had a typical story:

'Our Kenny got that farm and that wife the same year Tommy died, and our Margaret upped and left home the next autumn. So I'd been cooking for us all four, then I suddenly dropped to two, then to one and I didn't want to believe it. Quantity was my trouble. I went on buying a big joint instead of going down to chops. Sometimes the butcher would say did I want a smaller cut, and I'd wonder why.

'I went on buying all the wrong things that our Kenny and our Margaret used to have special like. The worst was OGGIE, that were Kenny's favourite. It's like black pudding except it's white and he liked it fried, our Kenny did. Well, I went on buying it for months. I didn't like it myself so it was a terrible waste.

'Some days, I'd go into the sweet shop, to perk myself up. I'd be tempted to buy this huge piece of white chocolate, because our Margaret liked that. She said it tasted like condensed milk so she wouldn't touch the brown. I humoured her but personally, I can't think of white chocolate as real food. If a food is white it doesn't mean anything to me. I'd bring home this white chocolate and I'd think, what have I done that for, she's no longer here. Then I'd think my Tommy will have a good laugh at me for that. Then I'd think, he's no longer here, my Tommy isn't here, and I'd want to cry. I'd eat it then. There didn't seem much else to do. I'd sit and eat all Margaret's funny white chocolate. They were hard times. They made me feel worse about white foods.'

What many women miss is the other person's appreciation. Eater approbation is such an important element for women that sufficient approval may often make up for lack of participation in the cooking chores.

These comments from Eileen, a retired botanist recently widowed, were characteristic: 'People should eat together, it provides a basis for getting friendly. Eating with someone else is natural. I don't enjoy eating alone, I have to force myself to eat, but if someone is there to appreciate it I don't mind how much cooking I have to do.'

I asked Eileen if her husband had cooked. 'He was *able* to cook,' she said. 'If it was an emergency he could do a lovely bacon and egg, and I've known him twice cook a Welsh rarebit, but of course I didn't often ask him to do it. He was always so busy. Yes I know I had a job too, but that didn't matter because he was appreciative every time. At every meal he'd say, "Thank you darling, that was very nice." Of course if there was something he didn't like . . . Eileen paused for a long time, then went on resolutely: 'Well, there were things he didn't like, and he didn't praise me then, far from it. Like when I cooked the porridge too thick, so he wouldn't touch it. In the end I never cooked anything he didn't like, and he was always appreciative.'

For Eileen meals were bound up with conversation and leisurely evenings. 'I miss talking to him over our evening meal, that's what the meal was, a place to talk and let the evening slowly draw in. We used to talk the most over cauliflower cheese. But I don't make that now. There's no point. The only time I prepare food is for my ecumenical meetings which we hold here. I enjoy cooking little things for my friends who come regularly.' She sighed wistfully, 'But I wouldn't do a cauliflower cheese like I would for my husband.'

Another curious change which results from widowhood or desertion by a male partner, is the licence to get fat.

Fifty-year-old Jessie, known as Jelly Bean, wobbled with laughter as she told me: 'Widowhood has really changed my eating habits. One consolation has been my glorious Mars Bar days! I never could have had them when Willy Bean was alive. It's not a joke, Sal. Nowadays I buy eight to ten Mars Bars every week, then if I wake up one morning with the Craving, and feel that I don't want anything but Mars Bars all day long, that's exactly what I have, with tea loaded with sugar. When Willy was here, bless him, I'd be worrying about him not liking me fat. He never said he minded but I knew. It was in my head, and it was in those magazines: *Woman*, *Woman's Weekly*, *Woman's World*, I had them all for years. They all put the point over about not getting too heavy. As for Willie, not a word did he say but I could see his twinkling eyes on my little tum.' She patted the tum affectionately. 'Chocolate's always been my downfall. When Willie was alive I would slip away somewhere secret, slice up a Mars Bar and pop piece after piece in my mouth. Nobody knew. But from when he died I didn't worry about those things. I do what I want. Now that I'm on my own I can eat all the naughties without feeling guilty. I'm a size 18 but free as a bird on my Mars Bar days!'

Desertion can have the same effect. Listen to Joanne, an Essex accounts clerk: 'When John was living with me, I had to remember the whole time that the way to a man's heart is through *his* stomach *not* through yours! When we were eating, John's eyes were always on my tum and my tits. If he thought I was packing it away he told me. Every time I cooked a big meal and he thought I might pick, he made up a little tune he got me to sing over and over: "Tum and Tits, Tum and Tits, remember them and don't eat the bits!"' Then one night after chicken suprème and sauté potatoes he just walked out and never came back! Of course I was shocked and didn't eat properly for a week but now I'm back to packing it in and I never have to sing that hateful verse again!'

Men control our bodies and our lives with the power of stigma and approval and we try in turn to control our bodies with our food intake. But when the critical male gaze is removed the food patterns may change.

That food provides a context for relationships is seen also in the changes in eating habits that take place when, for example, a hitherto faithful wife has a secret adulterous affair.

Robin, a thirty-five-year-old secretary from Essex told me: 'Obviously, with Dick, my husband, we'd be seen at the pubs and wine bars our friends frequented. Eating out was pleasant but routine. When I started the affair with Tony, who was married to a girl in Dick's office, food assumed a great significance in our lives. It was almost more of a thrill than the sex!

'We'd phone each other at the beginning of the week, pick a restaurant about twenty miles away, then drive separately to the rendezvous, parking in different streets about quarter of a mile from what we called base food camp. I'd get there first, and order avocado with prawns – always the same starter. I used to dip my fingers in the garlic dressing, and pour it slowly over the prawns, thinking about him, and imagining what we'd do. Then I'd rub the dressing over the avocado and wait for the phone call. He phoned the restaurant after he'd parked his car to make sure no one had spotted us. If I said it was all clear, he'd arrive just as the waiter brought the second avocado. Sometimes he would feed me small pieces from his spoon. It was all so intense and special. Eating had become something private between us.'

A similar view in a comparable situation, but where the woman was not married, was expressed by Philippa. 'When I first got involved with a senior admin. man meals had to become secretive, clandestine. When I took up with him, his wife was in another town. I've never had any of those messy on-the-doorstep situations. The men were already estranged from their wives. Our meals had to be private but they weren't messy. It matters to me that things aren't messy.

'In the past food had not played a noticeable part in my life. But eating was the focus of our affair. We always ate in, we were never seen in public places, the food was covert, the time private. Every meal was special because it couldn't be shared with anyone but him. Even cooking a simple steak and grinding real coffee became a romantic act.'

Less documented is the effect of a change in sexual orientation either from heterosexual to lesbian or the reverse. The key words women used to describe these situations were clandestine and mysterious. The emotional intensity attached to eating had a heightened charge.

Gillian, a senior civil servant, who after seven years as the live-out lover of a well-known politician suddenly, at the age of thirty, began a relationship with a woman in her own department, describes how it altered her eating habits: 'When I was with Frank, we ate out a great deal, and I entertained lavishly for him. It was part of my public role as his official woman friend. Meals with Frank were routine, public, before or after the pub, part of an everyday steady relationship that people approved of. Then suddenly I had my first homosexual relationship with somebody who couldn't bear to be known about, so I went underground. There was no way we could eat out together. My social life completely changed. So did my feelings about food. I stopped entertaining. She cooked for me and I cooked for her, quietly, with great love. Cooking for her and with her was real joy, a mark of affection. I had never found that before. Sitting quietly over an ordinary stew and a bottle of wine and candlelight in the kitchen was the pattern of three or four nights a week. It was an end-of-the-day pleasure to come home to. Those meals certainly weren't routine like the ones with Frank. I remember the foods I ate with Edith because of the intensity of feeling.

'I think the mystery comes because in a first homosexual relationship you have to go to ground; eating becomes a positive thing you do together, rather than a passing way of doing other things. That relationship only lasted six months but it changed the pattern of my ordinary eating. It gave me, with those meals, an intensity of feeling I have never experienced again.'

Although heterosexuality, in this society, is an approved, indeed increasingly mandatory, lifestyle, when a lesbian woman changes to a heterosexual relationship, heterosexuality in her group is also taboo, so she too feels the need for secrecy.

Linda had been involved in women-only sexual relationships since the age of seventeen when she left school and got a flat and a job as a printer's assistant, and began to take an active part in the city's gay scene, often eating in restaurants and bars with her women lovers. At twenty-three she had come out to everyone at work, but not to her parents who were pressuring her about marriage.

'Mum and Dad often saw me eating with my women, but never thought anything of it. They never realized how much eating together is part of your sexual relationship. But Bristol is a small place; word was getting around and I didn't want someone else to tell 'em I was a dyke. Ten to one they'd tell 'em all wrong, and Mum would have a collapse and Dad would throw a wobbly. I knew how important I was to them, and I reckoned I'd got to be bloody sure I was a dyke for life, and would eventually settle down with a woman and have a proper family and cooked meals and everything, before I told 'em. So I decided to have one more bash, the first in six years, with a bloke. I started going out with this orl right fella, which pleased Mum and Dad, but I couldn't be seen out with him where my mates went. I'd have lost all of my street cred! So I had to go underground. For the first time in years, I ate in. We had quiet evening meals at my flat, with lots of wine. I must say the secrecy gave it a thrill. Meals seemed different. I even started cooking, all these genuine fancy foods. There I was, a well-known dyke, cooking for this man. He was nice enough, took his turn washing up, made a reasonable chicken curry, but it didn't feel right. I was always wondering if he really approved of my dinners. Me? Who didn't care a sod what other people thought! I was buying all these carrots and fresh sprouts and making gravy, ready for our Sunday meal, just like Mum did. Well I had to stop that. So we started going out to eat, and sharing the bills, but even then we didn't eat in the city centre, it was always some remote pub. It didn't last more than three months, but it did have quite a special feel, because of the secrecy I suppose.'

For so many women, from Eileen and the cauliflower cheese to Linda making gravy for her temporary male lover, eater approbation is all important. For women in traditional domestic situations this means that men and children have to approve of the food.

Gina, who has three children under five and whose husband is a shift worker who keeps unsocial hours, summed it up: 'I've been pulling the dinner in and out of the oven making sure it will still look good for him, while the kids are driving me mad, and I've laid the table all nice. Then if he says, "What's that lovely smell?" when he gets in, it don't matter how late he is, I know I'm on the right track, and I don't mind that I've been all hot and sweaty in the kitchen for three hours with the kids screaming under my feet.' As in Eileen's case, male appreciation is often sufficient substitute for very little male support.

In lesbian feminist households where two or more women operate a consistent policy of shared cooking, shopping and preparation, eater approbation usually works as a mutual system of approval and praise. Interestingly, where two women live together but only one does the cooking, the approval and praise of the woman who had *not* cooked is just as avidly sought as when a woman lives with a man. If one woman is the wage earner, even if only temporarily, this too can affect the cook's need for approval.

Jilly, who is a painter and works in a studio behind the house she shares with Bunty, a schoolteacher, explained how it works for them: 'At present Bunty teaches, and earns a lot more than I can, so as I'm on the spot I cook weekdays for us, and I give the two children tea when they arrive home from school. What is curious is that though I am a good fast cook, I am so concerned about their approval, that I often spend far longer than my work can afford in the kitchen, knocking up treats for the kids, and making sure our meal is garnished properly and smells beautifully.'

She laughed as she added, 'I've really bought into the notion that she who goes out to work, needs to be greeted with a properly cooked dinner! Never mind, next year Bunty's on sabbatical. She intends to do the cooking and I can play at being an executive artist with a briefcase and paintbrush and rush in from the studio ready to give my verdict on the night's meal!'

That lesbians are far from immune to the hankering after male approval is shown by Linda's story and my own, very funny experience. Many years after I had split up from my second husband, and was living with Ba and the girls, Larry came to our house to rescue some of his music manuscripts which were still in my possession, lurking under rubble in the garden shed.

Although he and I had not lived together for a very long time, and rarely ate together, I spent that morning before his arrival in an agony of conflict between my badly suppressed and desperate desire to bake his favourite walnut cake and run up a spectacular lunch, and my ardent political determination not to boost his ego in such a stereotypical manner!

After an amiable couple of hours rooting through the past in the shed, drinking coffee which I resolutely served without walnut cake or any other, it grew nearer and nearer lunchtime, then well past it. We both became edgy with hunger and fatigue. 'I'm a little hungry, honey,' he said gently. I stifled my own hunger pangs and ignored the remark. After another hour he said mildly: 'Are you getting hungry, honey?'

'No,' I lied severely. 'I'm rarely hungry at this hour.'

A short time later we found ourselves wandering hopelessly into the kitchen. He looked around desperately. 'I'm pretty hungry myself,' he said, still politely.

By now I was very hungry but still ludicrously determined to act towards my ex-husband in a way I certainly shouldn't have acted towards the merest passing stranger. Finally I burst out: 'There's *no* lunch and I'm *not* cooking!'

He looked faintly surprised. The years had patently changed me. Then he said agreeably: 'Well, let me take you out to a Chinese.'

I thought of refusing – but you can't win them all, and I do think it important to redistribute patriarchal wealth whenever possible! It was a delightful lunch. It is not, however, insignificant that my amusing memories of that particular meal have attached a positive and humorous meaning to several Chinese dishes, in much the same way that Eileen's memories linked cauliflower cheese with loss, and Robin's memories added eroticism to avocado prawns in garlic sauce.

Memory and emotions colour our views on food. Male approval or fear of fat control our patterns of intake and choice of menu. Each society marks its own group or class with particular food rituals, but regularity and routine are cross-cultural constants. Any disruption of food routines is disturbing, radical changes in an individual's life mean changes in eating. And in this society it is women we see as maintaining stability and offering us a sense of security through the meals they make. Food as I have discovered is considerably more than fuel, for women even more than for men.

THREE
COMPULSORY CATERERS, DISCRETIONARY COOKS

In Britain, in the late eighties, the women's movement has reached maturity. There is the rhetoric of equality in the air. Dutiful diatribes deny discrimination. Lip service is paid to equal rights, as politicians begin to erode them. I expected the world to be different from the world of the sixties, when, as a successful paid worker, my place was still in the kitchen. I wanted the world to be different. I have written and taught and worked for the world to be different for fifteen years. But the data I have uncovered on cooking and catering suggests that the social world we inhabit is not fundamentally different. I had hoped that women's role at home had undergone profound alterations but I have discovered that although there are changes, they are only cosmetic.

The issue is still that women should be in the kitchen, preparing the family meal; that women's proper role is to service men, directly with the food we prepare, indirectly through the food we manage. According to the women I have interviewed this remains true even when men do some of the cooking, and even when women go out to paid employment.

Although there has been a small shift (in certain households where the discourse is on egalitarianism) towards women and men sharing the practicalities of cooking or shopping, the underlying obligation about meal provision is the woman's.

In many marriages (or heterosexual live-in-lover structures) cooking is seen as part of the emotional, not merely the practical, fabric of the 'marriage'. For many women, cooking is bound up with nurturing and caring in a way that cleaning and ironing – seen simply as chores with no emotional overtones – are not. A characteristic story comes from forty-two-year-old Denise, who looks back on her first marraige whose pattern echoed that of her childhood.

'Because my father was in adult education he was often home in the day, away at night and could share chores like shopping. He was a good cook. He once won a prize for making rock cakes. But it wasn't his responsibility. Even though there was some equality between my parents, I still learnt from my mother about what men should do and what women should do, about the rights and duties within marriage, how you compromise, you give up things. You make whoever you live with comfortable, particularly with food. So when I married Gerald, a much older man with a prestigious job in an art gallery, although it was a revelation to me that he couldn't cook at all, I just got on with doing all the cooking. I was expected to give three dinner parties a week. Elizabeth David's *French Provincial Cooking* was my absolute standby. I also did all the cleaning because that wasn't what men did. Gerald was very kind, very gentle, but rather inflexible. He saw marriage as a series of rights and duties. Before we were married he paid a women to do his washing and he could have afforded to have someone clean, or even cook, but I was expected to do all that, despite the fact that I was an architect with a full-time job. Gerald's washing was really phenomenal. Two clean shirts and two lots of cotton underwear a day, vests and knickers, that's fourteen lots a week. Having done all that, I must say I did expect Gerald to turn a hand to cooking when things got difficult, but the fact that he didn't did not become an issue because in the first flush of marriage you do all those things, it is part of what you do when you are married, it is playing house. I can remember being more irked by the cleaning than by the cooking. The cooking was irksome but it seemed right. So did the planning. I accepted it as part of the rights and duties of marriage.'

What wives are expected to do differs substantially from what girlfriends are permitted. This is Dale Spender's experience: 'I hate cooking and refuse to do it. Before we were married my ex-husband would come round to my flat, and he'd say, "What's for supper?" and I'd look at the fruit bowl and say, "Oranges, apples, bananas, chocolate biscuits, what do you want?" He would laugh, think I was sweet and unconventional, and say tolerantly, "Let's have a chocolate biscuit, then we'll go out to eat." Then we got married. The very next day, he came back from work and said, "What's for supper?" I looked at the fruit bowl and said, "Oranges, apples, bananas, chocolate biscuits, what do you want?" and he called me a bitch. Obviously wives as distinct from girlfriends are supposed to provide proper meals and I wasn't doing my job properly.'

Molly, a round bouncy woman in her fifties whom I met in Cornwall, found cooking for her family deeply satisfying. She tucked into a hearty slice of lemon meringue pie and effervescently described her early influences:

'I tell you, Sal, give me trifle or queen's pud and I'm in heaven. Puddings are my beloveds. Father was most particular about Mother feeding us proper puddings but girls had to be careful. It wasn't until I lost Maurice and became a widow that I felt free to eat them. Before that I did everything properly just as Mother did. I learnt from Mother that was the way to make a family happy. Mother always cooked, that was her pleasure. She was in charge of all the budgeting, all the planning, that was her worry. Only father had the right to complain but fortunately Mother was a wonderful cook. Liver was her best. All our village heard tales of Mother's liver. Father was proud of her.'

Father dominated the family with his stringent beliefs about homecraft and the appropriate role of wives and mothers. He was not a man his family challenged. 'A very forceful person, Father was,' Molly said, still sounding a bit in awe of him. 'A Royal Artillery man. You don't argue with them. Father said a good table was the most particular thing and it was Mother's job to plan for it. If we were short of money she had to plan to keep us in good food. Planning wasn't for Father. Of course he didn't cook at all. There was never a question of Father doing anything.

When Mother died he was absolutely beaten. I had two elder brothers in the navy, but they didn't cook. I was the only girl, so at the age of ten, when Mother died, I had to carry on.

'Right from a little child when I stood on a wooden stool by the sink because I wasn't big enough, I had been Mother's little helper. It was always me.' Molly's voice was enormously proud, and her eyes filled slowly with tears.

'Father and the boys had never helped Mother and I didn't expect them to help me. I expected to take Mother's place and I did. I've always been a rebel, and for a girl I defied Father a lot, but I never rebelled about what's right in a marriage, or what's proper in a family.'

When Molly left home she worked full-time as a nurse, but when she married Maurice she did not allow her job to interfere with her notions of a proper woman. 'Maurice was modern, not like Father, and he would help me wash up in a friendly way, but of course I didn't expect him to cook. That wasn't the way. I never asked my children to cook or wash up, not even the girl. I did it the way Mother did and we've led very happy lives.'

To what extent are cooking and planning shared in what Molly calls a 'modern' marriage? Do men participate equally? What happens in the kitchen when men cook?

American mystery writer Joy Magezis assured me: 'Today sharing the cooking and the planning is symbolic of the kind of relationship a couple are in. In America there's a new category of couples in which men and women out of political or social consciousness set up a relationship in which every domestic chore from cooking to cleaning to child care is shared fifty-fifty.'

I was delighted to hear it. Certainly Joy and her writer husband, Bob, have established a firm relationship on those lines for their household with two teenage children. They even have a rota to implement it. Computer time, childcare time, cooking time, and more significantly planning time are all worked out for the week and divided up in equal shares. 'I've lived with Bob since 1968 and for twenty years I've ensured he has done fifty per cent of all chores,' said Joy. She thought his leftist background was partly responsible for his willing participation. 'His parents were in the Communist party, and his mother had feminist ideas. She had two boys and she damn well wasn't going to be a slave to them. So she taught them to cook and even better she made them wash the floors. I'm a terrible cook, the kind that throws condensed soup over tinned pasta, so Bob probably cooks to keep sane. But he makes wonderful meals and nurtures me with his real spaghetti. It means I'm happy to take my turn.'

Many women would be happy to take their turn in that situation, but unfortunately Joy's delightful experience turned out to be rare.

Cheryl Lean's artist husband Graham Metson, another expert cook, did more than half the cooking and planned for the meals he made. Like Bob he cooked for pleasure and from a desire to show affection. 'Graham nurtures me and shows off to all my friends with his brilliant meals and I really appreciate it, because I'm a lousy cook,' Cheryl told me. 'But he often makes a mess in the kitchen and he doesn't see himself as in charge of overall planning and budgeting.'

Many women knew men who made special meals, or show-off meals, and several women with paid jobs had partners who did a dutiful amount of discretionary cooking. Very few men, however, cooked every day as a matter of routine. Most women had to tidy up the mess.

Cooking is often the unpaid family task which men most readily take on for its creative aspects and because they receive praise.

These were typical comments from the women I talked to:

'Mum tends to do the everyday cooking and hates it. Dad does special meals and enjoys it, but he makes a fuss about it and we all pay attention, it's not a routine thing.'

'My boyfriend often cooks, especially if friends are coming for supper. The food is smashing but I have to clear up after him.'

'I've always had nurturing men around. They've all liked cooking for me but most of them never cleaned up as they went

. They produced some splendid meals and I felt very cared
~ven if I did have to tidy up later.'

'My father sold processed food, so food was his line of country.
He liked cooking, never looked down on it, so that gave me a
positive role model. But he only cooked when he wanted to, like
Sunday breakfast. When he took over the kitchen, he never did
the washing up and everything had to be just right. He would go
up the wall if he didn't have the right ingredients or if the pans
weren't where they should be. That was all my mother's job.'

'My father hadn't a clue about cooking. Mother did it all. Just
occasionally he washed up. As we got older there was more in
the papers about men helping so he washed up a bit more.'

'My first husband wasn't averse to learning to cook, but he
wanted to do the really complex things. For some reason he
thought making sauce español was the mark of a good cook. This
bloody sauce took about three days, you have to get the bones
and boil them down. Then finally a brown gravy-like substance
ensued. The mess was unbelievable. And I had to clear it up!'

'Adam never cooks for me, even though he could, he just
makes out he can't. He is completely hopeless. He is too
pampered for words. I asked him to make the Ready-brek this
morning and you should have seen the panic. He went "Ah Aah
whaat?"'

'All the men I've been involved with have done the chef's bit
and insisted on a female assistant. That was me for years! When
my husband deigned to do a curry I spent the entire bloody
Saturday in the kitchen chopping and preparing and the entire
bloody Sunday clearing up. He spent one hour stirring, tasting
and prima donna-ing and everybody said not only "Oh what a
wonderful meal" but they actually turned round to me and said
"Gee you're lucky to have a husband that cooks."'

Cooking, it seems, is still at men's discretion. What about
catering, planning and overall responsibility for food?

Because responsibility for food tasks is still seen as part of a woman's proper role, many women trying to perform fulfilling professional work find they are putting their jobs second.

Listen to Imogen, wife of sales executive Max, and housing manager for a large inner-city housing co-operative: 'I love my housing job. I'm good at it. I know I could reach a higher grade if I put all the "anxiety-hours" into it that I still earmark for domestic chores. When I wake up, the first thing I think about is food. Not with pleasure but with a shuddery feeling – a kind of nervousness mixed with irritation. What had I planned to give them today? Will I have enough time before I leave for work? Do I need to shop in the lunch hour? I lie fretting, I make shopping lists in my head, before I get up and scramble through the breakfast, so that Max can take the twins to school.'

Imogen's late nights in bed are a replica of her early mornings. Max worries about his work, Imogen frets about their food. 'Max lies there reading his reports for tomorrow's sales schedule. I ought to be planning the agenda for a crucial housing meeting, but I am planning supper for tomorrow because I am bound to be late and though Max will willingly cook, he won't sort it out. That is my job. He is keen on equality which is a big relief. We do equal shares over the cooking but I have all the responsibility. That is what I fret most about. That and making sure they have *hot* meals. Max doesn't feel the family has been fed properly if it's cold flan, even homemade. It's true, on Fridays when I have a co-op meeting I degenerate into sandwiches and salad but to make up for it I slice the tomato and grate the cheese and carrot before I leave for work. That way Max just has to assemble it.'

Imogen is not resentful about her double burden. She accepts it as a legitimate part of the proper role of wife and mother even if the 'anxiety hours' could be more usefully spent. Imogen is grateful that Max is 'keen on equality, which is a big relief.' Max's keenness, however, does not extend to shouldering the underlying accountability.

Esme is a ex-teacher with two young children, married to Hugh, an energetic town planner who, like Imogen's Max, has encouraged his wife to take advantage of equal opportunities and, assuring her of his co-operation in the home, has made it possible for her to return to full-time studying.

'He does help, yes he does,' Esme told me. 'But he doesn't plan. Planning is the most anxious-making business. Some days I enjoy the responsibility but at other times, if I've got an essay to hand in, it is the last thing I want. But that has never been Hugh's task. Part of his job is to cook quite often as he's better than I am. He takes infinite care and spends longer than I do and doesn't mind if we all wait. Even when I cook most of the meal our guests praise the bit he did. But traditionally the final responsibility for planning is mine.'

Esme had found this responsibility easier before she became a student, when she was a full-time teacher. 'I used to come home earlier than Hugh, so it seemed more reasonable as I had more time.'

When pressed she admitted, 'It's true I have done it when I haven't had more time, or even any time. Other women have talked to me about re-allocating our chores and our roles, but our finances are set up for me to do all the shopping and organizing. Actually I'd be very loath to say to Hugh "I want you to do it" because he would find that too burdensome. I think he would feel I had failed. I couldn't say, "I want you to do it because I can't manage," because I've been doing it all these years, so obviously I can. If I said, "It isn't fair for me to do it all," then he'd say, "Now look here, I haven't got the time. I don't stop for lunch. When could I possibly do it? I don't leave the office till seven." Hugh might be angry underneath but he would make it sound so reasonable. We have always tried to run our marriage in a reasonable way, compromising where necessary.' Most of the compromises have been Esme's. Like most women I talked to, Esme believed that women must accommodate more within a marital or cohabitation structure; and accepted that a large part of negotiations will be over food.

'I think in any relationship you make accommodations. To do it over food the way we have is traditional. I definitely see it as something that is my role even though I have another role now as a student. I've taken on a kind of picture of what a proper woman does. So even if Hugh cooks midweek, he cooks the food I have bought.'

I asked what would happen if she tried to make major changes over food provision. 'Oh goodness,' she said in alarm, 'if I were to try and change our shopping habits and thinking habits over food that could really be a source of great dissension. Perhaps it's because I realize this that I've always shied away from it. If I did work myself up to say something about change, Hugh would say, "Some things are all my responsibility, some are all yours. You do nothing about the car." That would sound all right but I don't know how reasonable an argument that is, after all the car doesn't need daily thinking about, the car doesn't adversely affect his work the way food does mine!'

Despite apprehensions about her imminent exams, Esme was unable to contemplate what she saw as disastrous consequences which would follow any changes to the food habits that structure their marriage.

There are good reasons why women like Imogen and Esme should spend less 'anxiety hours' on compulsory catering and more on studies, training and job skills. Women in the eighties who shoulder professional roles outside the home (as well as unpaid ones within it) still receive less power, prestige, status and control than do men who work in absolutely comparable jobs.

Women, I am sure, will not be surprised to learn that in 1987 in Britain, womens' earnings were 66% of mens' earnings and of people who earned £500 or more per week, only 6% were women. Despite legal changes in Britain on grounds of sex discrimination the situation still exists that while women compose almost half the country's workforce, they make up only 10% of its general managers, 8% of its chartered accountants, 7% of its senior civil servants, 3% of its judges, and 2% of its surgeons. There are infinitely fewer women than men who succeed as scientists, editors, politicians, conductors, financiers, philosophers, train drivers or even chefs.

Ironically however it is women on the lower rungs in all these public occupations who still do most of the work inside the home. And most of that work has to do with food.

Today in the almost 90% of British households where the woman does the washing and ironing, or in the 75% where she does the cleaning, it is established that in 70% she also makes the supper and in almost every household in which there are male and female adults it is the women who are in overall charge of organizing the food.[1]

In the USA too, where 70% of married women who have full-time jobs outside the home, and who for the first time in the twentieth century provide a large part of the domestic financial support, it is the women who suffer a similar inequality over catering and cooking.[2]

Several recent studies confirm that the well-documented in-equalities women fall victim to at work are sadly paralleled by the domestic injustices they meet when they return home.

Dr Janet Reibstein, a psychotherapist and researcher at Cambridge University, found that couples who both had professions, managed a balanced relationship in the home and kitchen until the birth of their first child. She said that the couples 'coast along happily with the idea of equality until a child comes along and throws it up in their faces. They then become much more traditional, with the woman cutting corners in her career, and much less sharing of the cooking and shopping and housework.'[3]

Sometimes there is so little sharing that the woman gives up her career in despair. Frankie's story is characteristic. Frankie came from a traditional farming family where she learnt from both parents that the kitchen is the focus of family life and the wife is the major source of food provision. 'Because Mother went out into the farm and Father was always coming into the house there were no clear boundaries. He was always nipping in blue with cold saying, "Can you make some coffee, these people have arrived with sacks", or "Please rustle up some food, the sheep have got out and when we've rounded them up all the men will want feeding." Mother and her stove were always on call. She was always available. Father actually assumed her labour was his to use. The good side was that she and her food were valued, and her provision was crucial to the running of the farm. But the responsibilities were utterly one-sided.'

This inequality affected Frankie's marriage to Richard. 'I was left feeling I must provide for my man and for our children singlehanded. As long as we were both working there weren't many problems. But two pregnancies made me vulnerable and though Richard helped me before the first baby, he never helped afterwards. I had to shoulder all the chores as well as my job. For years every row started with food and the unfairness of our roles. I'd always had a powerful sense of injustice since I was a child but it seemed there was nothing I could do. Finally I gave up my job, and just did it all. It meant I was even more dependent on Richard for approval of my cooking and catering because that's who I was. Every time the thought of going back to work crossed my mind, I found myself spending another week, another month, another year spooning food into babies' mouths, then cooking teas for small children, then shouting at teenage girls to help me.'

Sheila Kitzinger, a leading British authority on childbirth and breastfeeding, understood from her own personal experience Frankie's conflict and the difficulties in resolving it. 'Since my marriage, I must have cooked 11,648 meals, and that does not include snacks and toddlers' treats, for my husband and five daughters to consume. I never felt I had a choice.

'I'm glad I don't have to make three meals a day any more. It is not just the cooking but the whole business of preparing food, clearing away, washing pans, planning ahead, making lists, checking what's in the fridge and the cupboards and the freezer, the trek through the supermarket and the limbo of waiting to get through check-out and then heaving the stuff into the boot of the car and heaving it out again. A repetitive, exhausting kind of servitude, in which women are trapped day in day out, because that's what mothers are supposed to do.'

A social anthropologist herself, Sheila Kitzinger pointed out:

'In traditional cultures women did not question this role, but they were not alone with such tasks. They did them in the company of other women. In the Carribean, I've seen women enjoying tedious things like shelling nuts or coffee beans, or stirring food in a big pot over the fire, while they talk, exchange news and laugh together, shooing away the chickens, nursing the babies, and sharing out the chores. Compared to that most women in the West are isolated from each other, each on her own treadmill.'[4]

Frankie decided to step off her treadmill, and save her sanity, by forcing changes through her household. 'I'd had it, I really had. Proper roles or not, I had to teach Richard to cook. Oh the rows. Oh the awful weariness. But eventually he did just about learn and took on some of the cooking though at first he made the most almighty mess. It was his way of manipulating me. Finally when he realized I wouldn't abide by tradition and I no longer cared whether he approved of me, he grudgingly began to pull his weight.'

The biggest shock came when Frankie discovered the same tiring pattern was occurring with her children. 'I had to go through the same fights with them as I had with him. Fights over cooking, shopping, mess. My own kids! I could hardly believe it. Fights over food, that is what being a mother was to me. Battles over planning, that is what marriage was about. I still remember the sense of bloody despair when I woke up each day. I put on weight eating cream buns, which I knew I shouldn't have, to console myself, and because I was angry. There is no doubt in my mind that having children helped imprison me in the role of cook and provider.'

Frankie's predicament illustrated the conflict contained within women's 'proper role'; they must provide nourishment for their families whilst being expected to refrain from indulging themselves.

Susie Orbach enlarged on this dilemma: 'There are deep political implications in the need that has been imposed on women to feed others. What we can see over the last forty years is this centrality of women feeding others, and feeling that they themselves are not allowed to eat. There is this complex relationship: food for others is nourishing, good, full of love, whereas for themselves it is dangerous, something they should not be having, something they fear.'

When women break this self-denial, or abnegate accountability for food provision, they are seen as not fulfilling their proper roles.

Frankie's perception that pregnancy, vulnerability, the need to be a good mother and the desire for male and child approval (all paralleled in Esme and Imogen's stories) had served to increase the inequality in the household, was matched by dozens of other accounts.

In every case, no matter how little practical help the men gave their women, they expected consistent, untiring emotional support. Shere Hite, in her new study *Women and Love* reports that of her sample of 4,500 women, the overwhelming majority said that men were unsupportive in the home while simultaneously demanding women's emotional backing. One woman who performed 85% of the childcare and 100% of the catering and housework, told Hite: 'The few times I've gone to a meeting at night and left my son with my husband, I'd come home to find my husband asleep on the couch in front of the TV. He was supposed to remind our son to make his sandwich for school the next day. So I always come home before the boy's bedtime. If the sandwich hasn't been made and I ask my husband about it, he is very hostile to me. At other times, to my son's credit, he has remembered to make his sandwich.'[5]

Hite's research corroborates what I found, that neither husbands nor sons are expected to prepare their own food. It is still the woman's job, and if men and boys do it, we regard it as to their credit.

So while cooking may be discretionary, though not always at the women's discretion, catering remains compulsory. What is even more extraordinary is that many women seem incapable of leaving their families to fend for themselves without a major bout of catering before they set off. Virginia's story is characteristic:

'When Mum went into hospital for a fallen womb, even though it was painful for her to stand for long periods, the week before she went she stood for hours at the cooker, stewing, casseroling, roasting and baking my dad dozens of different meals. She packaged them, labelled them, and put them in the freezer. She even sorted them so that he could pull them out one at a time and have a different meal from the night before. She could have been in hospital for two months and dad would have been fine! When she came home, she opened the freezer and saw every meal exactly where she'd left it! My dad had had all these invites out. "Oh you poor thing!" said all my mum's friends. "Who's going to cook your supper?" Dad hadn't said, "It's already cooked and I'm going to stay home and eat it on my own." He'd just hung his head and looked pathetic and went out every night to a different woman's house to be waited on. It was awful the way Mum's friends, most of them widows, all nurtured him, all spent hours cooking for him. I mean it's not a very good advertisement for them is it? All those women whose husbands had died, what they wanted was a man to put his feet under their table, not under their bed, and they'd feel fantastic! Poor Mum, she wasn't just cross, she was deeply hurt, she said she felt utterly rejected. All that physical energy she couldn't afford. All that catering, all that emotional investment, just so he'd be well looked after. I tell you one thing, she'll never do it again.'

I listened to Virginia's story and suddenly found I was red with embarrassment. I had behaved just as her mum had when I was married to Larry. The first time I was to be away for a week, I cooked seven different meals, wrapped each in tinfoil, then stuck on typed labels: Monday, Tuesday, Wednesday through till Sunday, as well as explanatory labels with the contents (chicken and duchesse potatoes, baked halibut with petit pois, etc.) Then I typed a list of the days and meals and pinned it up by the cooker with heating instructions. Did I think gastronomic incompetence a prerequisite of musical talent. Or did

I have a submerged need to keep a highly autonomous powerful man dependent on a skill I was proud of. Whatever the reason I drove off for my 'free' week satisfied that I was a 'good wife'.

When I returned, not only were the seven packages untouched, but Larry said he had forgotten I had cooked them, he hadn't noticed the list, he had gone out for three expensive Chinese meals, he had accepted two invitations to dinner with sympathetic friends, and twice had got my eldest stepdaughter Carol to come and cook for him. I felt not only deeply hurt, not only that my status as a wife had been gravely wronged, but that my role as a stepmother had also been severely tested. What upset me most was wondering if my efficient caring stepdaughter had believed I hadn't catered properly for her father. My catering for *assumed* male helplessness occurred in the mid-sixties, but Virginia was talking about the late eighties. It seems that women today no less than yesterday are not merely stuck with the ultimate responsibility for food management but also take it upon themselves where it isn't necessary.

This unnecessary responsibility, which operates on a twenty-four-hour-a-day shift, straddles social classes, cuts across continents, and occurs in different cultures.

The most extraordinary example of this can be seen in a recent Japanese film called *Tampopo* which glorifies food through its thesis that meals are for men to appreciate and criticize, whereas cooking and catering are ancient forms of slavery which proper women in the late twentieth century still enter into willingly. Tampopo, the vigorous, widowed heroine, is a rebel against food convention. She energetically attempts to open and run a fast-food noodle restaurant in Tokyo, to prove herself the world's best noodle-soup maker, before an army of cynics (including her own helpers) who believe firstly that no women can cook noodles (or anything else) professionally; and secondly that female cooks should be tending their talents, their time, and their stew pots in private kitchens, not public restaurants. (Did my family put the director up to making this film I wondered?)

The most bizarre but relevant scene, shows a man running

home to his wife's deathbed. She is quite past human aid when he arrives, becomes distraught, anguishes for a way to revive her, and finally shouts: 'Get up and cook! Get dinner ready.' Slowly and unsteadily, she rises from her bed to prepare the meal for her husband and children. With infinite patience she stays alive until she has served it. Then, duty diligently performed, the director allows her to keel over dead.

The wife is cold, the meal hot, the children frightened and forlorn. They begin to wail, but their father, griefstruck though he is, rallies sufficiently to shout: 'Keep eating. It's the last meal Mom ever cooked. Eat it while it's hot.'

Extreme, yes. Amusing possibly. But as a cultural image it mirrors a basic and bitter truth for women in Western no less than in Japanese society. Though cooking may be shared, catering, women's ultimate responsibility, continues in sickness and in health even unto death!

To my amazement I discovered that in some cases catering for men continues after death. When I met Roma in St Ives, her husband had recently died, but with great vivacity she showed me a huge set of photos of the funeral spread which she had prepared singlehanded.

'Look at those topped-up plates,' she said proudly. 'There's his ham, there's his chicken breasts, there's his cut turkey slices. It was all there for him just as it has always been. Forty years we lived in this house and he never peeled a spud. Never turned up a knob on my stove. Never planned a bugger. Always expected me to be in charge of his dinners, to do all our thinking for the family meals. No different when he died really. First thing I thought when we got the news was, what kind of spread will the old man expect? Worried right through the funeral in case we didn't have enough and he came back to complain! My son took the pictures so we've got a remembrance like.'

I admired the photos, and I admired Roma, an indomitable woman with a big cracked grin across her craggy face. Suddenly she twinkled at me, and taking me out of earshot of her many children and sisters and brothers she whispered: 'I got my own back. I did him a cold spread. Bloody grand it was, but cold. He'd have asked for a hot!'

Is there no liberation from this endless round of catering? I had hoped that politically conscious, or very rich, or highly successful women might have avoided this trap. I had already discovered that feminist awareness does not automatically help. Now it seems that neither money nor status necessarily has a liberating effect on women's domestic roles.

American researcher Bebe Moore Campbell, in a new book called *Successful Women, Angry Men*,[6] studied one hundred couples involved in liberated-looking high-achieving marriages. She discovered that 'many men admitted that although they'd been committed to an equal relationship at the beginning of their marriages, they find it difficult to maintain an egalitarian stance.' The women had all carefully chosen men who had promised to aid and support them while they strove for professional achievement; but the sad fact was that most of the husbands withdrew their support just when the wives needed it most.

Even very rich women, those who lead superficially enviable lives, appear no less immune than the rest of us from this perception of our proper role.

Take for example that glittering group, the Ladies, an extraordinary American club of rich and role-conscious women, every member of whom is a glamorous ex-Hollywood wife. The initials of the club's label stand for Life After Divorce is Eventually Sane; and having found sanity, the former wives are planning a cook book called *Leftovers* of ex-wives' favourite recipes. When interviewed this year for television every one articulated a sense of relief at no longer being judged not only in terms of her husband's success but also in terms of her own food management.[7]

President and founder of the Ladies, Patti Lewis, former wife of comedian Jerry Lewis, explained that being a proper wife means being on constant menu-call, fashionably fastened to food preparation and meal organization. Patti informed us that there was no respite from the responsibility for food and nurturing, not even at night. When this proper wife had improperly tucked herself up, exhausted, in bed, Jerry Lewis would get a faint rumbling in his comedian's stomach at about 11 pm and, doubtless with a witty smile, would demand his favourite cheese-and-tomato sandwich.

'He always used to say: "No one makes it like you do", so of course I got out of bed to make it. Being a wife is a twenty-four-hour-a-day job,' Patty reminded herself with a flicker of fatigue.

As I listened to her wistfully explaining that she had been on that job for more than twenty years, until Jerry decided to exchange her for a younger cook with perhaps a fresher line in late night snacks, I thought, if this is the glitzy role of proper women in Hollywood, it does not bode well for the most mundane among us.

Of course Hollywood wives, even ex-wives, with all the desirable creature-comforts and help in the home, in no way suffer the practical restraints of suburban women living on economical budgets or social security in Britain, and in that respect comparisons are meaningless. Nevertheless, this group of women perceived the crux of their womanly roles in the same way as the majority of the women I interviewed. Moreover they feel it necessary and appropriate to present themselves as women who endlessly service their menfolk with food.

Does one more cheese-and-tomato sandwich made by one more woman, any woman, matter? Yes it does. Every time one of us jumps out of bed to serve a sandwich to the man we love, or fear, or the man we no longer notice, when we could be lying comfortably composing sonatas, writing blockbusters, planning buildings, or getting some sleep before a shift at the factory, or performing a heart transplant, or getting the children's breakfast, we are consenting to the silencing of our own better interests. We are agreeing with the idea that women's time is of less value than men's, and acknowledging that the labour of one sex is of less worth than the labour of the other.

It is on the backs of women making cheese and tomato sandwiches, or egg and chips, or huge roast beef and Yorkshire dinners, when they could be doing something else in their own interests, that patriarchy is built and maintained, step by step, dish by dish.

Patti Lewis's account, like Frankie's, Imogen's, Esme's and Roma's, shows us that men sometimes cook, sometimes wash up, sometimes shop, as favours to the women they live with. They do it as losers in a struggle over domestic chores when both partners work outside the home; as part of a new fair-deal rhetoric. They do it because they enjoy it. As a group, men still do not do it as of right, or because of social expectation. Many women confirmed that when men do cook they make a mess, they make a fuss, they make it harder for women to rely on them. This means that for dual-career wives and women-friends, discretionary cooking is a highly problematic improvement.

Nor have men taken on fundamental answerability for food preparation and provision. In the eighties as in the fifties this is still the role of the proper woman, which is why when men undertake food tasks, their 'contribution' (and the very word illustrates the partial nature of their share) is received with surprise, pleasure or praise. Women's share is expected and barely acknowledged. Women's role is not to contribute, it is to organize. When women's work does receive notice is when they fail to cook or to manage, or when they are 'bad' cooks. Then they are seen as not fulfilling their role as 'real' women. The sad fact is that 'real' women are not far removed from excellent servants. In 1914 Emmeline Pankhurst said: 'It was rapidly becoming clear to my mind that men regarded women as a servant class in the community and that women were going to remain in the servant class until they lifted themselves out of it.'[8]

Women have not done so yet.

FOUR
STOCKCUPBOARD SYMBOLS, SUPER MARKET SERVITUDE AND SELF-ESTEEM

If men expect women to act as caterers, then shopping and stocking, even more than cooking, lie at the heart of women's domestic role. It was not hard to discover what women do, so many of us live up to men's culinary expectations. But what do women feel about the importance of this mandatory food provision in our everyday lives? What do women feel in particular about the centrality of shopping and stocking? Is it only a cause of worry or does it bring a sense of satisfaction?

I peered into a great many women's larders, opened a great many cupboard doors, and walked up and down aisles in countless supermarkets talking to women pushing trolleys. I wanted to know what stocking-up means. I wanted to know why some women always keep cupboards full and others just as decisively leave them empty. I wanted to know what emotions flood over women who shop at supermarkets.

I started with the stockcupboard because decisions to stock up are as much internal moral strictures or expressions of emotional need as they are practical policies. For many women, security stems from a full larder. Sometimes a stack of jars of homemade chutney or neat rows of tinned baked beans fill an emotional gulf women may be hardly aware of. One woman told me: 'Sometimes when I feel dissatisfied with my life – but there's no real reason; after all, I've got a good husband, always in work and enough money to feed us on – I bake a batch of cakes and pile them up in the larder and I feel better. I stock up with damson jam, or I put by a dozen jars of beetroot and apple preserve and it makes me feel useful.'

Some women regard stocking up as a necessary part of family life. That certainly is how I saw it, and not only when I catered for a horde of hungry children. In Liverpool, when seven-year-old Marmoset was a weekly boarder and I shared a flat with my friend Margrit, I still insisted on buying in bulk to keep our cupboard full. Margrit, exasperated at my silliness, would say, 'You're being ridiculous, Sally, it is quite unnecessary. After all we are not a family.' The truth was, I wanted us to be. I wanted to be part of a 'proper family' as my unconscious actions revealed.

For other women, stocking up is a way to 'do it right', or to avoid male displeasure. The phrase 'doing it right' was one that occurred consistently, interview after interview.

Nettie, a twenty-four-year-old Londoner who feeds three children, a husband, and an elder brother, focused on the safety that the 'right' actions bring.

'There's got to be at least four tins of soup in the cupboard, I don't mean packets, they don't count, do they? There's got to be six of baked beans, four of tinned tomatoes, and your tin of meat for best, then if you've done it right you feel safe. I always put a frozen cream sponge in the freezer and a packet of those chocolate rolls. I know I mustn't eat most of it but it's there for them others, and him of course. Then you feel you can do your teas safely. You're not going to get caught out.'

Rita caters for four children and a dependent ageing father. 'I have to keep the fridge and the cupboard full because there are so many people to feed. I shouldn't worry for myself, we aren't meant to eat much anyway. I worry for those others. If I ran out of milk, bread, or toilet paper, it would finish me off. At least I've done right by stocking it up.'

This mixture of constraints and temptations is echoed in virtually every issue of every women's magazine, where there are, side by side, articles on how to prepare and provide for others, and how to deny ourselves. Babies need feeding, families need nurturing; tasks for women simultaneously instructed not to feed themselves.

This conflict fills some women with dismay. For others, like

Violet, the unease is about male criticism, which she believes a constant supply of suitable food will keep at bay. Tired at fifty-five, Violet spends her time alternately shouting at and trying to please her two sons, one on the dole and one an invalid, and her husband, who has just been made redundant. 'With that idle lot, mate, you've got to fill it up. Moan, that's not the half of it! Two tins of beans in my kitchen cupboard? You're joking, more like twenty mate, that's the way I've been brought up! I've always done it like me mum did. I always like tins of salmon and tuna and corned beef stuck in there cos after all you've got to have your cold meat in case you haven't got your hot for him. You might be hard up one week and before he complains well you can get it all out nice just as if you'd been shopping. Not that he's got any right to complain, or them idle others, but that's what they're like. I have to keep the freezer full an' all, so there's always enough in there meat-wise for next week and the week after even if it's only two chickens, some turkey steaks and of course your cream cake in case there's company. He wouldn't stand for it if I ran out of meat. So if you've got your meat and your cake for tea they can't say nothing.'

As we shall see in Chapter 5, Violet and Nettie were not the only women who mentioned saving meat for men and freezing fattening foods which they did not allow themselves 'for company'.

Stocking for company is done by women irrespective of their relative wealth or poverty. Cait, from a large Irish working-class family, told me: 'We were incredibly poor and Mum had to shop a little bit every day. But even though she never had anything in her cupboard she always kept a tin of salmon in case the priest came round.'

Lucy, twenty-two, unmarried, who has lived with Alan for two years, reminded me that a major part of women's role is to ensure men need not plan.

'I don't cook for Alan, I burn everything, so I try and make up for it by keeping the storecupboard full so he always has something to rely on. Then he doesn't have to think out a meal.

If it's empty I'd feel guilty and insecure. We haven't got children yet. When we have I'll have to try and cook and go to Tesco's because he will have done his share.'

Janie, an American computer programmer, suggested that keeping cupboards full was more of a worry for British house-wives because so many shops close at 5.30 pm. 'I never used to worry in Brooklyn, where the neighbourhood store was open twenty-four hours a day, seven days a week, but living in Bristol I've taken on all that British worry of figuring it out in advance. I figure and plan and worry more about that than about my programme.'

Certainly when British women do not plan in advance it seems to be shame that they feel. Angie, a dance teacher, spoke for many: 'I am getting so naughty now that my corner shop stays open late, I often don't plan in advance, don't keep the cupboard full, I feel quite ashamed. I know other women disapprove of me. I don't feel so bad because Pete doesn't live full-time with me. If he did I expect I'd change my habits just to fit in and feel secure.'

Eva, a fifty-year-old community care worker, has spent twenty-five years trying to fit in her work around the needs of her three daughters and husband. She hates cooking and stocking so much she has finally gone on strike. 'I have found it impossible trying to do my work properly while never being free of domestic responsibility. Mathew used to appreciate my meals, so I tried to be creative. I dug up delightful menus, because he cared. Italian risottos, chicken in cream sauces, baked halibut . . . I did it all. Then Mathew stopped noticing. In twenty-five years he's never once cooked us a meal. But he went on expecting the cupboard to be filled with an infinite variety of foods so that I could make anything he suggested. As for the girls, they don't like this, or they've gone off that, they only help if you nag. I who loved cooking so much have learnt to dread it. Nobody helped and nobody cared unless the stockcupboard was empty. Then they cared all right. Finally it ground me down. I want to fill bookcases with penguins, not cupboards with Laughing Cow biscuits because the girls won't eat any other kind. It's taken over twenty years of stocking up and suppressing what I felt. Sometimes I'd crumble up all the Laughing Cows, shove them in my mouth crying with rage and frustration, then I'd have to go and get another packet before they came in from school. I suddenly thought, 'Why am I bothering? Now I'm fed up. I never want to see another Laughing Cow. I am sick, sick, sick of food, sick of thinking about it. So I've gone on strike. I don't get anyone else to do the cooking. I just don't do it myself. The rows of course were terrible, but not more terrible than the endless responsibility, so I've stuck to it. I haven't made them a meal in six months, and the cupboard is often empty! I am beginning to feel like a free woman.'

What do women feel about shopping at supermarkets? For most women I talked to, the topic engendered highly explosive and contradictory emotions: pride was mixed with anger; fear and hatred overlaid responsibility. Again the women felt they were 'doing it right', but doing it in a place they saw as a jail.

The women's responses were strong, the images they used compelling. Sickness, tyranny and prison were consistently evoked by women who saw no release from an odious but 'proper' task. The few women who had freed themselves from this domestic hell, felt that in some way they had failed.

Listen to Shirl, aged forty, who lives in Cambridgeshire with a sick husband, two girls and three dogs to feed.

'Gets on your bloody wick it does, all that hassle and queueing, you can't get near the checkout, all those others with more money than you, not that there'll be any difference at the cash till, no one's going to put me down for not spending enough on food for my lot I can tell you! But with all that to worry about you feel quite faint and ready to have a turn by the time you wheel the bloody trolley out. There's many a time when I dream of not doing it properly; and just pushing the cart into their faces and walking out free. Well I suppose I might take the dogmeat with me, after all.'

Catherine, a London office worker in her mid-twenties, is married but has no children: 'Whenever I'm in a supermarket I feel very unwell, as if I'm going to be sick. I know most of my women friends feel like that, but it never occurs to any of us not to do it, I mean we are all married or living with men so there isn't any choice. I see it getting worse when you have babies.'

Even women without men in the home to approve or criticize still cling to the idea that proper housewifery should involve the misery of mammoth marketing. Anthea, a divorced research worker living with her daughter and two cats, spoke for many in similar positions:

'Every time I go into Sainsbury's I get a feeling of claustrophobia. I keep wondering if I'm going to be sick. All those people, most of them women, all that food. It makes me feel hot and heavy. I want to rush out. But I can't, there's my daughter to think of and the cats and the feeling that at least I'm trying to do it right.'

Women with very low incomes or living on welfare, who might have been economically better off shopping at supermarkets, were amongst those who expressed the greatest anger, in some cases rebellion, and in all cases a perception that others would see them as failing.

Pamela, a single parent, lives on social security:

'I can't handle Sainsbury's or Tesco's and watching people spend more than sixty pounds at one time. It's obscene. Even Budgen's makes me feel faint, and the Co-op just depresses me. I feel trapped by the trolley and by the memories of my mother's full storecupboard. She still wants me to do it properly but it makes me feel I'm in prison. I did try, I used to try quite hard when I lived with Tony. But since we've split up and I live alone with my small daughter I rely on the corner shop. It's not as economical when you have to watch the pence. We frequently run out of bread and jam and I know other women think that's disgusting because I've got a kid and you always have to have bread and jam. They don't see me as a proper mum any more because my storecupboard is empty and I won't go to a supermarket. I don't care because I'm a lot freer than they are.'

Rita, who had told me that not having a stock of milk, bread or toilet rolls would 'finish her off,' elaborated. 'Because of the massive amounts of loo paper and bread that have got to be put in the cupboard I force myself to go regularly to the supermarket. It's like driving voluntarily into jail.'

A few women did not feel hatred at the store itself so much as envy for the men who shopped there. Lana, (thirty-four, living with three children, three cats, and a male lover who has his own flat but eats with them) summed it up:

'Every time I see a man wheeling a trolley alone, I look at his basket and he's usually got a load of booze, some exciting frozen flans and trifles, something jolly from the deli, and absolutely no washing powder! Lucky sod. You can bet he's got a women doing his washing. I feel real envy and hatred because my trolley is never like that. It's piled high with disposables, cat lit, cat food, Persil, baked beans and the giant ketchup.'

Eva, who struck against cooking and Laughing Cows, has not yet struck against supermarket shopping but her plans are made. Already she has a fantasy of retaliation against the tyranny of supermarkets. 'I'm still doing it, hating it even more than the cooking, it has been nothing but drudgery for twenty-five years. But not for much longer.' Eva's well-modulated voice rose to a shriek. 'Nothing in my life was worse than supermarkets. They interrupted my work. They came between me and my life. I hated watching women with vast trolleys piled high, paper towel rolls falling off, cans of peas clanking like chains. It's gross. The women looked like slaves but instead of carrying burdens on their backs they were trailing them behind their bums.

'What I've always wanted to do was go to Sainsbury's and stuff a trolley to the very top, till it's brimming over with the most expensive foods in the store: smoked salmon, fresh trout, bottles of champagne. Then I'd walk round the store watched with envy by all the women piling theirs up with catfood and washing-up liquid. Then with a huge fat grin I'd trail it to a far corner and just leave it. Abandon the lot! I'd run through the cash till. For the first time in years I wouldn't have to open the car boot. I'd be absolutely free. I'd be able to drive home with my boot empty, my heart singing and all that awful food stuck in the trolley waiting for some poor soul to unload it. But for once it wouldn't be me.

'I've spent the last six months fantasizing. One day soon, I'm going to get up the nerve and do it. I'd thought about stealing the food, but I didn't want to get caught. So I've decided to desert it. Just walk confidently out. "Whose is it?" they'll say. "Where is she?" they'll wonder. "Has she actually gone?" and I shall have! I shall have walked out a free woman knowing I am never going back!'

Supermarket shopping overwhelmingly produced negative reactions, such as feelings of sickness or images of imprisonment, while filling up stockcupboards generally provoked positive feelings of security, safety and the desire to nourish others. Both, however, were seen as essential parts of 'doing it right', and for these women that meant doing it right in men's eyes.

Although eater approbation is valued, whoever the eaters may be, there is no doubt that the approval of the menfolk is courted most – while disapproval from that quarter is by far the most dreaded. Compulsery catering makes us anxious; at the same time, it can be a source of self-esteem.

Remember housing manager Imogen's 'anxiety hours' and student Esme's view that planning was an 'anxious-making business'? Fortunately these were offset by architect Denise's pride in the 'rights and duties of marriage' and the satisfaction that pudding-lover Molly received from 'doing everything properly just as Mother did.'

For many women, however, worry outweighs pride. The anxiety of catering for others utterly dominates their lives. Frankie, who longed for years to force changes on Richard and their two children told me: 'For several years supermarket shopping made me so anxious I was physically sick. For years all food made me ill with anxiety. The constant buying, putting away, pushing food at the kids, eating it up when they didn't, clearing it away when Richard wouldn't. I thought I was going crazy with endless food. IT WAS MY LIFE. All that buying and stocking was my total life.'

Edie, a sixty-year-old grandmother, has cooked and catered for eleven: 'There's never been anything except washing t'pots, peeling potatoes and counting them out so there'd be enough for his Sundays, worrying myself sick. His meat dinners were the worst, and puds for them young 'uns. And when I'm not at the stove, I'm buttering paste sandwiches an' crackin' on the biscuits.'

Listen to Gwyneth, a twenty-six-year-old married Welsh woman with two toddlers and a baby. 'Food is my life. I can't see anything beyond spoons of purée and slop on the floor or burning his mince with him being late. There I am fretting and fraying, eating cold custard and drinking sweet tea to put myself right.'

This was Hettie, fifty, giving advice to her newly engaged daughter: 'This is your life, Annie, his teas and his dinners are what you are about now, don't you forget it.'

The most moving story I heard came from Mary, mid-fifties, with a big laugh that lit up her drab, grey-striped dress. Mary who has brought up five sons and now has to care for Kenny, her invalid husband, talked first about her mother's life. 'There were seven for Mum to cook for. She was always in a state about teas and dinners, some days it was so bad she shook. I've grown up shaking just like her.

'Mum would by frying mince in the big earthenware pan, and my Dad would come in and yell at her: 'I can see the gristle! I can see the gristle! What kind of sodding meal is that?' My mum's little white hands would shake at the stove as she pretended not to hear him, and we all hoped it wouldn't get any worse. He'd knock her about for much less than the gristle. One day he sent her flying when the parsnips had boiled too long. When my big sister Maggie tried to stop him he knocked her about as well. Sometimes my mum's hands shook so bad she couldn't lift the big pan off the stove. I can tell you it didn't have a very good effect on me and my sisters.

'I remember us girls helping get the gristle off the mince, which isn't easy on a cheap cut, before he came home. Once I stuck up for her and said the mince was all right and he got the belt to me. You had to be careful after that. You had to watch what you said to Mum as well. If you so much as said "There's some gristle" she'd start to shake. One day she moaned about her life and the mince and that being all there was. I can hear her now: "This is your life, Mary," she said, wringing her hands, kind of crying. "This is your life, Maggie and you lot. It's all mince and gristle going wrong. There isn't anything else" Then she began crying and we got frightened because he'd be home in a minute and the tea wasn't done.

'Then we'd try and comfort her. All we could think of was to open the tin and hand her the sweet biscuits. I'd be buttering the end of a loaf, cutting it off. Another sister would put by some slices of hard cheese and toast it for her. When she was comfy with the biscuits and the toasted cheese, I'd do some more slices for us. Maggie would brew cocoa. Then Mum would stop moaning. If we were lucky her hands would stop shaking enough for her to finish the mince before he came home.'

This story is sadly neither unique nor extreme. Many women's lives are like this. Mary's Mum was cooking her mince in the fifties. Three decades later, Hettie is teaching her daughter that his teas and his dinners will be her life, will represent what she is. Gwyneth, a young mother, has already discovered that slop on the floor and burnt mince are her daily routine.

As I listened to these voices, I remembered Esther Sussman, the fat, sloppy heroine of Fay Weldon's best-selling novel *The Fat Woman's Joke*, for whom catering and cooking had become the totality of life.[1]

When Esther lived with her husband, food set the pattern of

their days. 'All day in his grand office Alan would sip coffee and nibble biscuits and plan his canteen dockets and organize cold chicken and salad and wine for working lunches, and all day at home I would plan food, and buy food, and cook food, and serve food, and nibble and taste and stir and experiment and make sweeties and goodies and tasties for Alan to try out when he came home.'

On the first morning of a diet to reduce his mounting paunch, Alan was conducting a seductive but businesslike tête-à-tête with his slim secretary, Susan, a girl conscious of her youth and beauty 'which indeed shone like a beacon in a boozy beery world' and who therefore wore a very short skirt and a very skimpy jersey and who certainly had no need to diet! Just as Alan's trembling podgy paws slid over Susan's slim breasts, his fat useful wife Esther phoned to inquire, in her ever-helpful manner, about his evening's dietary requirements: 'Did he want a herb omelette and a tomato, separate, or the tomato cooked in with the omelette?'

Esther, no fool, knew by his voice that his secretary was 'sitting there exhibiting her legs to him under the desk'. Well, wives fat and otherwise do know, don't they? 'Day one of the diet was a horrible day for me,' says Esther who, long-suffering in the matter of food, is now dieting herself to fit in with Alan. Perceptively she adds '. . . although no doubt it was a delight to my husband.' For Esther enough is enough. Catering for husband and children is over. 'Marriage is too strong an institution for me,' she says. 'It is altogether too heavy and powerful.'

Weary and worn out she gives up planning and cooking. She certainly gives up dieting. She decides to live alone in a grimy flat in Earls Court. Food, however, is still the centre of her world. 'During the day she would read science fiction novels. In the evenings she watched television. And she ate, and ate, and drank, and ate.

'She ate frozen chips and peas and hamburgers, and sliced bread with bought jam and fishpaste, and baked beans and instant puddings, and tinned porridge, and tinned suet pudding, and cakes and biscuits from packets. She drank sweet coffee, sweet tea and sweet cocoa and sweet sherry.

'This is the only proper holiday, she thought, that I have had for years; and then she thought, but this is not a holiday, this is my life until I die; and then she would eat a biscuit, and melt some ready-sliced cheese on top of it, remembering that the act of cooking had once been almost as absorbing as the act of eating.'

For Esther and Mary's Mum, both eating toasted cheese and comforting themselves with biscuits, the constant catering is both the trap and the escape.

Fay Weldon talked to me about the trap. 'I think the key to it is when she says "this is not a holiday, this is my life until I die." I think the feeling that makes you eat more, is this sense that this is your life until your death, that there is nothing you can do to change it. Esther feels, as women do feel, that she is trapped in her circumstances and therefore she will take what pleasure the day brings her, and pleasure is in eating things which are pleasurable to eat, and you don't care about whether they are good for you, or whether they will bring about the event of your death rather sooner.'

When Weldon wrote this novel in the early sixties, and portrayed the predominant emotions of her heroine as those of total obsession with food, unremitting anxiety about cooking and catering, and life itself as an unending vista of food rituals, she was revolutionary is believing that what women felt about food was proper stuff for literature.

In the late eighties, the women I interviewed revealed feelings remarkably similar to those of a fictional character created more than twenty years ago. When I discussed it with Fay Weldon she said: 'When I first started using food images in my books they were simply not considered a fit subject for literature. Only the things that happened in men's lives were important enough for print. But food is a woman's world, it is an integral part of every woman's daily life, it often holds the key to the meanings in her life. Perhaps those meanings have not altered substantially.'

For the women I spoke to, like Weldon's Esther, depression

can be bound up with catering and overeating. And yet consolation can be obtained by more of the same. Like Nettie, Rita and Lucy, for whom full cupboards represented security, Esther admits: 'She had not felt so secure since she spent her days in a pram.'

Fay Weldon suggested that: 'Feeding others has a lot to do with controlling them. The way women feed their children involves control. The way women used to keep men out of the kitchen was a way of saying, you depend on me for your nice food; just as the way men keep women out of (or down in) the workplace, is a way of saying, you depend on me for my nice wage packet. Kitchens are far from neutral places. Food is a weapon of control.'

Unfortunately full stockcupboards often give women an illusion of security and control, for as I have discovered, women control food because they cannot control their lives. Mary's mum's misery over the mince is very much the worry of a woman not in control of her life. Inevitably it had spin-offs for Mary herself. 'What happened with Mum has left me the anxious sort, so if my Kenny or the five lads are in my kitchen it can set me off. It's worse since Kenny's accident. With him permanently laid off there's honestly no pleasing him. I have to keep his mind on other things to prevent myself getting the shakes like my mum. I never asked him to cook any more than Mum would have dared ask Dad.

'I brought the lads up to eat hearty and to keep out of my kitchen. Being turned off meat and fries by what Mum went through I've concentrated on puddings. I used to feel satisfied with what I turned out but the same everyday routine of it, and never finding the time to do it properly has ruined all that. The worst is trying to find the right food to suit them all. Not one of the lads will eat the same food as the others. Jack won't touch custard, Harry wants steamed jam roll on Thursdays, Ben only wants what Dad has but wants it at a different time. The two youngest always bring their girlfriends for meals and it's no chips for one, too fattening she said but she was like a wraith; and the other said avocado surprise was her favourite. We gave her a bloody surprise! You don't see avocados down ours! On his money she must be joking!' Mary laughed loudly.

'I used to try and do it creative but I soon gave that up. They hardly noticed and no matter how much time I put in one of them would moan. When Kenny was on the building site he always needed his meals at a different time from the lads so often as not I'd be doing three teas. They are good lads but they never seemed to notice I might have other things to do apart from cook for them.'

Mary's sentiments were shared by many of the housewives Ann Oakley interviewed about the satisfaction or displeasure they received from housework, cooking and food preparation.

'Cooking, for instance, recognized as a potentially creative activity by the majority of housewives, often is not, because husbands and children demand certain sorts of meals at particular times during the day, and the housewife also has to meet a mass of other demands on her time.'[2]

Thirty out of her forty housewives said they found cooking and similar tasks monotonous. Thirty-six reported feelings of fragmentation. This was largely because the work was seen as a series of unconnected tasks, none of which required the women's full attention. Half of the group said that any satisfaction they might have had was decreased because they had too much to get done during the day. Indeed almost every housewife mentioned frequent time-limits as a big source of dissatisfaction. Catering and cooking need not be monotonous or fragmented, but for many women they are. Monotony, fragmentation, and excessive speed are often cited as sources of job dissatisfaction for industrial workers, yet women are expected to accept this as part of their informal job definition.

When Oakley compared the incidence of these unsatisfactory experiences between groups of housewives and groups of factory workers she discovered that housewives experienced considerably more social isolation, fragmentation and monotony in their unpaid labour. Industrialization has changed the roles of men as well as women; but for men it has enlarged the world outside the home (chiefly by expanding their range of possible jobs) whereas for many women, even today 'our window on the world is looked through with our hands in the sink.'[3]

Women are still in captivity. There they are, day after day, busy with household budgeting, family food preparation and unending meal-making. Indisputably they are at work. Yet these jobs are not perceived publicly as 'work'. It is considered low status and unimportant, yet it is utterly essential to the running of a 'good' family. It is no wonder that women like Mary need the praise and recognition of the men who consume their food; no wonder that they are confused by their inability to feel satisfied with the food tasks they take on so willingly. It is no wonder that anxiety is such a predominant emotion.

Fortunately, the other side of the coin is self esteem.

As I wrote this the telephone rang. It was Enid, the recently widowed mother of a friend. 'Hello dear, are you all right? I've had such a difficult week. I've been cooking for the bods. I expect you would call it entertaining, well it hasn't felt very entertaining! It's all such a worry, except on the other hand, it does make you feel proud.'

Had Enid been taking a peep over my shoulder? Certainly her phonecall bore out my words: 'Glenys and Ted came for supper. Oh what a pickle!' she said, still excited at what had happened. 'You know what a good cook Glenys is. *You*'re supposed to be, aren't you, dear? But it does mean making a meal for them is a positive nightmare. Like being had up before the headmistress. I made that casserole I'm quite good at; not as worrying as fancy chicken, but of course I burnt the sprouts. Well, there they were on the doorstep, dreadful smell of burning, my heart thudding, my apron still on. What could I do?'

What did you do? I asked with real interest, having often been in exactly the same situation. 'I answered the door and made a bad joke of it,' she said proudly. 'I said I thought a burnt edge would add a certain flavour!'

Did they mind? Was it OK? I asked. 'Ted's a real gentlemen. He laughed and laughed.' Then she added confidentially: 'I expect it was his criticisms I was worrying most about. I knew Glenys would understand, not that *she* ever makes mistakes. But Ted kindly ate it all up, even praising the casseroles, though I saw him sneaking the fatty bits and a particularly burnt sprout to the side of his plate. I could hardly eat at all, though I put on a good show. I didn't relax until they had gone home.'

Cooking for others offers women a self-esteem that is elsewhere largely denied us. But this self-esteem is inextricably tied into our need for eater – which for many women means male – approval.

As Enid relived her anxieties, there was more than a hint of pride in her voice. 'You have to do it, Sal. You have to go through all the miseries, but I think it makes you feel satisfied.'

These conflicting emotions are subtly portrayed in Virginia Woolf's *To the Lighthouse* when Mrs Ramsey, wife of an egotistic philosopher and magnificently imperturbable mother of eight children, is about to serve dinner to fifteen guests, amongst them William Bankes, childless widower, sterile botanist, who smelt of soap and who 'would prose for hours . . . about salt in vegetables and the iniquity of English cooks'.

Mrs Ramsey, a beautiful and generally serene woman, is worrying about how her dinner will be received by a dried and shrunken scientist. 'She wished the dinner to be particularly nice, since William Bankes had at last consented to dine with them, and they were having Mildred's masterpiece – Boeuf en Daube. Everything depended upon things being served up the precise moment they were ready. The beef, the bayleaf and the wine – all must be done to a turn. To keep it waiting was out of the question.'

But of course it was that night, of all nights, that her husband, her children, and the countless visitors came back late and the food had to be kept hot. As the guests finally straggled in, horror of horrors there was a smell of burning! 'Could they have let the Boeuf en Daube overboil, she wondered? pray heaven not!'

She serves the soup, feeling like an alien at her own dinner table. 'But what have I done with my life? thought Mrs Ramsey, taking her place at the head of the table and looking at all the plates making white circles on it . . . she waited, passively, for someone to answer her, for something to happen. But this is not a thing, she thought ladling out soup, that one says.

'Raising her eyebrows at the discrepancy – that was what she was thinking, this was what she was doing – ladling out soup – she felt, more and more strongly, outside that eddy.'

Since she cannot bear incivility to her guests, to men in particular, she is civil and charming as she draws the men out and waits for the moment when William Bankes will taste the Boeuf en Daube. To her deep relief it has not burnt. 'An exquisite scent of olives and oil and juice rose from the great brown dish . . . And she must take great care, Mrs Ramsey thought, diving into the soft mass, to choose a specially tender piece for William Bankes. And she peered into the dish with its shiny walls and its confusion of savoury brown and yellow meats, and its bay leaves and its wine, and thought, This will celebrate the occasion.'

My own heart was in my mouth as I too awaited Bankes's judgement. I knew just what it felt like! It is impossible for at least women readers not to empathize with Mrs Ramsey.

Finally, 'It is a triumph,' said Mr Bankes, laying his knife down for a moment. He had eaten attentively. It was rich, it was tender. It was perfectly cooked. How did she manage these things in the depths of the country? he asked her. She was a wonderful woman. All his love, all his reverence had returned, and she knew it.

'It is a French recipe of my grandmother's,' said Mrs Ramsey, speaking with a ring of great pleasure in her voice. Of course it was French. What passes for cookery in England is an abomination (they agreed). It is putting cabbages in water. It is roasting meat till it is like leather. It is cutting off the delicious skins of vegetables . . . Spurred on by her sense that William's affection had come back to her, and that everything was all right again, and that her suspense was over, and that now she was free both to triumph and to mock, she laughed, she gesticulated, till Lily thought, How childlike, how absurd she was, sitting up there with all her beauty opened again in her, talking about the skins of vegetables.'

Mrs Ramsey proudly accepts William's accolade, just as Enid bravely retrieves the tricky situation of the burnt sprouts and deserves Ted's praise of the casserole. Both women share the anxiety felt by every woman I know over meals made to please others, and they share in that great feeling of glory when they have successfully achieved it.

Enid, Mrs Ramsey, Mary with her five sons; all trying to please men and to avoid male criticism, all of them striving to excel in the one role we are unambiguously allowed. And a great many women thinking that even the worry is worth it.

FIVE
PROPER MEALS,
IMPROPER OCCASIONS

Remember Dale, who offered her husband fruit and chocolate biscuits and was called a bitch for not fulfilling her wifely role? A proper woman's job is to provide proper meals. But what exactly *is* a proper meal?

Remember Roma, who organized the funeral feast on lines her dead husband would have approved of, but retaliated by serving cold food instead of hot? Why do so many women serve men hot food in preference to cold?

Remember Violet, who stacked up tins of corned beef because she believed 'you've got to have your cold meat in case you haven't got your hot for him . . . He wouldn't stand for it if I ran out of meat.' Why do so many women indulge men with meat even at times when they cannot afford it?

Why do busy housewives shun food processed and tinned to save them time, and continue to believe that meals made from raw ingredients are better?

All the women I talked to had very clear ideas about what constitutes a 'proper' meal. It became clear that 'proper' is by no means synonymous with nutritious, although the terms sometimes overlap – for instance, they were adamant that proper vegetables were fresh, not tinned or frozen. Raw vegetables, like salad, however (though in fact retaining vitamins cooking partially destroys) are not proper – perhaps because lack of cooking implies lack of time spent, and therefore of emotional commitment. Baked beans, for all their nutritional value, are not proper because they are tinned. The dominant message was that hot food made from raw ingredients, centred on meat and served by women makes a proper meal. Alternative sources of protein – cheese, eggs, even fish – are not highly regarded. It became plain that 'a cooked', which was how working-class women referred to the meals they felt bound to provide for their families at least three times a week in order to keep them healthy, did not simply mean hot, fresh food. 'A cooked' is meat – preferably roast – with potatoes, gravy and other vegetables. Chips do not appear in a 'cooked'. It is worth mentioning Roisin Pill's observation in her study, 'An Apple a Day', that 'the evidence leaves open the possibility that a significant proportion of women do not perceive food as particularly relevant for health or the prevention of illness.'[1]

It also seemed important to explore whether the kind of meals we cook have something to do with the kind of relationship we find ourselves in. Does romance or depression dictate the ingredients we choose? Does mutiny turn a gourmet possibility into a makeshift menu?

In the course of research I discovered that, yes, the food we serve, is symbolic of the relationship within which we cater. But it is also based on the firm belief, shared by women and men, that hot food is 'proper' and cold food is not. Daphne, a newly wed, reported: 'Soon after the wedding day his mum came to stay. The first thing she said was, "What do you give him for breakfast?" I said: "Well I don't. We're both rushing to work and we get our own. There's always fruit juice and cereal in the cupboard." She was horrified and said "A man can't go to work without a cooked breakfast. Men need cooked breakfasts. That's one thing you must do dear." Nothing would change her attitude. What was worse, my husband, who had never minded at all, began to get quite indignant towards me as if he thought she was right.'

Anne Murcott's investigations into food and gender, which focuses on married couples, show that women believe meat and hot food with fresh vegetables are part of women's responsibility towards the men they service.

> Essentially, cooking is important in that a wife is to provide the meal for a man's return from work. It is proper that as often as not a cooked dinner is ready for him and it is proper that preparing it is the wife's work. In this light being a good cook does matter.[2]

This conclusion matches my discoveries. Cait, one of eleven children whose mum saved a tin of salmon for the priest, bore this out: 'We hardly had any money but Mum saw to it that Dad always had better meals than us because he was working. Even when each of us went out to work and brought her our wages it didn't make any odds. I'd come home from my first job and there'd be Mum frying delicious liver and bacon. "That's yer dad's," she'd say. "Yours'll be fry-up and bread and jam." Sometimes Mum would get a tiny piece of steak and beat the hell out of it and make it more, but only for him. He only thought her meals were good if they had meat in them.'

Just as a girl's upbringing influences her subsequent views on her role, it can also affect the choice of menu she sees as suitable.

Molly, who was proud of the reputation of her mother's liver, explained further: 'Mother wouldn't do best liver without gravy, and it had to be fresh vegetables for a proper meal. Best of all was the Dippy. That was when Mother cooked the liver in a tin in the oven. When it was ready the tin was put in the middle of the table and we were all given freshly baked bread to dip in and get the goodness out. We loved the Dippy. All in our village knew Mother's Dippy. It didn't matter that she was always tired because us children were happy and Father was satisfied.'

The views of Molly's father about what was fitting food for families established the household menu. 'Mother would have to ring the changes to please him because he was a Royal Artillery man. We always had to have certain things on certain days. Monday was mashed potatoes, cold beef and red cabbage, because it was washday Monday, and because meat was particular for Father. Tuesday you'd go on to pork chops which Father had to have with his gravy and vegetables. She wouldn't think of using a tin, not for his dinner.'

When Molly married Maurice, she worked full-time as a nurse but continued her mother's tradition of proper meat meals. 'I made the Dippy for Maurice because liver in gravy is a real man's dish and I wanted him satisfied. I'm proud to say it's always gone down well. So have the pork chops I used to make for Father when Mother died. Like Mother I would get tired (being a nurse is very tiring even if you are not married) but all my childhood Mother made the most marvellous hot meat dinners and kept us happy so I wanted to do the same.'

Molly's socialization into her proper role is accompanied by such happy memories that for her the constant tiredness and perpetual food surveillance is merely part of the natural order of family life.

That exactly the same 'proper' family foods, set in a similar background of unequal distribution of labour, can produce a very different, less happy response is shown by thirty-year-old Sheila's story:

'Don't give me pork chips or liver and gravy, they bring back terrible memories. Most of my childhood I watched Mother come in worn out from her job in the local canteen, having done the housework before she left and the shopping on the way home. Dad of course never did any of it. Then she'd cook dinner which had to be meat and gravy for him and she had to make sure the veg were fresh or he'd moan. She was afraid to say anything as there was always this fear he might not come home. Some nights she was sick and couldn't eat the meal and Dad got in a rage. That's what marriage was to Mother, making sure he had his meat and we had it too because that's what families do.'

Despite the unpleasant memories, Sheila dutifully repeated the menu in her own marriage. 'I just followed Mother. I did all the shopping, planning and housework and of course the cooking. Jim's mother hadn't taught him to cook so there wasn't any choice. We had jobs in different offices in the same street. I tried to hurry, so I could be there first to get something on the table for him. Even when I came in tired I'd do liver and gravy or pork chops with fresh veg then I'd feel sick and couldn't eat. Jim said he didn't come home to eat on his own and if I didn't cook real dinners and eat with him he'd go elsewhere. It was just like my childhood.'

Wednesdays was Jim's half-day off but not once in ten years had he begun the cooking before Sheila got in. 'Some Wednesdays I was so done in, and underneath so angry, I'd have liked to use frozen veg or a tin of meat but I knew I couldn't. Jim was like my Dad, he had to have a proper dinner.'

Sheila's anger and sickness, like that of many women I talked to was less with the content of the meals they prepared than with the unfair content of their mother's marriages which they had replicated. The type of food itself seemed mandatory.

The women Anne Murcott interviewed similarly stressed the importance of what they termed a 'cooked dinner' which was a meal 'reportedly proper for a husband's (and children's) home-coming'. These cooked dinners, exactly like those described by Molly and Sheila, pork or liver with potatoes, cabbage and peas, symbolized the home, a man's relation to it, his woman's place in it and their relation to each other, which, as in the cases of Molly and Sheila, were far from equal.[3]

Nickie Charles and Marion Kerr, who investigated the attitudes towards eating expressed by women dependent on state benefit, discovered that no matter how poor the family was 'for a meal to be considered proper it has to consist of meat (or fish) potatoes and vegetables, be consumed by a family, usually mother, father and children, and be cooked by a woman. A meal which consists of chips, baked beans and sausages . . . is not usually graced with the term proper, it is regarded as a lower status and less desirable substitute.'[4]

These women felt that families whose diets did not include a regular consumption of proper meals were not proper families. Charles and Kerr point out that because the dominant food ideology accords meat a central place and the highest value, vegetarian households would definitely be considered improper. Many women I talked to bore this out. Donna, whose mother was vegetarian, told me: 'Mum always tried to serve us healthy vegetarian meals but Dad got furious if she gave us salad. He said it wasn't a proper meal. If it was hot food he relaxed and felt he was being looked after. If it was cold, particularly if his eye fell on lettuce, he felt his needs were being ignored.'

Even Imogen the housing manager felt she had 'degenerated' when she served her husband salad. Anne Murcott's research has produced similar reports from women who saw salads as 'insufficiently filling for men'.[5]

Women's views on nutrition are also influenced by social categorization, so women believe that 'improper' meals cannot constitute an adequate nutritional diet and no amount of positive nutritional information can convince them otherwise. This means that women who lack sufficient money to provide what they see as proper food feel they are failing their families.

Pat, a single mother with three children, told me: 'I've had to cut down, I've stopped taking sugar in my tea and I don't buy them clothes, but it's when I have to give them pie and chips, I feel bad.'

Margie, whose husband has been on unemployment benefit for many months, told me she tried to cut down on everything else before she cut down on food. 'Since he lost his job we've got to pay the bills first, but with what's over I try and buy them pork hocks or a cheap cut of meat so at least they're still getting their meat.'

Despite Roisin Pill's proviso, that it is possible many women make little connection between food and health, both she and I found that many do have particular views on health which influence their attitudes to meals.[6]

Fiona, a Scottish divorcee, has three teenage sons. 'It's been a lifelong job getting them to eat, making it balance. What with them wanting beefburger and chips and me wanting to do them a cooked, you know potatoes and gravy for their health, it's been nothing but worry. If they leave it on their plates I think I've failed them because you've got to look after their health, haven't you?' Fiona, like other women I talked to, and those in Roisin Pill's study, sees herself as in charge of her family's health. This means she must balance her children's desire for 'unsuitable' (often fried) foods with 'a cooked'. Although some women do not go 'all the way' with roast dinners, they are convinced that hot meals containing meat are 'healthier' than hot meals without, or even cold meals with.

Listen to Megan who brings up two boys on her own: 'I feel I am responsible for my family's health so I have to use fresh things. We haven't got a freezer and I don't use tinned. I spend hours balancing what my loved ones want with what I feel is good for them. The children want junk like fish fingers and crisps. I think they should have what's fresh and not cold either so I put up hot casseroles.'

Even though Fiona and Megan are divorced their ex-husbands' views on what is appropriate healthy food for their children are still taken into account.

Megan told me: 'Actually I'm a vegetarian, but because their father thinks I should give the boys meat, he says growing boys need their meat, I do a veggy casserole for me and put meat in a separate one for them. Strange, isn't it?'

At first I did not think it was strange, until I listened to a number of similar accounts and realized how strong an influence the wishes of even absentee males can be. Fiona's story was remarkably similar. 'He has the boys alternate Saturdays and often takes them to Wimpy bars. Well he's out to please them, isn't he? But he doesn't think it's right that I should. He says it wouldn't be keeping them healthy, and they must have a cooked at home, so that's what I do.'

Remember Max, who insisted that Imogen made hot meals, not cold flan for their children? Remember Hugh the town planner who wouldn't share the food planning but who decreed that their family should eat a balanced meal, and that getting the balance right was Esme's job? It is always the women's task to organize that balance. It is always wives, girlfriends, and mothers who are in charge of the family's health.

Esme, deep into her studies, said sturdily: 'Because I agree with Hugh that we have to have a balanced meal, I do it. Because we haven't enough money for me to say "Sod it, let's have a carry-out", I do it. Anyway there's the problem of Hugh not thinking a carry-out is healthy enough.' A trifle wearily she added: 'Now that I'm in my final year at college it's a real trial but I can't see any choice. That's the thing about tradition, women are brought up to do the shopping and have charge of the family's health. Hugh and I have begun to change the rules a little, but there are some you can't break.'

In most homes today there is the conflict that regardless of who is the wage-earner, the woman is expected to spend time in the kitchen, symbolically and practically providing the nurturing through food and being held responsible for the health of the household.

The most important thing is not how 'healthy' the family meal should be but that the woman should be in charge of its organization.

You can produce statistics proving that there is more nutrient value in meals from MacDonalds or takeaway fish-and-chip shops than there is in the average British meat and two veg but the woman who sends her children regularly to MacDonalds is seen to be falling short of the required standard.

Fiona's agreement that she should not take her boys to Wimpy bars although their father does, bears this out. In Esme's line, 'There's the problem of Hugh not thinking a carry-out is healthy enough,' there is a half-conscious awareness that her motherly role, not the food's nutrients, is on the agenda. Similarly, Imogen was caught between her role as good cook which would ensure her cold flan would be healthy food, and her position as a good mother which decreed only hot food is fit for 'proper' families.

These accounts show that though women are nominally in charge of the household's health, it is often men's decisions about which food is healthy that count. Chris Wardle quoted the conclusions of one mid-seventies researcher on why nutritionists were having only slight success in improving the average British diet. 'Many still believe that mothers decide what their children eat. However, today it is actually the husband who has the greatest influence over what food is eaten in the home. Ironically he is the member of the family who knows least about nutrition.'[7]

He is however the one with the power to enforce decisions, a power often masked by the rhetoric of diet-as-morality. Who has power, whose is the responsibility, in the following story of food and health?

'Jane, my elder sister, had been married for years to Ken, a self-indulgent man with a red complexion and a temper to match. He made it plain from the start that a good wife cooked to please her husband. Jane certainly did that. In her lunch hours she bought him treats, on bus rides to work she planned luscious, often fattening meals he considered proper. They always included meat, and plenty of cream cakes. Of course he put on weight and so did she. Although he called her a fat cow, he never allowed her to cook simple, unfattening meals. He demanded syrupy puddings, lots of cake, butter in his mash.

'Last year the doctor discovered Ken had a heart complaint and told him to reorganize his diet. The first thing Ken did was to shout at Jane and blame her for his heart disease. He said she fed him the wrong foods. Very distressed, she began a new meal plan of salads. He got even angrier and said they weren't proper meals, and it was obvious she had stopped caring for him. Some evenings when I was there I heard him scream at her for not baking cakes, for docking sugar in his tea, or for giving him smaller pieces of lean meat. Poor Jane got increasingly nervy with his conflicting demands. If she served him fatty foods he abused her, if she didn't he teetered on the edge of violence. He told me he thought Jane was trying to kill him! To look after his health realistically she would have had to deny him what he saw as proper meals and she couldn't do that. It never occurred to either of them that his health and his eating habits were *his* problems. The rows were terrible. He refused to change and attributed his worsening health to her. After months of worry she cracked up and had a nervous breakdown.'

Even in the areas delineated as women's province, such as health and food, male management and male wishes circumscribe women's choices. Again and again women are caught between these prescribed roles of being good cooks and good mothers, as much to men as to children.

Even women who were not mothers saw cooking as a 'motherly' process, a way in which they could express affection, caring, and responsibility. Full-time housewives saw food as the crux of their womanly role and placed a particularly high emotional investment in preparing proper meals.

Frances, a London mother, considered herself a *good* mother, as well as a good manager. 'Cooking a meal for my three children is an act of giving. I give them love when I serve them. That's why I always start with raw ingredients so that my meals show effort. Pulling out a Marks and Spencer packet never shows effort.'

Jenny, who had no children, but who catered for her husband and elder brother who lived with them, saw herself as the right kind of motherly woman. 'Andy, my brother, has a very hard time at the petroleum works, so weekdays I wouldn't dream of just doing a sausage fry-up like I would weekends. He needs my chops with a good gravy when he comes in. Bill is on the road selling all day, and bad-tempered with it, because daytimes he has to make do with plastic sahnies from the caffs. When he comes home he has to have his grill even if it isn't a roast. You have to mother them a bit.'

This attitude leads women to feel both needy of male approval and vulnerable if the meals are rejected. Jenny said: 'Sometimes Bill has had such a foul day he just tells me and my dinner to piss off. I'm never sure if he means it but I want to cry. I look at the chops going greasy on the plate, and I just hate myself and can't eat them.'

And here is a snippet of a typical interview in Shere Hite's *Women and Love*: 'If he criticized my cooking (adversely) I used to get very hurt. Of if there's a bad family argument and no one eats the meal I'm very upset because I think "Here I slaved cooking this meal and here's the thanks I get.' "[8]

Megan the vegetarian (who served her boys meat at her husband's dictate) confirmed: 'I get a feeling of impotence when the boys won't eat what I've cooked. It's like I've become sexually sterile.'

For many women the possibility of rejection is preferable to the guilt which occurs if they do not cook proper meals for their families. After her divorce Nancy spent many years cooking for and being rejected by her two girls. 'They used to be so faddy and make such a fuss after all the hours I had put in that I couldn't bear it. So now when they rush home from school saying, "I've got to be out by seven, isn't there anything to eat?" I have started to reply: "There's food in the fridge, just get your own." The trouble is I've swapped feeling rejected for feeling guilt-ridden.'

This was an emotion I understood perfectly. After many years of catering for the likes and dislikes of teenage girls, Ba and I finally decided that at least once or twice a week the adults should get a break. We instituted the MAKE-YOUR-OWN syndrome. The problem was that when Vic or Marm or Cas got in from school and expected to rush out again after a meal already prepared by one of us, their cry of 'Oh no! Not "make-your-own" AGAIN!' wrung my highly socialized heart with dreadful pangs. I never did decide which was worse: guilt or rejection.

Author Rosemary Manning, in her book *A Corridor of Mirrors*[9] reminds us of the other side of the picture, the child's viewpoint. 'Pain always returns too easily, even in its trivial form. I hurt my mother by refusing to eat the goodies she made. Food is an old temptation as far back as Eve's apple. I saw Mother's attempts to win me as a threat, as a preliminary to talk that I did not wish to hear . . . She was cooking and I was leaning against the kitchen table.'

Sheila Kitzinger believes that the notion of 'reject-my-food-reject-me' begins with the food bond established by breastfeeding.

'I think that to discover that sustenance, the very basic necessity of life, the thing which is going to make that baby grow up strong and healthy, is welling up from inside you and milk is flowing in fountains from your breasts, is a very exciting experience. It is truly life-enhancing. To feel the baby latching on to the breast, and then sucking in a very satisfying way, and knowing you can give that to the baby, I think is marvellous.

'But when a woman does that, when a woman offers herself literally as food, as a body, she is making herself utterly vulnerable to rejection by her baby.'

The feeling of rejection that can occur between mother and baby, can be translated symbolically into similar feelings between the woman and any other adult to whom she offers food.

'Food is heavily symbolic, it can symbolize celebration, a sort . of communion, but it can produce anxiety and can signify deep rejection. I think, later in life, women can feel very put down, desperately rejected, when other people, either children or the man in the family, refuse the food she is offering them, because it is like refusing the woman herself.'

Spare Tyre, the British women's theatre group, who run workshops after their shows for women to discuss issues of food and gender, have taken some very penetrating looks at women's food preparation and the emotional investment that goes into it. Founder members of the company Clare Chapman and Katina Noble agreed with Sheila Kitzinger about how this works for ordinary women.

'A woman has to prepare all that food, and if the husband or boyfriend doesn't like it, the woman herself feels rejected,' said Katina Noble. 'If the man is late, the dinner is left in the oven and burned. These things are interesting in terms of symbols of a relationship, of love, of loss, of abandonment. He lets the dinner burn, he has let part of their love wither away. He has rejected her food, he has rejected part of her.'

Clare Chapman added: 'Yes, and finishing up the children's scraps. How often have I thought, that chicken casserole, that was my achievement for the day, and no one wanted it. So I'll eat it all up myself because nobody else liked it.'

Being a vegetarian, the particular achievement I ate up for more years than I care to recall was my brilliant vegetable stew. I have to admit that if I was the only one in the house to say it was brilliant that simply wasn't enough to make me feel proud!

For some women proper meals are less tied into ideas of mothering and more tied up to concepts of 'wholesomeness' built around the word 'natural'. One woman summed it up: 'If the food hasn't been messed about with, if it's natural, then I know it will be a wholesome meal for the family.' I knew what she meant because I too have this need to prepare with natural plain ingredients, fresh vegetables and herbs, before I consider that the meal I have cooked is 'real'. For some irritating reason that I cannot comprehend I also need to spend time on it, even when I am late. For women like us, tinfoil trays of lentil roast (simply add cold water and mix with marge) or frozen vegetable lasagne (labelled 'a vegetable meal') are not in fact meals at all. And if I indulge in Uncle Ben's quick cook rice or packet cheese sauce I suffer a positive sense of sin!

My insistence on 'natural' ingredients seems to be shared by many women who have been mesmerized by the rhetoric that certain foods are wholesome, proper, and virtuous – in a word, natural, while others are not. That this is both a reasonable idea and a bit of a con can be seen in the difference between white rice, which has been 'refined' to the extent that it has been de-husked, and brown rice, which has some of the husk still on. The brown will contain more fibre and more nourishment, but when we buy it we have no way of knowing, for instance, what chemicals it has been sprayed with. Brown sugar is supposed to be unrefined, as opposed to white, but one always suspects that half of it must simply be coloured.

The rhetoric surrounds both 'health' foods and highly refined processed foods, and feeds on the presumed guilt felt by many housewives who consistently use convenience foods but believe they are not comparable in quality or nutritional value to foods which have been fully prepared by themselves. Researcher Paul Atkinson points out that 'The category of "natural" carries with it overtones of "purity" which is also captured in the closely associated notion of "whole" food.' Atkinson believes that contemporary foodstuff imagery reflects this when it suggests 'so-called "convenience" foods have been tampered with, adulterated, have had their "natural" nutrients destroyed.'[10] So consumers (mainly women) are gently led towards the contrast between the natural/healthy on the one hand and the unnatural/unhealthy on the other.

It is not only sensible, food-conscious adult women (which most of us like to believe we are) who are influenced in this way. Even teenagers hooked on oven-ready chips with tons of ketchup have bitten into the ideology of pure and natural. Certainly the four we brought up have swallowed some of the 'wholesome' wholesale!

Vic, now eighteen, recently told me about a weekend several years ago when Ba and I were away. 'Mum had left lots of fresh food but I couldn't be bothered to cook it so I bought a tinfoil dinner in a plastic pack. The potatoes looked really new and tempting but when I'd cooked it the whole thing tasted like powder. It was horrid. What was worse, Sal, was when I'd finished it, I was consumed with guilt. I felt I hadn't had a proper meal,' she said.

'What did you do?' I asked with interest. 'Did you cook up something else from raw ingredients or did you just drown your sorrows in a tin of baked beans?'

'Well, not exactly,' she said grinning. 'I went and cut myself some of that wholemeal bread and spread it with tons of peanut butter. At least I knew it was fresh and natural.'

This idea of naturalness as intrinsic to good food, consistently used by vegetarians and wholefood promoters, has now spread even to the processed food industry. In his study of the symbolic significance of health foods, Atkinson finds that a very wide

117

range of foodstuffs advertise their 'naturalness'; not merely stoneground flour, brown rice, or dried fruits, but also foods which are quite blatantly commercially produced.[11]

Anne Murcott pointed out to me that since the publication of Atkinson's article, even very highly processed supermarket products are hyped more and more in terms of 'natural goodness, old-fashioned wholesomeness and traditional fare.' Or in some cases even 'fayre'! All of which it seems appeal to the large number of women who stalk the supermarket aisles.

She reminded me that we can now walk into any British supermarket and buy a cereal in a sealed plastic bag which will stoutly state it is 'natural crunchy whatnots.'[12]

The labelling seems to work; many women undoubtedly choose the 'natural' bag in preference to a packet of cereal without such a label.

If the processed food adverts were accurate, many women I talked to could have lightened their domestic burdens or improved their financial state by serving canned or processed foods, but like the women interviewed by Charles and Kerr and by Anne Murcott, they did not do so because in their view processed foods do not carry the meanings of 'proper meals' suitable for men and children.

Anne Murcott found her interviewees preferred to prepare their own ingredients because that involved application, corners couldn't be cut, and women had to 'be bothered'. I discovered also that although processed and frozen food was often a very attractive alternative for time-pressed women and they bought it in consistent and large amounts, they saw it as 'morally inferior', because it took less time and effort, it involved less emotional investment, and it earned them a lower mothering accolade than hot meals made from raw ingredients. They did not say that convenience foods were undesirable because they lacked nutritional content.

Joan Dye Gussow and Mary Anselmino, nutrition educaters and researchers, (who found evidence that women's use of time has not markedly changed for the better since the introduction of

118

food innovations) studied womens' attitudes towards processed and convenience foods. They explored two key questions: firstly whether women really do hate to cook and are therefore eternally grateful for canning, processing and freezing; secondly whether there is any evidence that women's desire to get out of the household actually led to convenience foods.[13]

They point out that though most of us – even food professionals – have accepted the notion that 'convenience foods' have freed women from the drudgery of the kitchen, this notion may be flawed. Their research shows that changes in the food supply have not in the main liberated women for more delightful tasks, that many women do not view cooking as drudgery, and like the women I talked to many still view processed and convenience food with caution or dislike.

Anselmino discovered that 'the very attitudes among women that were supposed to have created a demand for convenience were actively promoted by the media . . . the food processors recognized the housewife as their most powerful rival. Because of women's positive feelings about their own work, early ads for processed foods could only hint that cookery was a form of drudgery.'

Joan Dye Gussow discovered evidence to show that even today 'many women failed to view cooking as old-fashioned, necessary drudgery or hard exacting work'. Indeed there were indications that women found some forms of food preparation 'a creative and enjoyable process' and in the few serious studies that had looked at women's attitudes to housework, one of the very few liked tasks was preparing food from raw ingredients. Many women I talked to did indeed find the actual cooking from raw ingredients enjoyable, what they disliked was the constant unending ultimate responsibility for planning and cooking.

Obviously there always will be women who hate cooking, but Gussow reports that 'there is no documentation that food preparation is or was a widely disliked task, just as there is no proof that a widely articulated hatred of cooking preceded the introduction of "convenience foods."' I met with a genuine suspicion of convenience foods, even from women who used them.

Anselmino's investigation pointed to 'the role that industry had in fostering negative attitudes toward food preparation' where cooking was portrayed as hard work and food was portrayed as raw material 'valued not for its intrinsic deliciousness but for its uniformity'. In other words, industry and advertising has asked women to celebrate the disappearance of seasonal vegetables and hail the uniformity of tasteless tomatoes all year round. As one woman living on state benefit said to me, 'Canned vegetables are such a disappointment after real ones. I try not to serve my husband them, even though it would be much cheaper.'

A tin of peas is cheaper than a pound of fresh peas. They don't taste anything like as good, but they require no preparation. Much of their nutritional value is destroyed in the canning process. Processed foods are intricately laced into the relationship between social class and health. DHSS findings confirm that the quality of food and health is a function of class and money, that the working class and the poor eat worse food and have worse health then those in economically sound middle-class jobs.[14]

Recent research shows that as the quality of food and health varies according to region, those of us in Scotland, Wales, Northern Ireland and Northern parts of England feed the greater number of our unemployed on larger quantities of more highly processed food and suffer poorer health accordingly.[15]

What those studies do not show, however, is whether factors other than health and money would influence women's decisions to use processed food, if economically they had a free choice. What came to light from my conversations with women is that this intangible concept of 'realness' is a major influence on their choice irrespective of the amount they are budgeting with. Margie, whose husband is on unemployment benefit, told me: 'Their dad would rather I gave the kids a few cooked veg than a tin of veg soup. He's right, you know, because if it's out of a tin it isn't a real meal.' The cooked veg would cost more than the tin, and take longer to prepare. They are the wish of a man. They are real. Fortuitously, they are far more nourishing.

We, the second generation of minute-rice users, may have been seduced by advertisers into *using* convenience foods but we have not yet been seduced into approving of it.

Processed rather than fresh ingredients were bad enough, it seemed, but to serve a packaged frozen meal indicated indifference. Erica sternly summed this up: 'When I eat on my own I don't mind frozen dishes, but I feel guilty if I pull something out of the freezer to feed anyone I'm fond of. I've been brought up to put *care* into cooking. Frozen food simply isn't adequate.'

Even students who had difficulty cooking for their boyfriends on bedsit gasrings felt this. As one Cambridge student put it: 'We'll use tinned food because it's convenient but frozen is taking it too far. We wouldn't do that to our boyfriends.'

Interestingly, it would seem that when a relationship ceases to be meaningful so does the food. Where women saw their personal relationships as lacking in love or changing for the worse, if they were sufficiently independent of male disapproval they 'degenerated' into serving frozen meals. If they were still constrained by male or child eater approbation they continued to make 'real' meals but felt their families or lovers 'deserved' frozen.

Clancy talked about the end of her affair. 'Cooking for your lover at the beginning of your relationship is like a golden bubble. Everything has to be just perfect. Very complicated, very real food from raw ingredients, decorated exquisitely, and somehow utterly different from cooking even a nice meal for a good friend. When the affair with Thomas was over, everything suddenly seemed unreal, so the food I made us could be less real too. Of course I went on cooking for him, but it no longer mattered that I bought a plastic meal or even pulled something out of the freezer. My memory of those last months is of cold cold food hastily shoved in the microwave and neither of us noticing.'

This is not only true of women's traditional attitude towards men. When two women live in a partnership the emotional commitment symbolized by carefully prepared meals appears to

be just as consequential, possibly more so. So too is the change
in the menu when the relationship fades. Monica, who had lived
with her women friend for seven years, told me: 'When our affair
was at its height, meals together were special and significant. We
always spent time cooking for each other, always used raw
ingredients. Towards the end, in the last six months, we no
longer cooked in that nurturing caring way. We took things out
of the freezer. We had hasty time-saving plastic meals and we
justified them to each other in terms of lack of time. We never
said what the new food pattern really meant. When she went I
carried on eating frozen food while she began cooking for a new
lover.'

If frozen foods signal the end of an affair, are there other kinds
of food which herald its beginning, or mark its progress? If
certain meals are considered appropriate for proper occasions,
are there particular menus and rituals for 'improper' occasions,
such as lustful nights or clandestine meetings? Remember the
piquant avocados with garlic sauce which spiced Robin's secret
affair with Tony; Philippa's 'simple steak' which became a
'romantic act'.

Just as the safe and steady content of meat and two veg
symbolizes women's roles as proper housewives, proper mothers,
proper women; so the exciting quality of specially inventive
meals, dedicated with extra care, symbolizes our sexual or sensual
longings. Interestingly, when the object of our affections is a
man, meat is usually on the menu, but it is often embellished
with a fancy sauce, and followed by a creamy or elaborate
pudding. Chocolate features strongly in romantic meals.

Listen to Susie, twenty-two, engaged to be married: 'Sometimes food can be a substitute for sex. But when you're in love,
there's something very sexual about eating. It has to be the right
food, the kind of meals men like. I always buy steak, and whip
up a cream and mushroom sauce. I always make a frothy dessert.
Something that looks difficult. My fiancé always buys me
chocolate creams with gooey centres. Like that Tom Jones film,
the food must be salivating and sumptuous. There must be no

possibility of rejection. Then when you're deliciously full you're ready to make love.'

Jancy, ten years older, told me: 'If a girlfriend comes to dinner it's OK to do a fry-up, but if it's a bloke and you know what he's got in mind, you don't want to remind him of his mum. So the right thing to make is very underdone steak, all that dripping blood makes blokes feel virile. After that I do a show-off pudding like baked alaska. Dipping slowly into that hot-and-cold creamy mixture and watching each other as you eat, you just know you'll be in bed before you've finished it. No man I know will be turned off a meal like that or turned off you.'

Sammy, who had been celibate for two years, used surprisingly similar images. 'When I was off it, I used to say I'd prefer a good meal to a good bonk. I'd certainly rather have a decent box of chocs, it's much less bother. But after two years I met James, who was so yummy I had to admit I preferred him to a Crunchie bar. Once I'd recognized that, I knew I'd have to spend hours cooking him special stuff if we were going to start doing it. Nothing frozen, nothing tinned, it just had to be pure steak almost raw, the blood makes men feel horny. But I topped it with this salivating mushroom sauce followd by a creamy dessert like chocolate profiteroles. We used to eat them with our hands, then we'd begin to touch each other. If he rejected a meal like that I would be pretty sure he would reject me.'

Even women who do not enjoy rich foods made from cream or chocolate nevertheless make it for men they are attracted to or care about. Penelope, a forty-two-year-old single mother, told me: 'I hate rich foods, but every man I've had a relationship with demanded orgasmic meals on those kinds of nights. I'd usually do a spicy borscht with sour cream because that really is orgasmic. I'd watch them lust first for the food then for me. Of course I always held back till the end of the meal, which was usually icecream with hot chocolate sauce. We'd let the chocolate sauce cool then take it upstairs with us.' She gazed at me in a considering way for a moment, eyes twinkling, and added: 'If you haven't time to make hot chocolate sauce, chocolate spread is nearly as good.'

I discovered that chocolate spread is extremely popular with men in romantic or sexual situations. A student called Pansy kept a dozen tubs in her college rooms. 'My men friends call me the Chocolate Spread Queen, because I never run short. I usually cook them veal escalope with a delicate sauce, then we finish with icecream, topped with double cream and cherries, and after that instead of mint chocs I bring out a tub of chocolate spread and begin to spread it gently over my lover's willy. It isn't runny so you have to lick quite hard to get it off. It gets you over any initial aversion, and it gets you into loving just that little bit more. I've always made meals like that for my lovers and I've always been very popular.'

I met only one women, Gilly, a teacher, who did not plan special foods for such an evening. She expected male lovers to cook for her. Usually she demanded pizza. 'I never cook before I am about to tumble into bed with a man I know well. It isn't worth it. His mind just isn't on food. And with a new man it's even worse. But after a bonk we're both really starving so I get him to make me a delicious pizza, drooling with mushrooms and green peppers and mozarella cheese. Sometimes I need pizzas between bonks. If I'm feeling too tired and don't really want to do it, I have been known to say, "OK, I'll do it if you cook me a pizza." Even if he won't cook, the very least I expect is that he'll go out and buy one!' One reason Gilly did not cook elaborate meals in sexual situations was that she had spent years watching her mother do so. 'After Dad left Mum, every time she was starting an affair, she'd scrimp and save to buy steak, then she'd spend hours slaving away at a really complex pudding. It just seemed ridiculous.'

It does of course seem ridiculous. But many of us will admit to similar behaviour. Looking back over my chequered culinary career, I cannot compete with confessions in quite the same way, if only because I cannot take refuge in an anonymous name! But I can confirm that a romantic affair breeds the desire to put on a gastronomic spectacular, whether for a man or another woman. What springs to mind is the romance with Terry, which is usefully coincident in several key ways with these other accounts.

It started when we began a correspondence. Initially just a few postcards, then more regular communication. I have to admit that the regularity was entirely one-sided. Mine. Terry was tall, aloof, moved in mysterious business circles to which I had no access, was usually too busy to answer letters or to buy food. Terry lived in a rented palatial apartment with gracious furniture and a woman who cleaned. I lived in a small house I cleaned myself on the days I could not write. I had recently come out of a longstanding relationship. We started to have meals together, sometimes at the elegant apartment, sometimes in my small house. We cooked in turn. I was delighted to take more than my turn. Terry seldom shopped. Too overworked, too full a life. Domesticity hardly a part of the mysterious business world. The fridge in the apartment stayed empty, which I found distressing. Did I want to fill Terry's life? What I did was to fill the fridge! I began to leave food parcels on the doorstep of the flat. Was I falling in love? I expect I was falling into something, and love has a more mature ring than infatuation.

One night Terry arrived with a bottle of champagne. Pure Bollinger. Nothing wishy-washy or second-rate about this offering. The occasion did not seem sufficiently momentous to merit the uncorking. 'Save it until Saturday week,' Terry said suavely. I shall come round then. We shall make Saturday special. Is seven OK?'

Terry strode out casually, memos to write, phone calls to attend to, meetings to chair. I began to plan a menu. Would next Saturday be special? We were after all still only 'good friends'. If it was going to be the start of something different, I had better organize a delicious repast.

Strangely the following weekend there was no phone call from Terry. During the week a further absence of phone calls. I pretended to myself there was nothing wrong. I left a few more food parcels on the doorstep, hoping it would not rain. There was no response. I went shopping on Friday, felt joyous, hurrying in and out of crowded foodstores. On Saturday I prepared the elaborate meal, the kind designed to look as if it had been thrown together in twenty minutes, but to great effect. Several hors d'oeuvres, sole and spring onions garnished with seafood, a complex sauce, a sprinkling of brandy, fresh vegetables, an attractive side salad, all lovingly prepared as I played Vivaldi on the record player. Cheese and fruit would have sufficed for dessert as I did have another chapter to write, but I spent several hours making a complicated blackcurrant and cream mousse. Whipped. Then chilled. Then decorated. Only the candles were missing. I trudged down to the store where for 49p I purchased two bright red candles. A trifle Christmassy but better than nothing. I trudged back for the matching red napkins.

Promptly at seven Terry arrived, carrying tulips. Dozens and dozens. Glowing red and yellow embers burning their way through the paper. I did not have enough vases. I did not have enough words. Inside the bag was a box of exotic, cream-filled chocolates. 'Just a little treat, dear.'

Terry had forgotten I do not eat chocolates. But I took it as a token that Saturday was indeed going to be special. Vivaldi was still playing in the background. 'How odd,' Terry mused. 'I have just been listening to Vivaldi on the car radio. That exact piece.'

Not odd at all. An omen. We were inevitably to become lovers. I sighed a big sigh of relief and looked at the dining table with contentment. Terry opened the champagne. Hardly a plop. Touch of the expert. Terry moves in Bollinger society. Would I soon become accustomed to opening Bollinger with hardly a plop? We chatted idly, sipping through the bubbles. Terry had spent several of the previous weeks hosting a foreign visitor, being kind and hospitable, driving the visitor places. Not any ordinary visitor, I was given to understand. Someone of rank and status. Someone of infinite attraction. 'The attraction of a strong character,' Terry hastily amended. The story went on and on. When were we going to talk about us? Was the visitor really attractive, I suddenly wondered. Could the visitor cook as well as I could? We had just begun on the hors d'oeuvres. The rest of the dinner was in the oven. Suddenly with a tearing flash of insight I said: 'That was who you were with last weekend, wasn't it? You have become lovers, haven't you?'

We did not finish the hors d'oeuvres. We never started the remainder of the meal. It frizzled up in the oven. I had spent the day, or my life, cooking and preparing, and now my chapter was in small fragments on the study floor, my life was in small pieces on the dining-room floor, my futon was ready for me to sleep in alone on the bedroom floor. Food and disorder everywhere.

After Terry had departed, I froze what was left of the courgettes. The fish dish was ruined. I tried the seafood sauce the next evening on my jacket potato, but it had a bitter taste. Some sauces do not keep. I also found Vivaldi a little hard to listen to that week.

Terry's last words had been: 'I am sorry. Truly I am. I know how you feel.' Did you, Terry? Did you then? Do you now? Does one ever really know how somebody else feels when they are being rejected? If you had known, you might have tried to eat some of the fish!

I saw my life measured out in recipes. I saw anger and rejection through a thin film of food. That incident, like so many I have listened to this year, does not merely illustrate the kind of ornate meals a proper woman makes for what she hopes is an improper occasion; it shows us yet again, the power that food has to be so much more than fuel in our lives.

For women, food is built into each sexual contract, attached to the process of each affair. Food is tied into romance, fastened into security. We date over dinner. We lust over lunch. We toy with each other's affections as we toy with our tea. This symbolism goes back to something I discovered earlier, that when we give food to other people, we give up a part of ourselves, open ourselves up, lay ourselves on the line. The connections between loving and feeding start with the breast and continue throughout women's lives. And if we are to offer ourselves, of course it must be with a proper meal.

Given women's emotional attitudes to frozen and processed foods, it comes as no surprise to find that women are actively hostile to the container-type food with which astronauts were originally provided and which many of us use for camping and caravanning with children. Space-age victuals, which come hydrated or compressed, fitted no one's definition of real food.

Paula, saving her clerk's wages to go hang-gliding, is keenly interested in all aspects of space travel; but her reaction to their provisions was sympathetic rather than enthusiastic: 'After I'd watched those TV programmes about space I felt really sorry for them. I kept noticing their dinners came out of packets like toothpaste. It was weird the way they had to suck them out. The only way you knew it was pork and spuds was by the label. It didn't seem like a dinner to me. You've got to see your meat not squeeze it and it's got to smell like your childhood and people have got to think you've taken some effort.'

Several middle-class women felt meals were places to linger and talk, and that the appearance of the food counted a great deal.

'Talking over supper is what matters. You wouldn't want to linger over a tube.'

'You couldn't put containers of food on the table, it wouldn't look right, and nobody would be impressed.'

'You can't put paper napkins by the side of a tube, or light it up with a pretty candle. Space age stuff is like putting an open tin of sardines on the dinner table.'

Many working-class women felt meals were occasions to fill your belly, and there was a general emphasis on quantity.

'You've got to fill the family up with your teas and all those tubes have got the same amounts in. No, it wouldn't do for our lot.'

Many women mentioned smell. 'My husband and children like to come home and smell the dinner cooking, then they know I've done a proper meal. They're even funny about fish and chips from the chippy. Although they enjoy it Fridays, they always say it hasn't got the smell or the taste of homemade. You don't get any of that with the compressed stuff.'

All the women I talked to mentioned physical effort, emotional investment, and male approval as being lacking in space-age fodder. These were two comments:

'If I was an astronaut I daresay I'd be thankful for anything but there's no effort been put in it, so though I'd eat it myself I wouldn't serve it up to him.'

'In our house the children might eat it, give them a laugh, but Bill wouldn't touch it because it isn't real food. He'd still think he was hungry even if it filled him. That's because you've got to look as though you've spent your time in the kitchen even if you haven't!'

Only Katie from Canada had anything positive to say and even she was lukewarm: 'We've got to move with the new age. Compressed foods are just the beginning. It's a good idea but it does seem clinical.'

If food were nothing more than fuel, then women would not cavil at these containers of body-building material. One squeeze would give us two hours' energy. Time spent on elaborate preparation and cooking could be saved. Human tanks could be refuelled whenever necessary. The act of eating need no longer be a communal experience, it could become a basic and private act, such as washing or excreting. But women do not want to squeeze supper on to the plates just before doing their teeth. Indeed the fact that most of us find such a notion definitely unpleasant is an indicator of the strong psychological and social factors attached both to cooking and eating 'proper' meals.

If space-age food is ridiculous, surely the sublimely proper meal must be the traditional Sunday Dinner.

I have always accepted that the Sunday roast is still a very popular institution but I had never successfully analysed why. However after talking to women about what in their view is and is not 'real food', it is obvious that as long as family eating patterns are structured by our notion of 'proper meals', Sunday dinner will remain the archetype of proper family food. And women will still find themselves preparing it!

Hetty, whose food budget has been reduced by her husband's change of job, told me: 'Meat is the main thing on Sundays. Sometimes we go to Mum's, and some Sundays Mum and Dad come round ours. I used to always do a lovely big joint of beef or lamb, but now some Sundays we're down to chicken dinners. But of course I still do my roast spuds, and the kids still ask for Yorkshires. They say it isn't a Sunday without them.'

The women that Charles and Kerr talked to had very similar views. Meat is the central element of the proper meal and even in reduced circumstances it must still be there at least on a Sunday. One woman reported: 'Meat is the main thing. Every Sunday we go up to my mam's for our dinner. At one time I could get chops and steak and all sorts, but now we have things like liver and mince, the opposite to what I used to buy.'

Most women feel it as a hardship if they are not able to cook a traditional Sunday meal with the correct trimmings. Some women, short of money, who are unable to cook 'properly' during the week feel it is important to cook correctly at the weekend. This was a characteristic remark: 'When we have chops instead of a joint, it isn't the same. You need your Sundays, don't you?'

The permanent absence of a man sometimes produces changes in this conventional menu. Jilly has been a single parent for a year. 'Now it's only me and the children I don't have to get a joint. It isn't really worth it. At first it seemed wrong but we are all used to it now.'

Tricia, who lives with her woman friend and their children, told me: 'When Janet and I started to bring up our kids together we changed to a vegetarian diet so of course we gave up Sunday dinners. The kids were surprised at first but they soon settled down and we are all thriving on new kinds of food.'

For Tricia and Janet the alternative lifestyle brought with it a radically different food ideology which no longer placed a special value on the preparation and consumption of traditional meals highlighted by a Sunday roast.

My own experience was similar. In the life I shared with Ba and our girls, for some years after I became a vegetarian we would both cook vegetarian meals during the week, but she would make an elaborate and traditional roast beef dinner with brilliant Yorkshire pudding on Sundays. (I have to admit that I never gave up eating the Yorkshire pud – all that gravy – with my vegetables! Was it the taste of Sin that gave it that added spark or was it simply that I hadn't cooked it?)

Then one day Ba decided it would be liberating for all of us to give up the roast. That first meat-free Sunday we told the girls to Make Your Own, and set off for the pub. The girls were outraged at this audacious flouting of tradition and did not accompany us. Indeed two of them lurked sulkily in bed and did not eat lunch at all! We bought lagers and hearty sandwiches, then looked around. The pub was absolutely packed with *men* comfortably smoking and drinking while their wives and girl-friends slaved over hot stoves basting the meat and waiting for the Yorkshires to rise. 'This is more like it!' Ba said. 'Why haven't we thought of doing this before?' The following Sunday the girls joined us.

Having been very proper women making very proper meals for more Sundays than I feel like counting, at first we thought the heavens might fall in as a punishment for our improper food behaviour. But they didn't. Not that I want to give all you women still out there slaving away on a Sunday any ideas . . .

SIX

TABLE MANNERS
AND TYRANNY

'That boarding school you sent me to, with its all-female staff, was just as tyrannical as *you* were at home!' said Marmoset, in one of those conversational tones, that can only lead a mother into trouble. I decided it might be wiser to avoid the issue of home, and to concentrate on school discipline.

'Tell me what you remember,' I encouraged.

'Well, they were ever so strict,' she said. 'We had to eat everything on the plate or we wouldn't get seconds. If we wanted more we had to leave our knife and fork on the plate in a triangle shape and if we didn't want more, we had to place them together. I remember the little cheeses in plastic packs. Two of my friends didn't want to eat theirs so they unwrapped them, dropped them on the floor, and ground them into the wood with their shoes. They were forced to scrape them up and eat them. They were sick later. No one stuck up for them and I was relieved that I liked cheese.'

'That's barbaric!' I said self-righteously. 'That's a real abuse of power.' Marmoset looked at me with a hint of amusement. 'Lots of people you wouldn't expect abuse power,' she said knowingly.

I could see it was certainly going to be safer to stick to the education system, where, according to the women I talked to, keeping your elbows on the table or your mouth open when chewing were but minor transgressions in an escalating series of deadly food felonies. My daughter was far from unusual in recalling school food as a primary part of an authoritarian structure.

Shirley, a young playgroup organizer, told me: 'I think my

first and worst school memory was being forced to eat dried haddock that flaked in your mouth. I must have been quite little, because I remember hanging on to the belt of Mum's plastic mac as she walked away, leaving me in the hands of the teachers. I felt betrayed. The teacher in charge of dinners used to come round our table straight from writing on the blackboard. She'd deliberately shake her chalky fingers into the dinner. Then she'd stand and watch us try to swallow flaked fish and blackboard chalk dust. Sometimes I nearly choked and wondered how my mum could have left me there. Even today when we have haddock I suddenly see her plastic mac shining and I remember how I gulped back the tears.'

Beryl, a primary school teacher, had a similar recollection. 'I still sweat when I see thin strands of fat round the meat. At school I used to wrap the gristly meat in my hanky and stuff it in my pocket. Then I'd sweat with nerves through afternoon lessons in case the teachers found out. One day I was caught. This big woman towered over me. "Take that precious morsel out of your pocket!" she bellowed. "You ungrateful little squirt. *Take it out.*" I didn't know she'd seen me. Eyes in the back of their arses they had! Well the meat had slipped out of the hanky and had stuck on my tweed tunic pocket. It was covered in fluff and hairs and dirt. "I can't eat that," I said. The teacher looked positively triumphant. "You should have thought of that before. Eat it!" she said. "And don't put your elbows on the table while you do so." I ate it of course. Then I was sick in the loo.'

Despite her vivid memory of that unpleasant episode, Beryl admits that today she regularly patrols school dining tables to ensure that children eat up 'everything on their plates'. 'It is my responsibility,' she said seriously. 'It's as much a matter of health as it is of disciplining their spirits. I'd feel I'd personally failed if they didn't eat it up. School dinner discipline is not like other school rules, because so much more is invested in it.'

I found this an interesting parallel to the accounts of emotional investment and potential rejection offered by women cooking up 'proper meals'. The significance of Beryl's account was heightened by forty-year-old Janice's interpretation of the attitude of female teachers towards food control. Janice still recalls with horror sticking her gristly meat under the chair then lying to save her skin when she was confronted. 'Food was such an important issue to the women who taught us. You almost had to lie so as not to let them down.' Though male teachers also exerted authority at mealtimes, Janice recalls the women as having greater effect. 'It was the tone they used. Something about the tone. Sometimes they were angry with us but there was a lot of other emotion behind their voices. You felt it was because it was about food. Eating up school dinners wasn't an ordinary school rule, to them it was really important. It meant something, so generally we did it. It was like you were doing it for them. That's what was in their tone.'

These accounts of school meals complemented the evidence given by women on proper meals, in showing this curious connection between women's emotional and symbolic attitude to food and the fact that women have access to food in a way they do not have access to power. The school meal material also raises new questions about the use of power wielded by women in the area of food provision.

In schools, as in comparable institutions like the army, food is part of the power structure. Meals are part of the package like uniforms, plimsolls and rifles. Children and troops may not like their dinners, but at least they quite literally know where they are with them. The food, so quickly familiar, provides stability. Meals linked with such autocratic institutions have (as we saw in Chapter 2) little to do with nutrient value, but a great deal to do with the power invested in and despatched by those who cook and serve them. Certainly many children's meaningful relationship to food has been perverted by those in charge of it.

So many women revealed school to be a ripe repository for nerve-racking food recollection, it seems singular that the discipline attached to school dinners, administered largely by female staff, has figured as little in books on the sociology of food, as has the authority women wield over children through meals in the home.

Why do women appear to abuse this particular and limited power? Why do women do so consistently in their own domain of food? These are highly significant questions, which I recognize are difficult for women to answer. They are questions I have been reluctant to put to myself. I thought back to my daughter's provocative statement: 'Lots of people you wouldn't expect abuse power.'

I had thought this chapter would be easy. That was my first mistake. Nothing personal to put in. Just a few minor problems to sort out. I decided to voice them aloud to my daughter. That was my second mistake.

'I see no problems,' she said in the cool, wise voice of twenty-two years old. 'Table manners and tyranny, a very simple theme. About how parents, usually mothers, as well as teachers, use food to abuse the power they have over children.'

'That wasn't exactly what I had in mind,' I said with a respectable amount of patience. 'I was thinking about how men control women and children through the type of food they expect to be served, the times of meals they insist on, the money they allot women for food purchase. I intend to look at the aggression and tension that ensues when women are perceived to fail at food tasks. I thought I would tell the story of Tom Lass, the famous television personality, and the difficult time he gave his five children.'

Marmoset exploded. 'Typical! Absolutely typical! Your version of what is true. Of course men do it, but it is not just men. It is not just fathers. It is mothers. It is mothers like you. Tell them about what you did to me. Tell them about the cabbage behind the washing machine and the two days' tyranny you exerted over a small child. Now there's a story you can't feel proud of!'

My third mistake was in not leaving the room then. As it was I stayed relatively calm and reached for precision.

'It was fish,' I said imperturbably. 'It was not cabbage. It was at most a couple of hours, not a couple of days. I had excellent reasons for insisting you ate it up. Tyranny is a grossly exaggerated term. It was a radiator not a washing machine. We did not own a washing machine then. In any case the object you stuffed the food behind in that disgusting way is as immaterial as is that ancient anecdote to this new chapter.'

There is no doubt about it, my lofty tone indicated I was rattled. The ensuing wrangle over who remembered what, was almost as fiery as the original incident, which took place in Knowsley, Lancashire, when Marmoset was seven. I gave in, when she reminded me of how much respect she used to have for my public pronouncement that one should 'tell it how it really was' no matter how hard it is to do so.

This time it is hard. How it really was is a matter of selective memory. Hers versus mine. My remembered version is that as a small child Marmoset was fussy and difficult over food. (Today I feel this may have been partly because, with my agreement but not through any choice of hers or mine, she was a weekly boarder at a school several miles away, and only ate with us at weekends.) I recall worrying both about her not eating enough, and about her table manners. I used to insist 'for the good of her health' she ate up everything, especially protein and fresh vegetables. I remember occasionally saying she could not leave the table until her plate was cleared. I have only a vague memory of the incident in question, but feel sure I had prepared delicious grilled fish, which my daughter had refused to eat, and when my back was turned had secreted somewhere, probably behind the kitchen radiator.

Marmoset's version is slightly different. She remained adamant it was cabbage, that she always disliked cabbage, that I rarely took her preferences into account, that if she didn't eat it at one meal, she was offered it again at another. Finally in frustration she said she had plasterd it behind the washing machine.

Naturally I find my part in her version both extreme and hard to credit. After struggling with my conscience for longer than you would believe possible, I decided to look through my correspondence, as I recalled Marmoset had written me a long letter containing her early food memories.

I found it. Selective memories indeed! To my chagrin the daughter comes off singularly better than the mother. But there are some surprising changes.

> Dearest Mummy,
>
> You asked me to write to you with my early food memories. My memories of food include hating SWEDE and being forced to eat it. And when you went out of the kitchen at Whitestone Close I scraped it behind the washing machine. We later got rats and I felt guilty. I like swede now but I can never understand how I can allow myself to, all the trouble it caused me.
>
> I was once given SARDINES on toast in that house and I wouldn't eat them. You said I couldn't have another meal till I ate them. It appeared each breakfast lunch and dinner and [our friend] Thelma sat with me in the kitchen while I refused to eat it. The longer it was there the more the idea of it made me feel sick and I don't know if I ate it or not. Maybe it too went behind the washing machine.

Towards the end of her letter, Marmoset suggests that I should think about 'the punishments of those who don't conform and the abuse of power by those who make the rules and have no one to answer to even if they are teachers, mothers' friends, mothers' lovers, or MOTHERS THEMSELVES.'

Of course she is right. But what springs to mind nearly fifteen years later is the extent to which, as a non-conforming woman myself, in a less liberal era than now, I had acquiesced in being 'punished' by having my child sent away. It was in the context of that situation over which I had little control, felt unbearably powerless, that I used what slight authority I had left to exert an unnecessary autocracy over my daughter, through the medium of food, the one arena where I was still indisputably in charge.

That women still model themselves on patriarchal authority in this way is disturbing but hardly surprising; nor is the fact that women use as adjuncts to a borrowed control, the tools to which we have greatest access: food and meals.

Given the centrality of eating within the domestic world, it is predictable that women should describe conflicts relating to mealtimes, and the people they share them with in which not merely the meals, but the manners and codes which attach to them, are often the pretext for airing more deeply-rooted dissatisfactions and frustrations. Research shows that mealtime incidents crystallize underlying tensions within the family. M. K. V. Fisher in *The Art of Eating* drew up 'An Alphabet for Gourmets' and under F is listed: 'F is for FAMILY . . . The cold truth is that family dinners are more often than not an ordeal of nervous indigestion, preceded by hidden resentment and ennui and accompanied by psychosomatic jitters.'[1]

Cooking and food provision make up a vocabulary through which all members of a family, but particularly women, can explain their domestic circumstances. In my own case, during the period of enforced estrangement from my child, where my control was restricted and perilous, it is plausible to read into those mealtime traumas of swede and sardines (or cabbage and fish) the possibility that at weekends I was attempting to be 'father' as well as 'mother' towards a child who during weekdays possessed neither. It was a contradiction I lived out, but could not explain, that I attempted weekend parenting in the problematic 'fatherly' ways of a nuclear family world which I myself uneasily fitted. It was a further contradiction that I continued to do this despite the fact that during the weekdays, through my first tentative steps into feminism, I was starting to struggle against such 'fatherly' lines of authority.

As a publicly radical feminist mother in the late seventies, encouraged by a supportive partnership at home and a firm background of women's movement politics, I was able to restructure my domestic domain and rethink food patterns on less masculist, less autocratic lines. But in the mid sixties and early seventies, like other women of that era, with few alternative models, I was only beginning to feel a way forward. Today I must live with and learn from those inconsistencies and contradictions to which many women today are still subject.

Very few women offered me accounts of how *they* tyrannized over their children through an imposition of table manners or mealtime stringency; yet a great many showered me with data about how their mothers or grandmothers similarly controlled them. Not for one moment do I believe that such a striking social phenomenon got wiped out in a single generation. Perhaps for reasons of time, the research became focused on some important issues, which necessarily omitted others later thought to be equally important. Perhaps interviewees told me only those parts of their own truths which were accurate but which left them with some street credibility. Whatever the reason, it is nevertheless extremely relevant to look at typical accounts women give of their experiences as children, to see where they mirror my own material.

Often a childhood food trauma can in later years undermine the strongest of adults. Jacqueline, a forty-two-year-old television administrator, was a tall, proud woman who held herself with dignity, had a forthright manner, and organized her staff of twenty with a whiplash tongue. I was very surprised when one day she admitted: 'If I as much as think about sago and tapioca pudding, I crumble with nerves. It puts me right back into the nursery which Mother ran like a concentration camp. She treated myself and my brothers like prisoners. It was Mother's duty to administer sago, and our duty to eat it up. We were forced to sit in the nursery until it was finished.' She shuddered and seemed to shrink in height as she repeated: 'Sago, ugh, it makes me feel quite helpless, as if the food was putting me back into place. I've organized my whole life since I grew up to stay in control.'

When I learnt more about Jacqueline's life, I began to understand why. 'Father wasn't around much,' she said. 'He came in quietly for meals, insisted they were to his choice, at the time he preferred, then he slipped quietly out again. He was often frustrated at work and angry at meals. Later my brothers and I found out he had a mistress. But she didn't cook for him, he still insisted that was Mother's job. Mother couldn't or wouldn't do anything about the situation. She was too proud to appear to take any notice. She never spoke about the mistress, she just got on with running her house and running us.'

If Jacqueline's helplessness over her childhood experiences led her to admit that she organized her adult life to stay in control, we may reasonably speculate that Jacqueline's mother, equally helpless, equally proud, similarly tried to keep at least one area of *her* life under her control.

Fifty-year-old Jennifer came from a strongly matriarchal household ruled over by her grandmother and a regiment of aunts. 'Grandmother had long ago been deserted by her husband, so she surrounded herself with a severe posse of maiden aunts. The eldest and crossest was stern Aunt Bean, the youngest and frailest was Mother. She too had been deserted by Father long before my brother and I could remember him. Grandmother and the aunts would sit us in front of large bowls of stewed apples with instructions not to move until the bowls were emptied. How I hate stewed apples. Those horrid hard bits in the centre. We were told it was good for our health but we knew that meant it was good for our souls! Grandmother, stern Aunt Bean, and the others sat in front of us while my brother and I pushed the apples around our plates. Then one by one they left us alone in the long chilly dining room, for what seemed like hours. Neither of us dared to move. Finally we got on with it.'

Jennifer and I discussed the reasons behind this stringency. At first she suggested it was due to the practicality of wartime. 'Healthy food like apples were at a premium and waste was not encouraged.' Then she suggested it was due to the strong puritan ethic by which such upper-class families lived. 'We all believed that what you disliked most must be good for the spirit,' she said, then added, thoughtfully: 'Also in the absence of men to rule, the women had the floor to themselves.'

Later however it emerged that after her father's abandonment, her mother had had a serious mental breakdown. 'She wasn't able to look after us, so for some time my brother and I were sent to a day care place. I suppose it was a benevolent institution but it didn't give us the same security as you get at home.' When their mother had sufficiently recovered, the two small children were brought back to the grandmother's house to continue life with a mother they were unfamiliar with, under the wing of a stern family. By this time Jennifer had become a diabetic and, like her mother, was considered delicate and a constant source of anxiety. 'Yes, it was all a bit precarious,' she said. 'It is not surprising that Aunt Bean and the others felt a rigid need to impose control on the household.'

Two women did give me personal accounts of how they exerted unnecessary control over their children at mealtimes. Both were Canadian. Kanny, in her early thirties, had been training to be a sculptor. She had left college, given up her art, when her husband Joe felt she was not paying sufficient attention to the needs of her home and the dietary health of her children.

'We lived in the city. I guess the kids ran a bit wild. I didn't care too much if they snacked on French fries and tomato sauce. My energy went into my work. But Joe objected. He never felt my work was as important as his, which often frustrated or angered him. Certainly my work wasn't as important as the ideal home of his dreams. He was an architect, could get work anywhere, so one day he moved us out to the country, upstate New Brunswick. We had a load of chickens and goats, a huge orchard and a field for the kids to play in. Healthier for them, he said. No one artistic for me to exchange ideas with for miles around!

'Every day I'd clean this large house, tidy up the kids, sort the animals, roast a chicken, make a soup, or maybe buy fresh fish, then I'd gather the apples and bake an apple pie for supper. I lost my energy, was always tired, had no time to paint or sculpt. No one to talk to. After a while Joe began working longer hours, and wanted the kids fed and put to bed before he got home. He'd arrive back tired and discontented and demand my immediate attention. The kids were so used to packet food and running wild that they didn't take at all to those new regime of wholesome homebakes and regular hours. I was at constant war with them. One day Junior was modelling with some new clay and he refused to sit down at the tea table. He kept saying: "Hold it Mom, I don't want apple pie, I wanna finish my model!" Suddenly I flipped. I dragged him to the table where the other two were sitting and I sat over all three of them forcing mouthfuls of apple pie down them. They were all three screaming. Inside, I was screaming too. But I couldn't let up. I couldn't stop doing it. Why should he model when I'd given up everything for them? It was like the kids had to eat up every scrap I made or that dream I was trying to live couldn't come true.'

As Kanny told me this she was crying with rage and years of frustration. It was the same frustration I encountered when I met Lou, a thin, nervy woman of thirty-two with a tense manner and two long straggly plaits. We sat in her downtown untidy kitchen with its glorious view of Halifax harbour, and its muddle of unwashed plates and the smell of unchanged nappy. The baby toddled around in the nappy and not much else. The elder boy sat silently on a window-seat reading but keeping a watchful eye on his mother who prowled from one side of the kitchen to the other as she talked to me. Loud guitar music blared continuously from a cheap cassette recorder on the windowsill. Occasionally Lou would fling back a plait and yell irritably, 'Turn it down, Kid!' or 'Change that Babe, Kid!' The Kid looked at her resentfully but did nothing. The music continued to blare out. The baby yelled in discomfort.

Lou continued to prowl as she told me: 'I'd been brought up conventional. I tried darn hard to live the way the family wanted. But it didn't work out. All I wanted was music in my life so I broke away, ran off, got to playing guitar. Real well, some said. I was working nights in a band. Then I had the Kid!' She flashed the elder boy a weary but not unaffectionate glance. 'Not by anyone special. Never told him anyroad. I didn't do much in the way of domestic stuff. Just made us a lot of jello sandwiches or we'd dig into jars of peanut butter. The Kid would come with me nights to work. It was a fair old life.'

She broke off her narrative to yell half-heartedly, 'Turn it down, Kid! Change that Babe, Kid! He'll start to smell real bad.' The elder boy laconically picked up the screaming babe and left the room. He seemed to think this was a maximum effort so the cassette remained at full blast. Lou obviously didn't have the energy to deal with it. 'Darn it!' Her speech spurted like jets of water from a tap. 'One summer I went home to visit the folks. Shit can you believe it! I met this conventional real estate guy. Darn me I fell for him! He had this real hardpush job which gave me the heebies, but he offered to give me and the Kid a proper home. Mind you there was a catch. I had to quit playing guitar or working nights. I had to clean up the place and cook us all hot meals. I didn't say yes at first but then I got caught out with another babe, and no money. I was dead broke so I said I'd get hitched. He moved us to this real straight city. My guy said it would be healthy for the children. Harbour, boats, fresh fish, parks, playgrounds, beaches near by, the lot. He said while he was running his real estate business I could do things with some other wives (darn me I'd never met no *wives* before!) and cook this local caught fish and make this darn white sauce and never have to use another packet from the store!'

Lou's nervy voice shrilled in astonishment at the memory. 'Well I wasn't gonna tell *him* I'd never even got round to *packets* or that me and the Kid had done just fine on jello sandwiches. My guy was in *real estate*! He wanted me to lead a conventional life. He even promised he'd fix me a dream kitchen when he got rich. Jesus I tried. I tried to do it the right way. I tried to be a married lady with children who are cleaned up. I'd listen to his heebie real estate stories hour after hour. I put that shitty babe in real cloth diapers. I never had a disposable in the house! I cooked that darn fresh fish and made that real white sauce a million times and felt I'd died. Some days I wanted to kill myself. I just had to take it out on someone.'

143

She looked around wearily for the elder boy but he hadn't returned. 'Yeh, I guess it was the Kid. There were days I'd make the Kid sit in front of that fish hour after hour, until he darn ate it up. I just wouldn't let him get up till he'd stomached the plateful. I guess it's cruel but I couldn't help it. It's like my whole life now is a nightmare of white sauce and diapers. Sure I used to get the nightmares before, what woman doesn't, but the music and the jello sandwiches kept the nightmares at bay. Now they've gone too. There's nothing left but the bad dreams.'

Lou's narrative bears an uncannily close resemblance to an account of her life given by the poet and mother of two daughters, Anne Sexton, in an interview after she had won the Pulitzer Prize in 1966.

> Until I was twenty-eight I had a kind of buried self who didn't know she could do anything but make white sauce and diaper babies. I didn't know I had any creative depths. I was a victim of the American dream, the bourgeois middle-class dream. All I wanted was a little piece of life, to be married, to have children. I thought the nightmares, the visions, the demons would go away if there was enough love to put them down. I was trying my damnedest to lead a conventional life, for that was how I was brought up, and it was what my husband wanted of me. But one can't build little white picket fences to keep the nightmares out.'[2]

Like Sexton, Lou and Kanny attempted to subject their independent artistic spirits to traditional marital values depicted by the ideal-home dream of compulsory cooking and constant child care. Like Jacqueline and Jennifer's mothers, Lou, Kanny and I subjected our children to rigorous control through food. However, slightly different, though linked, factors are at work.

Jacqueline and Jennifer's mothers, themselves victims of oppressive domestic circumstances which reduced their personal power to nursery tyrannies of sago and stewed apple, had been sufficiently co-opted by this male-defined bourgeois dream to impose it on their unwilling children with high moral seriousness. They may have run the nursery or the dining room like concentration camps but they believed they did it in their children's interests. What was in their own interests was at that stage barely glimpsed, or considered less relevant.

The rhetoric of 'health', the morality of 'good diet' carefully effaced the underlying fact that what is eaten, who prepares the food, who gets whom to eat what, who insists everything is eaten up, is a matter of material and social relations, integrally located in a hierarchical social structure, where power, wealth, and freedom of choice are unevenly distributed; and where women have the least in all three areas.

Lou and Kanny, however, who gave up sculpting and guitar to reach for the same dream, imposed on their children a discipline through food they had no interest in cooking, as part of a model of life they were well aware they did not fit. For them, as for Anne Sexton, the dream had nightmare qualities.

Kanny told me, 'the kids had to eat up every scrap I made or that dream I was trying to live couldn't come true.' But it was her husband's dream of an ideal healthy home. Lou told me, 'My guy promised he'd fix me a dream kitchen.' Then the dream went sour and she revealed, 'It's like my whole life now is a nightmare of white sauce and diapers.' Anne Sexton, bringing up her children in the knowledge that she was a 'victim of the American dream', hoped against hope that those nightmares would disappear, if there was enough love to put them down. When there was not, she felt she had failed the white sauce fantasy. In 1974, she wrote in a poem called 'The Furies' the lines:

> Depression is boring, I think,
> And I would do better to make
> some soup and light up the cave.[3]

Some mothers' watch their hearts break as they carefully bake heart-shaped caked for rosy-cheeked children. Some mothers make soup and watch their step. That mother, a brilliant poet, committed suicide, when her daughters were still young. That is why I cannot easily dismiss Lou's lines: 'I felt I'd died. Some days I wanted to kill myself.' That is why I may not approve of Lou's keeping the Kid imprisoned over fresh fish, but I do understand it. That is why other mothers may not condone my keeping my daughter jailed to the swede but they will comprehend it.

In *Reflecting Men* we pointed out that women boost men's egos and service their emotional and physical needs often to their own detriment. This means that women like Lou and Kanny who have willingly subsumed their own interests and development to the needs of Joe the architect and Lou's conventional real estate guy, conceal or repress rage and frustration as they continue to support and cater to the men who have caused it. The anger of course does not disappear. It is often unfairly turned in another direction.

Earlier we saw how some women literally eat their anger with fattening food. Here we see how other women deflect their reasonable resentment by using children as receptacles for frustrations they dare not express elsewhere. As women 'force-feed' children with time-consuming hot meals, they reflect the male value-system that promotes the indispensable dream kitchen. What women like Lou, Kanny and Jacqueline's mother rarely question is the usefulness of systematically placing men's wishes at the centre of their attention.

Fran Ansley sees the emotional support provided by all women (but particularly wives) as a safety valve for frustration produced in husbands working in the capitalist system. Rather than being turned against the system which causes it, men's frustration is absorbed by the comforting, dependable cook-housewife, so that the system is not threatened.

'When wives play their traditional role as takers of shit they often absorb their husbands' legitimate anger and frustration at their own powerlessness and oppression. With every worker provided with a sponge to soak up his possibly revolutionary ire, the bosses rest more secure.'[5]

One can see a parallel between the way women serve as

sponges for men's frustrations at work and the way children serve as 'takers of shit' not only from women's own discontent at work, where they receive even less reward and status than men do, but also for women's disenchantment at home, under the informal control of male lovers or husbands. For men exert a powerful pressure on women in the kitchen. As one woman told me: 'Childhood was a series of frightening meals. Mother was always humiliated. Father shouted about the food, then my sister wouldn't eat, and Mother thought she'd failed. Because she felt pressurized by Dad who despised her cooking, she insisted we ate everything up. There was always a bad atmosphere at meals. You never knew how much he'd shout about tea being on time, or if it would get worse. Meals were dangerous places.'

Sometimes this male pressure is masked by the rhetoric of diet-as-morality which Kanny, Lou and Jennifer all mentioned. For the eat-it-up-it's-good-for-you theme is another aspect of the responsibility put upon women to be in charge of the family's health which we noticed in Chapter 5. But as we saw, it is male needs that dictate women's responsibilities in this area, and male control that enforces them.

We have seen sufficient evidence to establish that women who have scant material power in the public arena, and often restricted control within the private world, attempt to keep hold of it where it is most easily available to them, through food transactions. What has been substantially less documented is how little real power women have even in the social world traditionally depicted as theirs. The kitchen is women's realm but it is still men who make the rules. In almost all food areas women, like children, are still dictated to.

The mundane tasks of preparing food, cooking, eating, washing up, all central activities within any domestic regime, are curiously absent from existing sociological descriptions of family life. Sociologists usually suggest that it is the very taken-for-grantedness of the subject that has tended to obscure it. I believe it is the taken-for-granted fact that most of these tasks are done by *women* which has made it less worthy of sociological investigation.

As what happens to the cook and what happens at mealtimes tell us a great deal about other crucial aspects of the domestic world, it is fortunate that a few researchers are now attempting to fill in these gaps. Several studies have shown that in many homes men control the purchase of food by allotting specific amounts of housekeeping or shopping money; and the budget they set is inequitably operated in their favour.

Anne Murcott points out that the fact that men eat differently from and better than women and children in terms of both quantity and quality is more than a matter of the physiology of average differences in height and weight. She suggests that it also reflects cultural values about masculinity and femininity such that 'the privileging of men when distributing food is so well ingrained as to be perceived as "natural"'[6]

Whether most men *expect* to be privileged with larger portions or with good cuts of meat is unclear, but I found ample evidence that where money is short, where one person has smaller portions, eats scraps, or goes without, that person is the woman, not the man. I found no evidence that men in those situations object. Here are some women's views:

'Dad gives Mum her food money for the week. She says it's never enough. He won't let Mum waste any food but he'll go to the cupboard and open a tin of best ham she's carefully put by and have a large portion for his tea. Then he'll expect Mum and us kids to finish the rest up a little bit each day till the end of the week while he has Mum prepare his fresh meat.' (Norfolk girl, seventeen years.)

'When he wants to show me he cares, he tops up my housekeeping money. Then I buy him some steak and do him extra sausages and bacon to go with it. We have a good evening then.' (Harrogate wife, thirty-six years.)

'Our dad expects his Hot every day. Pie and potatoes won't do. It must be fresh cooked. He won't eat leftovers. He calls our mum the pig bucket and expects her to eat all the scraps. If his food isn't fresh he screams and hits out. Once he threw the pan of boiled carrots at her when she said there was only boiled ham for Tuesday. "I give yer yer bloody money, you give me my bloody dinner!" he shouted.' (Bradford schoolgirl, fifteen years.)

'When I do those individual Yorkshires with his Sunday he is real loving. I baste the pots just how he likes them then we're all cosy and set-up.' (Sheffield wife, forty years.)

'When we were short of cash, I'd just eat cheese on toast, but I'd still buy him meat. I suppose I knew he had to have the lion's share.' (Kent clerk, living with boyfriend, thirty years.)

'When we were on Welfare I learnt to eat real small. Cheese end, yesterday's buns, french fries with bacon pieces, even cracked eggs, but I'd feel guilty giving him those so I used every cent for deep fried chicken pieces for him and the boy. Sometimes I'd give them baked pork and apple, but not me or the girl. We had real small plates.' (Nova Scotian housewife, thirty-six years.)

'When my husband lost his job in that advertising agency, he got very depressed. I thought it a good thing to keep buying steak and little treats we couldn't afford to keep his spirits up. If I did salads he said I didn't care. I wasn't bothered about what the children ate.' (Cambridge mother of four, thirty-seven years.)

'The first time we went to the sea for our two weeks, we didn't have a proper cooker in the caravan, just a ring thing. I knew how important it was to him that I roast the joint, so I asked up at the local if I could buy into their cooker. They didn't mind a bit. I've been doing that for years!' (Norwich mother, fifty-two years.)

'When we were last on the dole, it was months, I couldn't make ends meet but he still expected his hot dinners. You couldn't give him sausage and mash, he'd wallop us for less than that. Give him his meat tea and he might keep his hands to himself!' (Leeds wife, thirty-eight years.)

'If I want him in a good mood, in the winter I do frozen turkey breast with bread sauce and fresh sprouts, if it's summer I do chicken dinner with my sherry trifle. He loves that and we all have a good old evening.' (London mother of two, thirty-eight years.)

Money is not the only food area that men control. Preliminary studies by Jacqueline Burgoyne, David Clarke, Anne Murcott, Rhiann Ellis, Cheryl Lean and myself[7] into the area of cooking and gender reveal that women are expected to prepare 'good' food on time for men; that the term 'good' is defined by men, and often means 'hot', that failure to cook what men want when men want it, frequently turns out to be the trigger for male contempt at best, for male violence at worst. Remember the woman who described meals as 'dangerous places'? The views of the other women I spoke to confirmed and extended all these findings.

Almost every woman I spoke to had something to say about the way her father, husband, or boyfriend ruled the household through strict table manners, types of food, or tone of meals. For some women, the discipline was extreme, the punishment immediate. Bouncy Molly from Cornwell gave a characteristic account.

'You'd expect a Royal Artillery man like Father to be wonderful with table manners. Oh yes he was! He always thought food and manners the most important things in our lives. It was for Mother to cook all that wonderful food and only Dad had the right to complain. He was always served first with the largest helpings and the best cuts. When we sat down it was a rule we said grace. One of us children had to say it, and you never broke that rule. You'd be too afraid of Father's punishment. Father wouldn't allow speech. Not one of us was ever allowed to speak during a meal. He used to say Mother had taken so long to do the cooking that we must all enjoy the food to the full by getting on with it and not talking. Not even Mother was allowed to speak, not even if she wanted to. There was no breaking Father's rules. You would be terribly punished if you spoke.

'If you had bad manners or defied Father or answered back you got hit. I answered back a lot, I got hit a lot. That was

Father's way. But I only tried talking at mealtimes once or twice. Then I was sent to bed and threatened. Yes I was defiant as a child, but I didn't try that again!'

Molly was giggling at the memory. Everything in her family life gave her a sense of pride and joy, which not even Father's iron discipline had ever subdued. 'You just had to put up with Father being a proper head of the family,' she explained patiently. 'Meals were something he ruled over, just like everything else.' Molly's biggest defiance came over her beloved puddings. She giggled again at the memory. 'I *was* naughty,' she said proudly. 'Father would never allow us to eat puddings if we didn't eat our first course. I was a real rebel. I would sit there and not eat on purpose because it was defying Father, even though I was aching for a pudding. So of course I was not allowed pudding. Father was not a man who ever relented. I was made to get down from the table and go away while the others ate pudding. Sometimes they'd have syrup, sometimes they'd have trifle, sometimes they'd have my best queen's pudding. That's why I love them so much now. I've had to wait so many years to eat them in peace. Because after Father, there was Maurice, my husband. I couldn't eat my puddings when he was alive, well not things like trifle, because I was afraid of getting fat. That was another hardship. I made them for Maurice but I couldn't be that defiant and eat them myself.'

And what about now, I asked her. Her lovely face suddenly looked sad. 'Now? Well now is different. There's no one left to defy. Now Father and Maurice are both dead, and I'm on my own, I eat what I like. I eat puddings whenever I like, I sit at table and behave how I like. I never feel guilty. There's none of my men left to say what goes on at my table.'

For other women punishment was not the issue. Patriarchal control was as fundamental as potty-training with consequences that were as long-lasting. This authority was exercised as fiercely through the type of food as it was through manners. Irene, a middle-aged headmistress, makes exactly this point.

'Table manners were bonged into us from the age of under-standing, so early it was part of being brought up, like toilet training. Father had a strong sense of authority. We had Victor-ian or even Edwardian values dumped on us when we were small. He couldn't bear us to eat sloppily, grab things, or eat out of the middle of a slice of bread. We had to start at the corner. Eating was sitting at a table with your place laid and real cloth napkins never being sloppy, never eating on the street, never being vulgar. If anyone was sloppy it made Father really ill.'

Father's illnesses controlled other areas of the family's food management. Irene explained: 'As Father suffered from ulcers, meals were always a problem for Mother. She might have liked to be a fancy cook, but meals had to be bland for him.'

These rigid Victorian rules kept Irene's own behaviour restricted for years. 'Even today I find people who hold food in the air, or who talk with their mouths full, utterly offensive. It took me till I was forty to learn to eat on the street. I did it for the first time last summer. I bought and ate a packet of chips, but I knew what Father would have thought and I felt guilty. I still have that taboo, that sense of shame, it seems so vulgar.'

Irene did not escape table restrictions when she married, for her first husband was even fussier about food then her father. His views on propriety controlled their sex life as well as their meals. 'Everything had to be properly done. You had to eat everything with a knife and fork. He couldn't bear picnics unless things could be eaten with a knife and fork. He wouldn't eat anything with his fingers, not even tomatoes. I would watch him cut them up neatly, then do the same. He hated having his fingers messy. It went along with other things in his character. Those kind of rigid manners controlled other areas of our lives. For instance I was never touched below the waist. It would not have been proper. Table manners became allied to all sorts of things he could and couldn't do, and then became things I must do or not do either. Yes, he was very fussy over food, and over bodies, yes very very fussy.'

A common report was that irrespective of whether the woman

was a good or bad cook, her meals were received with contemptuous remarks or sarcastic put-downs. Della, the daughter of a Canadian fisherman, told me a typical story. 'Dad's job meant he demanded hot food at ungodly hours. He was so particular, shouted so much, we were all frightened. Unfortunately Mum was a foul cook. She had this sense that you had to *tame* food by cooking it! So she burnt meat, overcooked the veg, or in desperation opened cans of vegetables. He wouldn't stand for that! Dad scorned her and her meals, and was snide at every mealtime. Mum got terribly hurt and weepy. So then I'd be hurt for Mum and praise her cooking even when it was lousy. It truly was bad cooking, but I'd eat it up just to be loyal. The lifelong effect on me was not to value food. I've a healthy appetite but I don't care what I eat, and I don't bother to cook, because I spent all those years persuading myself Mum's cooking was all right in order to defend her against him. I've taught myself not to care about food, to be totally undiscriminating. Now that I care so little, my favourite food is cold baked beans straight from the can.'

The experience of Mary Anne, an East Anglian librarian, was remarkably similar, even though her mother was an excellent cook. 'Dad shouted about Mum's cooking all the time no matter what she gave him. Her meals were brilliant but he told her they were no use, until in the end he reduced her to a kind of frightened peacemaker. When she made good, interesting meals he called them 'foreign rubbish'. He called her a 'lazy bitch' for not making roasts like his mother had. He put her down so often that finally she lost her nerve and just made cold joint and salads. This enraged him more and one day he hit her for not making liver and onions which he said was her duty. The paradox was he insisted we ate everything up but at the same time told us how bad it was. The effect on me was terrible. I lost my sense of taste, and can no longer discriminate between good and bad food.'

* * *

I listened to dozens of stories of the varying ways women are required through mealtime manners and controlled cuisine to make men feel good, to reflect male values, to avoid male annoyance. But there is one story which bears out virtually every finding mentioned by everyone I talked to.

It is the story of Tom Lass, the internationally famous television personality; the story which my daughter so successfully – and correctly – interrupted.

Tom Lass is a genial, smooth-voiced public figure, well known in several English-speaking countries as a sparkling broadcaster and trenchant interviewer. He is regularly quoted in the press, and frequently figures in colour supplements. His audience figures run into millions. So does his bank balance. In his mid-sixties, he is always described as having the youthful appearance of one who leads the poolside life of the enormously wealthy. Tom Lass, reported to drive a BMW and a hard bargain, considers himself both seriously rich and also a hard-working serious person.

Living and working now mainly in Canada, he was brought up in Scarborough, which he would earnestly praise for its good plain cooking. In many respects he still feels himself to be a good plain Yorkshireman; a captivating simplicity his public found hard to resist. From the public's point of view Tom Lass is an engaging man with an engaging personality. Those who know him privately have reported occasional displays of fretfulness if the well-oiled wheels are for once not turning the whimsical Lass way! In general, however, success has rendered him sunny and he has been caringly cajoled through any irascible moments by the bevy of warm-hearted women close to him. Chief amongst these has always been Milly, to whom he was married for more than a quarter of a century, and his five children, the eldest of whom in an excess of wit he had christened Bonny.

Amused and faithful viewers and friends thought how lucky Bonny, her sister and brothers, and Milly must be to have spent so many years providing their famous father with his favourite basic British fodder (indubitably improved, as the bank balance rose, by more and more champagne), the whole family sharing no doubt in Tom Lass's grateful appreciation of their services.

When I first met her in Canada, Tom's eldest daughter *looked* bonny enough. A small slight figure, one long shiny brown plait, gentle friendly eyes; but behind them was a strained wary look, and behind her well-trained sociable manner were years of bitter and nervous feelings stored up over the matter of her father's favourite foods.

'None of us could ever get it right,' she told me sadly, twisting the silky plait. 'Particularly not my poor mother, who tried the hardest. She spent her life trying to please Dad with food and never managing it. In the end it was one of the things that broke her up. They are divorced now but Mum still fears cooking, which is sad because she's a really good cook.'

The problem Milly faced was that Tom Lass's autocratic views on cooking controlled the type of food the whole family were compelled to eat. 'It had to be *plain* food, it just had to be,' said Bonny, her candid somewhat earnest face suddenly miserable at the memory. 'He hated everything that wasn't extremely plain. We had to make every sort of Yorkshire food, plain north-country cooking, nothing fancy, lots of bread and potatoes with everything. None of us could do it well enough to please him, but it was worst for Mum, she never got it right. Mother liked things like avocado and garlic, she really wanted to experiment, but he never allowed her to.'

I wondered if the charming and amiable Tom Lass had ever run up a little hot pot for himself? Bonny laughed at the very idea. 'Oh no! I and my sister and brothers helped, but really Mum did *all* the cooking. I don't think there was ever any question of him sharing the cooking. It wouldn't even have been considered. Mother was obviously deeply unhappy about a lot of that but it didn't come out for years. The problem was they'd become engaged when she was only eighteen so she stepped out of being a daughter straight into being just a wife. But even though she was deeply unhappy about a lot of it, I suspect she was trying to be even more perfect. Cooking was one way she tried. I remember Mum trying to come up with the ultimate and perfect Yorkshire pudding. Since Dad wouldn't stand for anything fancy, when it came to dinner parties, she eventually started to produce *two different meals*, one which my dad would eat, one which the guests would eat. Mother spent years trying with one meal to please him and with the other meal to please other people. I didn't take part in their dinner parties unless Mother was ill. When I did it was as a very worried substitute for my mother.'

Bonny shook away some of the worry with a toss of the plait, grinned, and reached for another memory. 'Once or twice when I was thirteen I had to do it, because Mum was doing something else which was a really dreadful sin. Of course that didn't happen often because Mother would not have dared to be not available. None of us would.'

Meal *times* had always been set by Tom and conditioned by his work patterns. 'In the early days when Dad had a regular job, he had to have his meals at regular times, so of course we all did too,' Bonny explained. 'It didn't matter what anyone else in the family was doing. That didn't count. Then when Dad became self-employed, and worked at home, things got more difficult. If he made irregular food demands they had to be met, everything had to change. When he became really well-known it was even harder. You couldn't even be sure that food would be there, it totally depended on what he wanted, when he wanted it. By then I and my sister were older, about nine, so we could do more for ourselves, like we made toasties. When you think that we all only ate what Dad wanted eaten, at his times, food really was a method of control.'

She looked at me in surprise as she said it, as if the idea was only now taking root. What happened when your father became a full-time public figure, I asked. 'It was dreadful,' she said, sighing. 'He would work through the night, and he had to be fed, and he had to have Mum there running things for him, being attentive, running the business, typing, sorting out accounts, cooking, always cooking. He couldn't cope unless she was there being supportive all the time.'

Milly's constant support through food as through everything else, did not bring her either appreciation or praise. Bonny told me: 'Her meals never satisfied Dad. There was never any praise, it was always criticism. No meal was ever plain enough or good enough for him. He shouted at her, he was always contemptuous of her food. That meant she could never do as well as she might have done if he had just approved a little.'

What it also meant was that Tom Lass's approval or more often disapproval set the tone of every meal, and all five children recall those meals as places of tension.

'When I think of food, what I remember are those tense occasions. Every meal made us nervous. Until I was ten or eleven, family breakfasts were deeply unhappy because they rowed over the food such a lot. Mum was always in trouble. My strongest memory is of Mum serving up all that food as part of her job, always in trouble because she got it wrong, always flustered because things were so bad. All that food always felt bad to me, no matter how nice it really was, because I was wondering how it would go between them. I worried what would happen just before and during every meal.'

I asked Bonny if she thought she and her sister and brothers had been made anxious children by mealtime traumas. She looked at me puzzled and said very sadly: 'I don't know what anxious children means, but I know I was bloody worried all the time about not being sure how the parents would be at mealtimes. I can't ever remember food as a cause of celebration. All us children knew that food and rows showed up the perpetual unhappiness in Mum and Dad's existence together, and when they constantly rowed over food, we knew there was something badly wrong in our household. We would all try and get through meals as fast as possible and not see them as occasions. All of us felt we had to rush away from the tension between Mother and Father. We have all five been affected in our food habits quite badly. It left us wanting to rush away from meals for years. I still consume food as fast as possible if I'm not thinking,' she said. Then she added anxiously, as if still the girl of ten she was recalling: 'When we rushed our food it didn't mean we didn't chew it up properly.'

I had shared several meals with Bonny, and was familiar with the way she jostled her food along as if catching a train. I had also noticed another strange food habit which she had not yet mentioned. If she was served anything green, such as fresh vegetables, tinned peas, or salad, she would scurry her knife and fork through every scrap of verdant material, pushing it and turning it as though searching for something. One lunchtime she told me the reason. Mealtime tensions in the Lass household had climaxed with what became known as the caterpillar catastrophe. 'It remains my most frightening meal memory,' Bonny recalled with a shudder. 'They'd had one of their rows at lunch. Everything was tense. She was already in trouble. He'd already yelled at her for bad cooking. She'd served us salad and from nervousness I was doing the usual kid thing of not eating what I should. One of Dad's rules was you had to eat *everything* AND HE MEANT *everything*. We all had to. Nobody was ever excused. He started to yell at me for pushing my lettuce around. So I began to hurry up and eat. Then as I looked down at my plate, there it was, crawling across my salad. This great big green caterpillar. It was big, I do mean huge, big and squidgy and soft and dark green with huge spots on. Ugh. It was darker green than the salad it was creeping over. I just didn't know what to do. I was very frightened. I daren't make a fuss about finding a caterpillar, I knew I'd just have to eat it up. You had to eat *everything* up on your plate, or you'd be in terrible trouble with him. Also I knew if I said there was a caterpillar, she'd get the blame. Mum was already in trouble. He'd been shouting at her through the soup. So honestly there didn't seem much choice except to eat it. Then I looked at it, oh what a big animal it was. I remember Mum consoling me afterwards and saying how big it was. I was worried about what would happen to me if I ate it, and I was worried about what would happen to me and to her if I mentioned it. I tried and I tried but I couldn't go through with it, so finally I said very quietly "Do I have to eat this?" Then of course Mother got blown up for not washing the lettuce, for not preparing the meal properly. The row was the worst I'd known and of course I felt guilty.'

I sympathized. It had been a dreadful predicament. Then Bonny said in that warm earnest voice: 'I still look at green things on my plate, salad and stuff, just in case anything pops out, just in case anyone shouts at me to eat everything up. You know I'd have eaten anything else on my plate to save Mum from another attack, but there are some things so big you can't eat them even to keep the peace.'

A protective and caring manner, the result of years of trying to protect poor Milly, is one of Bonny's most striking characteristics. But Milly, the patient Grizelda of the family's memories, is in fact very positively recalled by her children as a model mother. 'She actually was the perfect mother, cooking, serving, trying to please. She came from a background with lots of children so she knew what it would be like to be a mother of so many. If you went back to her old place for a Sunday lunch it was quite different from our home. Everyone was very polite and friendly. The food would go round and their rule was nobody could eat till we'd all been served. It made such a nice comfortable atmosphere, all of us eating together. But Dad hated that. He hated Mum's background, so his rule for our household was that you had to eat as soon as you got served. Of course he was served first and that was the whole point of the rule. He ate immediately every time. He never once waited. That meant Mother, who served herself last, wasn't even sitting down with us until he was half way through the meal.'

In the Lass family all table manners were dictated by Tom Lass, but not necessarily adhered to by him. 'He taught us how to use a knife and fork and if we didn't do it there would be great trouble. We had to sit properly at table and eat in a polite way.

Those were his rules. But of course he could break them. He was always using his power to break them.'

One day Tom Lass used this power to embarrass and upset a fat friend of his daughter's. 'I was twelve, and I had this friend, a vicar's daughter, who Dad couldn't stand because she was fat. He admired the vicar but hated my friend because she had so much fat from glandular problems that she wasn't very physically attractive. Dad was always making remarks about her fat. He called her unattractive and was determined to spoil the relationship between us. She did get very miserable about her size, and she had so much fat that at fifteen she had some of it sliced off her buttocks. Well, before she'd had any sliced off, I brought her home for lunch and Dad decided to have a real go! Mum had made soup. Dad started eating normally, then paused and decided to make use of his height to behave appallingly. He is six foot and I was quite proud of his height. Well he sat up at the table, then he put his long leg up with his heel on the seat. His leg was towards his neck. He put his arm round the top of his knees so that the arm was resting on the knee but the wrist was free so he could use an implement. Then he picked up the spoon with his free hand and started to slurp his soup into his mouth. It's an almost impossible way of eating and he did it to insult her. It was a deliberate act. He didn't like her because she was fat, and because she was my friend. He insisted we all had good table manners but he had the power to do what he liked, to upset whom he liked . . .'

Bonny's voice broke wretchedly at the memory. Determinedly she carried on: 'I felt very upset, very angry, because it wasn't how my father should have behaved. He was doing it just to make her look small, to upset us. I was so sure manners mattered because he had always told us they did that I made up excuses for him to my friend. I said he was well-known, that he was eccentric, I told my friend Dad's legs were so long that he couldn't get them under the table. I certainly wasn't capable of saying or even of thinking that he was a shit. Oh no, certainly not. Our whole household was geared to never saying, never thinking anything like that. I would have felt dreadfully guilty if I'd even thought that. It wasn't till I broke out much later and realized the extent of his control that I thought things like that.'

Even after Bonny had left home, her father continued to dictate the rules on table manners to his family, while he infringed them. 'He went on using his power to show people he could do anything and didn't care. One day when we were all grown up, the whole family went to a very posh restaurant. I took along the new friend I was involved with. Dad insisted on eating with his fingers just to show he wasn't impressed and could get away with it. My friend was appalled. The trouble is none of the family felt we could stop him.'

Today Bonny and her sister and brothers have tried by deliberate and conscious measures to change their relationship to food which their father's tyranny made so disturbing. 'We spend more time thinking about and eating food. We try to feel food is a positive thing, we try to make more interesting meals, none of that plain simple cooking. We try to spend longer at the table. I notice that all five of us have done it deliberately but we have never talked to each other about it. I suppose we had to try and change the thing that made our lives so uncomfortable as children. You see for us, food was never our comforter. There were not even biscuits you could help yourself to for a little comfort.'

The effects on Bonny particularly of her father's behaviour over food have been far-reaching as well as distressing, because the tyranny over table manners was symbolic of Tom Lass's control over his children in other ways.

'Dad didn't just choose our food, he chose everything. He even chose the training college I went to, and the course I did there. So I simply dropped out and became a market gardener. I left home and tried to fight him, but ended up attacking myself. Of course I did it through food. I simply stopped eating. Food had such terrible associations. Everything I ate got associated with not being worth much in my own eyes. The depression and the not eating got steadily worse. I would be feeling down so I wouldn't prepare food, I went long past hunger and got very thin. But when I went home Dad didn't even notice because he was busy being ill. There wasn't any time to pay attention to my sort of anorexia because he had diabetes and needed Mum to pay him proper attention. I suppose I was very passive where he was concerned. I don't know whether by not eating I was trying to get back at him, or whether I was so profoundly depressed there was no room for feelings like hunger.'

Fortunately two of Bonny's friends recognized the situation and began to feed her up and bring her back to the point where she took control of her own eating behaviour. However, even today if Bonny is depressed she stops eating. She told me: 'I'm not like my friends who reach for the cream buns if they are miserable. Food is never my comfort, far from it. Food has always been used as a weapon in my life, a very serious weapon. I don't want to blame anyone but I think Dad has a lot to answer for.'

I do not think that is in dispute. I did not see Bonny for some time after that conversation, then several months later we met again. 'I must speak to you,' she said. 'I've remembered something important. Could we have supper together?' We did, at my house. I made a simple meal, mainly salad with jacket potatoes. I hoped the plain country fare would not unnerve her. I noticed she was still picking up and examining every shred of lettuce. 'Are you still looking for caterpillars to spring out?' I asked humorously, hoping enough time had now passed for her to see the funny side. She gazed at me with that serious intent look. 'That's why I wanted to see you. After we spoke I remembered, it was not lettuce at all, it was cauliflower. Hot cauliflower. You might think it a miracle that the caterpillar lived but Mum only steamed vegetables very lightly, for a couple of minutes, so she'd saved its life, and there it was wriggling it out of the cauliflower. It was a great big . . .'

'I know,' I said gently. 'It was a great big green squidgy caterpillar and it was darker green than the surrounding cauliflower and your father shouted so much you thought you might

162

have to eat it up. And even though it was cauliflower you still scrutinize lettuce leaves. And cabbage leaves. And celery stalks.'

'I do! I do!' she said. 'I have to. It was a truly awful experience.'

It must have been. Like Marmoset and the swede (or cabbage), it is not the exact food that matters to the memories we hold so dear or so fearful, it is the loving or tyrannical behaviour that accompanied it.

SEVEN
DISTORT AND DISORDER

In every era there is an ideal of femininity that shifts in the wind of male approval and imposes a terrible tyranny on the women who try to attain it.

Writer Susan Brownmiller is characteristic of most women when she tells us that, as she passed through a stormy adolescence to a stormy maturity, 'femininity increasingly became an exasperation, a brilliant, subtle aesthetic that was bafflingly inconsistent at the same time that it was minutely, demandingly concrete, a rigid code of appearance and behaviour defined by do's and don't-do's that went against my rebellious grain.'[1]

Even the most rebellious women find themselves in an unceasing struggle to match up to each male-defined model. They do it because men's views on women's bodies carry more credentials than our own. 'Painted faces, shaved hair, uplifted breasts, blue-tacked smiles, stiletto heels, all these are body falsehoods which women invoke in the great male protection racket.[2]

When we fail at femininity we appear not to care about men, we risk the loss of their attention, their approval. Susan Brownmiller suggests that 'to be insufficiently feminine is viewed as a failure in core sexual identity, or as a failure to care sufficiently about oneself, for a woman found wanting will be appraised (and will appraise herself) as mannish or neutered or simply unattractive, as men have defined these terms.'[3]

Women's bodies have always been a screen onto which different values, such as receptive sexiness or fecundity, have been projected by men. What we know about the ideal women's bodies of the past has been filtered to us through the vision of

164

male artists. Look at the pictures: for hundreds of years, men admired the full fleshiness of the female figure. The round, reproductive, tummy-centred ideal was followed by one that was all bosom and bottom, emphasized by a narrow waist. At the beginning of the twentieth century, the full-blown figure lost favour. The new sensual aesthetic, particularly in Anglo-American culture, was a slender, almost tubular form.

Limitations of fertility and more overt sexual expression were suddenly important to women. The lean bean symbolized the sexual free agent. Women extricated themselves from restrictive garments and claimed the right to pursue their sexual destiny freed from the risk of pregnancy. The bean-lean body came to symbolize athleticism, non-reproductive sexuality, androgynous independence. But almost at once this symbol of liberation became oppressive to the majority of women who were not naturally skinny.

In other ages the tools of femininity were a bound foot, a hobble skirt, an iron corset, an hourglass figure, a rubber roll-on. Today the tools have changed but the goals remain similar. Femininity still demands impractical equipment (stiletto heels, pocketless pants, cumbersome clutchbags), femininity still demands we restrain our ambitions and restrict our shape to impossible ideals. We may laugh at the women who laced themselves into a whalebone cage, but we take very seriously the confines of the latest diet, the fetters of our fear of fat.

In this era, for women in the West, the prevailing standard and current tyranny is razor thinness. The fact that so few of us feel we can afford to ignore this stricture shows we have not yet shaken off our shackles, and points to the power of the critical male gaze.

In a consumer society where women's bodies sell commodities, as John Berger emphasizes, women are the seen sex affected by this insidious controlling inspection. 'A woman . . . is continually accompanied by her own image of herself . . . she has to survey everything she is and everything she does because how she appears to others, and ultimately how she appears to men, is of crucial importance for what is normally thought of as the success in her life. Men act and women appear. Women watch themselves being looked at. This determines not only most relations between men and women but also the relation of women to themselves.'[4]

Toni Laidlaw, the psychologist, believes that women's subjection to the male gaze adversely affects our self-perception and consequently our eating habits. 'In a patriarchal culture women are essentially defined as bodies. On the one hand we see our bodies as a source of power; if we can be this beautiful . . . and by beautiful I mean something that is defined not in our terms but in men's terms . . . then we think we have power. To achieve that power we eat or more often do not eat accordingly. If on the other hand we don't look like that ideal, we do not have that power. But in fact this is a very ambiguous concept.'

It is ambiguous because the paradox for women is that in theory our bodies are our most important assets, but in practice our bodies if uncontrolled can never be acceptable. Women are coerced into believing that if we don't want to lose out, we must lose weight, and that coercion is largely achieved through women's high visibility to judgemental male eyes. Our most vulnerable area is sexuality, once associated with a pleasing plumpness, but today locked into slimness. There may be safe sex, but there is no safe food. If we do eat forbidden foods (and which foods apart from the ubiquitous lettuce leaf are not taboo?) to do so confortably we are required to eat them away from the critical male gaze.

'Sometimes I want food more than I want sex, but I want to be thought of as sexual. So I tried to eat out of his sight, because seeing me eat would increase his irritation about my plumpness. If you're plump, you're against nature, you are not sexually available. I've got a barrel chest and a big pair of breasts and I knew I had to concentrate on my good legs if I was to be seen as a sexual person at all.' (Kitty, forty-two, twice married, several women lovers, no children, civil service executive.)

'Tim, my little boy's father, tried to be kind about my fat as long as I didn't stuff in front of him. He said, "You're a little plump lady, Lynne, that's OK, I can live with it, why don't you learn to accept it?" He thought he was being affectionate! What he meant was that some days I'm a lardy unhappy lump like a weight watcher's textbook, I get this horrific anxiety when I pull off my bra and pull in my huge stomach and see my tits hanging down to my waist. ACCEPT IT! How can I accept it when every time I remove my clothes I think, Here we go again, it's saggy tits time!' And other women will size up my body against theirs.' (Lynne, thirty-nine, unmarried, three children, chief librarian.)

Like Kitty, Lynne often prefers food to sex but still wishes to be rated as sexual by men. 'Fried egg and greasy chips give me ardent manic moments of pure joy. Butter, cream, soft fatty cheese, even *lard*, I love them all. Show me a pan of chips, hand me the salad cream, I'm a happy girl! I'll spread half the jar on the chips, eat every last one, and dip bars of chocolate into glasses of top-of-the-milk! Joy, sheer joy! You can't get that every time in bed. But then I start to repent. He knows I do it. He thinks it's gross. It is. It is gross. I look in the mirror, I see all that fat, I think bloat, bloat, bloat, that's all I did. Food is pleasure, intense incredible pleasure, but fat is crucifixion. He won't want me in bed, it's as simple as that.

'I came from a working-class family, chips with everything. Then as soon as I met this middle-class bloke I went on a diet. I knew I'd never get out of factory life if I was fat. I knew a middle-class 'chap' wouldn't go out with me if I went on eating fry-ups. Middle-class girls ate greens and fatless meat and had small portions. They didn't stuff chips and jam sandwiches round the tele in the front room like we did. They played tennis and ate lettuce and went to bed with men with posh voices and good jobs. That's what I wanted. There wasn't any choice. I had to get thin.' (Caro, thirty-four, unmarried, London schoolteacher.)

Compulsory slimness is not merely the consequence of a desire to be sexually attractive to men. It is more significantly the effect of a need to be approved of, to be taken seriously. Even women who understand this, and are politically aware, cannot escape this trap. Lynne, the librarian, told me: 'Being a feminist has helped me understand what's going on, but at the end of the day if I could have painless plastic surgery I would. The idea of a beautiful inside is crap. I'm still hung up on wanting to be a beautiful version of myself, on the *outside*. I want to eat normally! I want to eat anything! I want the happiness of eight stone! I don't ever again want to be called 'plump'. Frankly I want it all!'

Dale Spender is one theorist ready to acknowledge that we all share in the predicament. At forty-three she herself became an anorexic.

'Being fat is never acceptable. Women comment about it as much as men. Feminists are not immune. I'm certainly not. You watch women, even the fiercest, most politically ideologically correct, summing up other women when they see them running to flab. You see the signs as they say, "She's overweight, poor old thing, thank goodness I'm thinner than she is." It's a whole sub-language, a dangerous sub-culture. I know I haven't come to terms with it. I've spent my life determined to be thin. As soon as I don the bikini on an Australian beach, I think oh my god look at that stomach, isn't it dreadful, then I stop eating for days. At forty-three I reached the stage where the only thing that went on in my head was food. Every moment was a battle with food I wanted to eat and the shape I had to be. I would panic-eat, I would stuff, then I virtually stopped eating. I recognized I had become an anorexic. I had to go to a therapist to say "What is wrong with me?" I believe I am a rational, sane person, but every night when I got into bed the thought would lurk at the periphery of my consciousness that when I awoke I could well have become fat! Now how do you explain that?'

It is not easy to explain, for Dale, like Lynne and many other women, has a real knowledge of the workings of patriarchy, but from her story it becomes obvious that understanding how a system works does not necessarily prevent us being controlled by an ideological hold on our consciousness. Dale is an extremely *thin* woman, whose weight rarely rises above seven-and-a-half stone. She, like other thin women I talked to, is caught in the mythical fat trap.

Femininity in any age is a powerful male-defined aesthetic built upon an acknowledgement of women's powerlessness. Femininity in our age is gripped by this obsession with obesity.

To show you how this can work, I want to tell you The Story of O. Her mother had christened her Orana after an Italian heroine in a thin romance she'd picked up at the library. She put down romances soon after the child's birth. She put down the child, a fat child, for the next twenty-five years.

Well, that's if you believe Orana, about being fat or being put down. I do. Not because she *is* fat or because I think her mother is a beast, but because that 'truth' is part of Orana's story. It is HER truth. I see Orana as the crucial connection between ordinary women (like Caro and Dale) who believe they are fat when they are not, and fat women (like Kitty and Lynne) who believe they are failures when they are not. Orana is thin, thinks she is fat and therefore thinks she's a failure.

Though few mothers I have met have been beasts, many, consciously or unconsciously, have passed on to their daughters the message that girls are not important in this society, and that fat girls are least important and will be most derided.

It is not insignificant that nobody called Orana by her full name. Most of the time she was called O, as if her name didn't count for much. She said she preferred to be called O, but her preferences didn't count for much either. The name, she said, wasn't the best of starts and things did not improve.

'Mother never thought I'd make much of myself. No one did. I never did anything right in their eyes. Not like my brother. He's bright, at university. As for me, being attacked by that boy at school didn't help. Getting a head injury.' Her little face puckered up at the memory. 'Well, I couldn't go back to take my exams. So there I was, a few O levels, no real qualifications, and fat of course.'

Of course, I said sympathetically. O was seven stone and slipping when we met. The first thing I noticed was the way she kept pulling at her flesh, tugging at imaginary flab, twisting her face in disgust. She had a diminutive, pretty face spoilt by that strangely contorted expression and greyish bloated skin. When she was not pulling at her body, she was plucking at her watch strap, as if trying to wrench it off. She kept taking secretive peeks at the large luminous watch face.

I did not understand why time was so important to O. Frankly, during the first few weeks of meeting her I did not understand much.

After she had made several visits to my house, I noticed that she would not eat in front of me, but if there was any food around in the kitchen she would pull feverishly at it as if it was part of her arm or thigh, then glance over her shoulder to see if anyone was watching. Later we discussed it. She said: 'I'm like that at Mother's. I'll go in her pantry, grab a handful of cereal, a handful of biscuits, I won't take a whole piece of bread, just tear a bit off. That makes me feel I haven't had as much. Ten minutes later I'm at the other bit. I have to break biscuits in half. I'd never open a bar of chocolate, I'd break it in half. No more, I tell myself. Then the chocolate cake looms up. I start breaking off the bottom bit. Cram the creamy bit into my mouth. I tell myself it's not as bad as taking the whole thing. In the end I say sod it, and cram in the top bit too.'

As she talked, O's hands were working overtime, pulling at her stomach, scratching and plucking at her face, as her thin body writhed in my swivel armchair. She looked tinier than ever huddled inside the large leather frame. Her usually grey mottled cheeks had a greenish-white tinge that day. Had she been sick, I wondered?

'When I'm starving, I think of who to visit. I visit people to gain access.' She leant across and whispered: 'Access to food. Isn't that awful? Mother's is the worst place for access. I can't bear it there. She knows too much.'

Whenever she mentioned her mother, O's voice had a hard

strained tone. 'Mum puts things away, she would, she's sensible. She doesn't worry about being fat. She worries about whether Dad has got someone else. He probably has.' A secretive smile flitted across the greeny-white cheeks. 'She isn't happy so she has to be better than me. She has to be right about me, to bolster herself up. She has to make out I can't cope. But she doesn't know about me . . .' This time her voice held uncertainty, a tinge of fear. 'She doesn't know what I do, she knows I haven't any control over food. She watches me standing up to binge. I stay standing at the biscuit barrel, watching her watching me. When she goes out I reach into the fridge, snatch the cold custard, pour it into my mouth. Sometimes it's cold stew. I'll get handfuls, I won't use a spoon. When I'm actually doing it I'm comforting myself, but I'm hating myself too. I feel sick but I can't stop pushing it down.'

O's binges could take place anywhere. 'Some people know I'm a bit messed up about food, because I'm always standing, I can't sit down to a meal. One boyfriend noticed. I'll cook him a meal but I won't have a plate, just stand about and pick things off his.'

One day she cooked him a meal and they left for a party without clearing the table. With a hint of pride she told me: 'It was a proper meal. Vegetables, meat, that sort of stuff. The scraps were there when we got back, congealed gravy, half-eaten sprouts, greasy bits of meat. I had to go up to bed with him, but I crept down before he woke next morning and finished up that awful cold food. That time I did sit down, alone with the leftovers, well it was a proper meal. I've even gone to the bin where people have thrown food out. This is disgusting. When I lived with some girls, they used to tip stale teacakes, hard jam roll into the bin. I would wait till they'd gone out, then take it out of the bin and stuff it in my mouth. I was always replacing their food that I'd eaten but I wouldn't buy my own. I look at it this way: if it's theirs I won't eat as much as if it was mine. I haven't any control, I can't ever eat one of anything. Mother thinks I've got a problem, says I should go down the doctor's, but we don't actually get on well enough to talk about what it's really about.'

She looked at me uncertainly, then glanced at her watch. An expression of terror flashed across her face. Did she want to tell me? Did she know me well enough? 'Got to be home in a few minutes. Sorry, it's crazy. My body and weight are the most crucial things in my whole life. It's gone on since my childhood.' She did not return for several weeks.

O told me she had started weighing herself every day when she was fifteen. Tell me about being fifteen, I said. Were you teased for being fat? 'No I didn't get teased, it's always been my own thing. I was – not fat but overweight. Looking at photos I see me quite chubby. I gave up school dinners, had an orange. I had fights with Mother about dieting. She wouldn't do my special meals. *She should have!*' her voice rose in rage. '*I knew I was fat*. But it was no use. She kept them where I could see them, biscuits, fruit loaf, wicked things like that. It meant she made me eat packet after packet.' Her voice had grown resentful, her hands fretted around her stomach, then with one of those characteristic lightning changes of mood she smiled and said thoughtfully:

'I had an abortion when I was eighteen and the only reason was I didn't want to get fat! I was single, there was a boyfriend but that wasn't anything. I didn't want children, most of all I couldn't bear to get fat, I didn't have another reason really.'

After the abortion, O lost even more weight, and was still unsure what to do with her life. When she was nineteen, her father sent her off to train as a beauty therapist. 'Dad thought it would be suitable, beauty is what girls do. The place was bad for me in some ways because everyone was so concerned about their bodies. All girls together. We put on weight because the exams were hard and we used to go off and comfort each other with baked potatoes and chips. I went through phases of only grapefruit for lunch but it wasn't enough, I grew fatter.' She made a large O in the air to show me. Then she lowered her voice. 'I knew I had to think of *something else*.' She broke off the story and looked at me earnestly. 'Sometimes I think you don't believe me. I *was* fat. I must have been about 8 stone 10 lbs. Worse I *looked* fat, I had this really big round face. Looking back the only reason I got married the next year was because I felt fat and ugly. So I dived in and had this really SHORT marriage. Barry, he was the first one. It only lasted two years. He went back into prison. I wanted it short so I didn't mind. Marriage meant I could give up my job as a beauty therapist, where people look at your body a lot. Getting married meant I could go and hide. I had this really big round face.'

She repeated that phrase dolefully several times, contorting her lips with disgust. Suddenly her eyes lighted on my clock and she left in haste.

Sometimes she rang, said she would come round, then did not turn up. Sometimes we arranged to meet and she would phone and cancel. Her car broke down a lot. 'I sold my beauty business,' she said by way of explanation. 'I've given up my house too. Mum's bought it. I'm in a bedsitter. I'm going to try and study like my brother. Maybe I'll get to his university.' Once we arranged to eat at a Chinese restaurant, and spent an interesting time planning what to eat. She seemed excited. That morning she phoned with an excuse.

I never knew when to expect her, or what to expect. One day I told her I liked her face.

'DON'T SAY THAT!' she said fiercely. 'You must never say that. I hate my face. It's really fat. I can't stand anyone saying any of my body is lovely. Geoff used to say "You're lovely darling", looking at it. I hated it. I didn't believe him. I never believe anybody. I always think they've got an ulterior motive. I know they probably haven't. I am bright enough to realize but I still *feel* they have. I want to be bright enough to go to college, I want to be bright enough to stop feeling these things.'

Her hands were making those uncanny movements. 'You're pulling at your face,' I pointed out bravely. Was I hoping that if I could stop those disturbing movements I might change the line of her thoughts?

'I know! I know!' she said savagely. 'It's my body. I hate it so much. I'm always grabbing parts of it, I'm pulling at the bits I hate. Only my breasts are all right, I haven't got any.' A quick, bitter, satisfied laugh. 'I'm always feeling something, aren't I? I'm waiting for it to be smooth, like before I was seven stone. That isn't really thin, is it? But I didn't have the lumps then.'

Her gaze flashed by the wristwatch, settled on the stomach. 'I can't bear people to look at my stomach. I'll wear a bikini and go on a sunbed because if you're brown it's not too bad. But on a beach I don't relax. I sit hunched up thinking people are looking at my stomach. They're probably not. I've been thinking about having an operation on my stomach. I want the bottom bit cut out because I've got sort of stretch marks. They can cut the bottom bit off!'

Surely stretch marks implied pregnancy? O had always denied having children. Was Barrie anything to do with the stretch marks, if that was what they were? I wondered who Geoff was. O pulled at her memories the way she pulled at her flesh and her food. They were wrenched out of her grudgingly as if none of them belonged. All of them jagged.

'Geoff was the second one. He battered me, so food wasn't an issue then. I got pregnant by him when I was still married to Barry, before he went back to prison. I'd already got pregnant by Barry. I'd felt so fat and ugly that after I'd dived into marriage, I got pregnant immediately and got even fatter. I had a child straight away. It was wonderful afterwards because I breastfed and got back to being really thin. Six stone. It was pure joy. I could have married the second one if I'd have got a divorce. I did get a divorce later but I never married again. I don't want a man really, I prefer my freedom.'

She jerked to a halt midstream, and laughed wildly. 'You can see why Mum gets so righteous, she thinks I haven't made much of myself. But I did all right with the beauty business. I bought myself a house with the profits. Only I've handed that over now.' She looked sad. She suspected what I was thinking. She suspected some of it was a surprise. She was still half smiling as if a little surprised at herself.

'I never admit I have children. It's not that I'm ashamed but I shouldn't have had them. I hate the stretch marks they gave me. I wouldn't change them for the world now, I do love them, but it's mixing with younger people, younger bodies, that haven't had children. I gave up the children. Arnie, he's the boyfriend I've had since I gave them up, said "You won't be able to go out with younger people if you put on weight." He's only eighteen. I don't tell them how old I am. I don't *want* to compete but I try to. When I mix with his friends I can say I haven't had children because I don't have them now.'

She looked as if she might cry, or laugh wildly again. I asked how she'd managed with food during the years with her boys. 'I had them for three years and I was more in control over food then than I've ever been. I never let them have sweets or chocolates. I was keen on a balanced diet. OK I used to give them a meal and have nothing myself, I would pick bits off their plates or eat their scraps, but I didn't do anything else . . .'

She stopped, too upset to continue. Then she recovered and went on repeating her worn-down mantra. 'I was so slim when I was breastfeeding. The little one went away when I'd stopped breastfeeding him. I was so controlled when I had the babies. I didn't do anything else.'

I did not need to ask where her babies were now, but I did anyway. 'They went to my mother's. When I'd stopped breast-feeding, when I was working full-time, I gave them away to Mum. The eldest was three. She'd had them part-time when I worked four hours a day, but not full-time like now. I *have been a mother for three years full-time*. The way she talks you'd think she'd always had them. Mother tries to give the impression that I never coped with them but I have done.

'I suppose it's true that I'm not in control of that situation with my children, or over my house. But I don't mind. OK Mother has them now, but I haven't decided, not finally. Some days she wants to adopt them. Most days they don't feel like mine any more. If I visit I ask permission. Could I take them to the shop? Could I buy them a biscuit? I take the little one to the hospital a lot – he's handicapped. It's taken away some of the responsibility or all of it. So I get on with other things. I don't know where I'm going, I sit in this bedsitter and wonder. I want to go to university, but I don't think I'm going to pass. I might move to a different area. Sometimes I feel guilty about the children. People say "Oh don't you miss them?"'

'Don't you miss them?' I asked quietly. She spent a long time considering. 'I honestly don't. You get days when everything's gone wrong, I get a bit low, then I think about them. But I can't imagine getting them bathed, or to school or feeding them. Now when I get up in the morning I don't have to think about the babies, I think about my weight, what I'm going to do about it today. I'm a walking calorie book. There is hardly a moment when I don't wonder should I have some, am I going to be all right, can I risk spending time away from home, will I get back in time.'

'Tell me about the time, O,' I said gently. 'That is the worst bit isn't it?'

She seemed glad to be talking about it at last. 'Yes. Ever since I was nineteen when I first started taking laxatives to get rid of the food I've had to keep my eyes on the clock. I can't ever relax. I plan my whole life round the time I have to get back to my loo. It has to be the loo in my own home. I don't feel comfortable anywhere else. It is such a violent thing. Shitting away all that food, hour after hour. I get terribly ill after it. I'm doing it most days now. Though it's not always like this. This is quite bad. If I'm having moderate meals I only take about ten to fifteen tablets afterwards. Then I plan where I can safely go. I can't go anywhere for the next six hours because the laxatives will work.'

How did it start? I asked. Did someone suggest it? 'Oh no. I started at college. I just suddenly thought it would be a good idea. I thought I'd just do it once. But then I got into phases, having bigger meals when I might have to take sixteen or twenty, then twenty-five or thirty. Then I feel really ill. It's true, I am imprisoned by how long it takes to work. I'm not often caught by surprise. I panic if I think I can't do it in my own loo.'

Do you have to make up excuses to get yourself out of situations? I asked. 'Oh yes, all the time,' she said wearily. 'Lying is part of it. Of course you can't tell the truth.'

There are places O fears, and situations she can't afford to risk. 'I hate going on holiday with my parents because we eat all the time. So I have to take laxatives after every meal. Even then I'll put on weight so I actually have *not* to go places where I'll be forced to eat or where I can't stop eating like good restaurants.'

I remembered our cancelled trip to the Chinese. 'I was looking forward to it, I'd looked through the calorie books and found chicken and beanshoots three hundred calories, which is quite low, and I'd planned I wouldn't eat that day, and would take laxatives after the restaurant. But I went to see Mother, and you know what that's like. Unplanned eating so even with laxatives I couldn't take the risk of eating with you. I wished I could have told you, but I had to lie. I'm ashamed to tell anybody. You once said I hadn't got control over my life and possibly I haven't got control of that part of my life, and that makes me ashamed, but my method is to control my weight with laxatives, so I have got some control.'

The method is not one O finds pleasant or guilt-free but she cannot give it up. 'I feel so bad after a bout I always say this is the last time. I'll eat three sensible meals a day. I believe I'll never take them again. But I always do, I suppose it's a kind of addiction, yes it is, because I think if I don't I'm going to get fatter so I have to do it. I have to sit for hours on the loo waiting to get rid of the food. The pain is awful. I'm always looking in the loo. It's revolting, isn't it? I'm always staring down into the loo to see if there is any recognizable food which means it hasn't been digested. I have to keep looking to see if I need to take any more tablets. It is awful and I am concerned. But I have to know that I've rushed all the food through. I had forty tablets yesterday and I wasn't sure that was enough. The recommended dose is two a day. I've had several hundred recently.'

When O shared her house with women friends the precautions and lies escalated. 'I can't tell them so I can't spend too long in the loo. Just a few minutes, then a great holding in, and rushing away and rushing back again so it's not very obvious. I run the tap a lot. It's been a bad few days.'

O's worst problems occur when her supply of laxatives runs low. She reacts like an addict. 'I try and buy hundreds at a time, not always from one chemist. I don't want them to suspect. I get the biggest packets I can. But if I don't have any in stock it makes me feel deathly. Panicky, panicky. I have to go out and get more. I know every chemist for miles around that is open Sundays.'

O's other fear is of being caught in the wrong place at the wrong time. 'Once or twice I've been in someone else's house. It's scary. There's the smell to think of. I always carry deodorant just in case, then nobody knows. But the guilt and the shame are terrible.'

She covered her face with the roving hands, as if to prevent some of the shame leaking out. Don't worry, I said, lots of us do dreadful things to ourselves in order not to get fat. I told her about some of the things I had done, remembered how hard it had been to stop. She listened intently. 'I expect you had good friends who helped you,' she whispered. I acknowledged I did have. 'I was lucky,' I said. O is not yet so lucky. Her shame, her guilt, her understandable confusion, effectively prevent her from confiding in anyone who might be supportive.

'I can't afford friends, I don't like to tell them. I've sort of occasionally admitted to it, but as if it is in the past. You don't say it's still going on; you say: "Oh no, I don't do that any more." That's if you can tell your friends at all.'

There are only two people O thinks of as 'sort of friends', both men. Arnie is the eighteen-year-old who encouraged her to compete with younger bodies; Arthur is older and tries to be understanding. Telling me about them, O was on safer ground, her hands returned to her lap. 'They're both no use,' O said sadly. 'Arthur is one person who knows. I suppose he tries to be kind but it doesn't have any effect on me. I hate him because he is incredibly thin and fit, and because he knows. I don't even know what he feels about my body. Once he said: "OK so you're a bit fat but that's something that probably needs exercise more than losing weight." It hasn't helped, him saying that. I think he is lying like I used to think Geoff was lying. I can't talk to Arthur, now he knows. He follows me about. He used to look over my shoulder and watch me doing it, then grab the bottle. We've actually come to blows because he used to try and take them away from me. But he never once talked about it, not like I'm talking now. Once he said: "I'm only trying to help you;" but it didn't help. He says he is my friend but he's no use . . . its no use . . .'

Her voice trailed away despairingly. Perhaps she could count on Arnie? She gave one of her wild laughs. 'You must be joking! He's the first to put me down, you can't count on him for anything!' Arnie monitors O's weight with razor-sharp glances and insults. 'The whole time I went out with him he said terrible things about my body, so how could I tell him? The last time I saw him, I travelled right across England on a train to be with him. The first thing he said was: "You fat cow what have you been doing to yourself?" I think he only meant it as a joke, that's the way he talks to women. If he thought I was really hurt . . . well . . . but I don't give that impression, people don't think anything bothers me at all. But I thought about that remark the whole time I was there. It made me think I *had* put on weight. In a way, even though it hurt I was pleased because I thought, now I'll do something about it. So there I was back on laxatives.'

She looked at me with that half-crying, half-laughing expression. Was she aware that the extent to which she had internalized this phobia about fat had allowed her to accept Arnie's malicious jibes without showing anger or distress? I felt that somewhere she did recognize that, but it was not something she could admit to a woman. For O's repulsion about fat, particularly female fat, as well as her shame and guilt, alienated her from genuine friendships with understanding women. 'I can't feel warmth towards women friends because they're my enemies,' she said factually. 'We are in competition over our shape and size. I like them and envy them, but I hate them too. It is hard to have

women as friends. I think fat women are horrible. I think the fat
is absolutely repulsive so it is hard to see them properly. But
even though I am repulsed by it, I'd rather they stayed like that
because I feel better next to them. I can't help judging women
by their shape and weight. I always try and feed my women
friends up, so that they'll put on weight and I'll look thinner. I
don't exactly look down on fat women, no I like being friends
with fat people because it makes me look thinner. I do have some
women friends but no I can't talk to them.'

Did she like spending time with me because I made her look
thinner? I had to face it, I had not managed to break through O's
frightening social isolation, which had accompanied the seven
years of her spiralling disorder. During this time, O has managed
only a few short periods without laxatives. Often she recalls with
pride her three years of motherhood. 'Remember I didn't take
them at all then. I didn't have to when I was breastfeeding.'

But the improvement it seems was due less to the effect of
being a mother and more to the recording on the scales. 'If I am
near to six stone I never take them, and breastfeeding kept me
very near that mark.' It is obviously harder for O to contemplate
coming off drugs while she is living alone. 'I do it more now. All
I think about on my own is food. No I never enjoy it. It's sad
because food is the major thing in my life, but I just know I've
got to get rid of it. The way I feel about it at the moment is that
when I get back to my weight I shan't take them any more. But
that hasn't been true in the past so why should it be true now? I
just hope sometimes it will be. Yes food is the major preoccupation of my life, but my whole life is a mess because of it. And
I don't know what to do.'

I asked if she had thought of going to a therapy centre that
works with women with eating problems. She sat very still while
she considered this then shook her head. 'I don't think I could. It
is obviously a muddled mixed-up person telling you this. I think
in a way I have a bit of a problem but I won't admit to it. There
are some things I can't feel about, can't say. It wouldn't be any
use.'

Later that evening, with a characteristic change of mood, she became fierce and funny, stared at me challengingly, totally shifted her ground: 'I don't think there's much wrong with me or my life. I don't think my problem is that bad to actually warrant having help!' She clenched and unclenched the skin around her waist as if buckling a belt. I don't really know what problems I have at all. I am choosing to go to college, even if I don't get in. I chose to give my children away. I chose to give my house away. I choose not to have a man in my life. I always need one there but I wouldn't like to think it was permanent. I prefer my freedom to that!' She spat out the last words, and stared at me aggressively.

There was a long silence. I was running out of words. She was running out of time. We both knew she had to go home. Sadly, she said: 'Really I suppose I ought to, but I'd be frightened they'd want me to put on weight.' I suggested that they, whoever they turned out to be, might help her to accept whatever weight she was, even to see that it was not as consequential as she believed. But for some suggestions to catch on, the hooks already have to be there. For O they are not yet there. She resisted the words. She said, as she had many times, 'It *is* consequential. It doesn't make sense, but my weight is the most consequential thing in my life, you know that.'

I did know that. When she added: 'I didn't make up these problems, Sal,' I knew that too. Women like O are dealing with the consequences of those problems. But some of these consequences are scary.

I suddenly remembered the story of Rebecca Axelrod, the thirty-seven-year-old Connecticut eating disorders counsellor, who today has many joys in her life, but is missing part of her intestine and all of her reproductive organs, the legacy of her many years as a laxative abuser.[5] I do not want that to happen to O. Nor does she, but she knows it can. We met once more before I left for Canada. Her last words to me were: 'I have always thought I could get cancer of the bowel or something dreadful.

It's very likely, I know about these things. I know how the body works. Bad isn't it? Sorry, got to dash again.'

I was still thinking about O when I arrived in Canada to talk to women about food. Where did her story fit in? How unusual was she? Would another woman researcher, less emotionally involved with food, have been less affected by O? All women are emotionally involved with food. Talking to O would not have been easy for any of us. I decided to let the difficult material settle, to leave most of my questions unanswered until I returned from my trip.

One morning I arranged to meet Marly, a senior creative director of an advertising agency, for a relaxed lunch. I had no intention of interviewing her about food, although I knew her to be responsible for some interesting food advertisements. It was a splendidly sunny day, after one of those short sharp showers that miraculously clear the air. Marly and I met downtown in an outdoor restaurant. We sat sipping orange juice, the drops of rain still falling slightly. Suddenly we looked up and saw a rainbow.

'It matches your shirt!' I said. Marly was immaculately dressed in a powder-blue cotton suit with a translucent rainbow-striped silk shirt. Her hair looked as though she had spent the morning at the stylist's rather than attending to tomorrow's advertising schedules. Beside her, in my faded jeans and open-necked T-shirt, I felt like an earnest and somewhat substandard reporter.

'My shirt?' Marly said nervously. 'There's nothing on it, is there?' Her face was momentarily masked with anxiety. Nothing at all, I said reassuringly, wondering what the matter was. I had my usual lunch; a sideorder of potato skins and a very small green salad. Marly had three toasted bagels with lashings of cream cheese, a large salad, two chocolate brownies and the restaurant's speciality, ice-cream soda. Frankly I was envious. I should have liked the whole lot but I should not have dared. I glanced discreetly at Marly's figure. It was in even better shape than her clothes! A thought for which I chided myself severely.

It is her ads which are worth remarking upon not her body. 'Food is obviously not much of a problem for you,' I said, attempting to sound academic rather than envious; forgetting for a few minutes my years of research and the subsequent knowledge that there is not a woman for whom food is not a problem.

She smiled, then without answering excused herself and went to the bathroom. When she returned she looked slightly ruffled. We continued our conversation over coffee, with cream for her, without for me. Every few minutes she pulled out a handmirror and glanced at her hair, then at the neck of the rainbow shirt. Finally she put the mirror away and gazed at her pale blue shoes, taking off first one, then the other, peering at them closely.

I realized that this strong woman was suddenly close to tears. 'Are you OK? Can I help?' I asked. 'I have to check. Over and over again, I have to check. There is my job to consider.' The words jumped out. 'I am afraid. I am always afraid there will be specks of vomit.

'Sometimes it hangs on my hair or my shirt. Sometimes it clings to the toe of a shoe. I can't be too careful. I am so obsessive I usually go back to the bathroom again and again, just to check. But today I thought as I was with you, I could just use a mirror. Now I can concentrate on this afternoon's meeting.' She drew a big breath of relief and said decisively: 'You are right, I don't have a problem with food or with my weight. The only problem is the specks.'

Marly was a successful business woman with a highly-paid job, a husband who had an even better job in the same firm, carrying more status, making economic policy decisions that cut across her creative planning. They had a city house, and a cabin upstate. She spent her leisure hours canoeing and sailing in summer, ski-ing in winter. Her clothes were designer-made. She had help in the home, and no children to mess it up. At forty-two, she had a figure many young models might have envied.

In her view, she did not have a problem with food, or with weight; her only problem was the specks of vomit. She ate what she liked, when and where she liked. Twenty minutes later she vomited it all up. She was sixteen years older than O, but like her locked into obsessive and frightening food behaviour. Marly too was the prisoner of dangerous rituals, which she had been performing for more than two decades.

The name researchers give women like Marly is bulimic. Bulimia is a syndrome that is becoming increasingly well documented. The name I coined for women like O is laxativiac. Laxative addiction is a syndrome linked to bulimia, but as yet scarcely documented. Both women are fighting forces they see as beyond their control. Both are painfully struggling to control a single aspect of their selfhood. Their contorted food patterns are savagely coded messages which cry out to be fully understood.

I had not come to interview Marly and I did not stay to do so. She was having sufficient difficulty harnessing her poise and strapping on her style, ready for another tough afternoon. She did not need questions about her food behaviour to unnerve her further.

When I knew her better, I realized how much of her apparently enviable life was spent suppressing her resentment, frustration and anger. Her talents and skills, indisputably equal to those of her male colleagues and husband, did not gain her equal worth or equal rank. Her desire for a child had been submerged beneath her husband's desire for freedom. And she could never eat freely without regard to the physical consequences. For like many working women, Marly tightly conformed to the prescription of the successful advertising executive, where for women success is equated as much with a slim figure as it is with a sharp brain.

One day she told me: 'If I let myself go flabby, if I couldn't wear size 10 suits, there's no way the board would take my ads seriously. I shouldn't respect myself either. If I let go of that ideal, if I let the fat take hold, I'd feel I'd failed. I can't stop wanting cream and chocolate, I seem to need it even when I'm not hungry. If there's a big creative meeting, if I'm afraid I might be subtly put down publicly where I can't express what I feel, I have to binge beforehand. I make sure I eat alone. If I'm out, I'll have two pâté sandwiches and two lemon meringue pies at one café, move on quickly to another, have three chicken pies, a pineapple cheese salad, maybe four chocolate brownies, two milk shakes and a couple of icecreams. Then I'll go to the bathroom, ready to face the meeting. If I'm at home, I'll buy several charcuterie sausages, two or three pounds of pains au chocolat, and wolf them down together. Then it's the bathroom and off to work. I'm disgusted with my greed, disgusted with myself, but I can't control it. What I can do is to keep making myself throw up.'

Many women's stories were like Marly's. They show how striving to achieve this media-manipulated ideal is at the root of women's self-estrangement. It comes as no surprise then that as the number of reports of bulimia and anorexia increases the 'right size' for women decreases. It has in fact been decreasing yearly since 1965. Marly's fanatical need to fit into a size 10 suit was shared by most women I spoke to. In Britain today size 10 is offered as standard, and size 14 once the 'average woman's size', is considered large.

It comes as no surprise either that the super-thin goal of the binge purge exponents has flourished largely in affluent cultures and in times of increased political and economic freedom for women.

'It was after the flapper era that anorexia began to be commonly reported,' said Dr Marlene Boskind-White, author of *Bulimarexia: The Binge-Purge Cycle*[6]. 'In the late sixties and seventies when the feminist movement was emerging, the female ideal went from Marilyn Monroe to Twiggy. It was out of that milieu that we began to get cases of bulimarexia.'

Marlene Boskind-White, director of the out-patients eating disorders programme at St Alban's Psychiatric Hospital, Radford, Virginia, believes that pursuit of this mistaken goal causes irreparable physical and mental damage. 'Women are rebelling against their biology. We were *meant* to have certain fat levels. They are important for menstruation, pregnancy, and lactation. And if you go five pounds below the minimum level, your body is going to fight back. This ideal body is impossible to maintain over time, but meanwhile there are a lot of women and girls profoundly malnourishing themselves.'[7]

Susie Orbach, author of *Hunger Strike*, a new book on anorexia[8] thinks that the contemporary skinny image has a direct and frightening relation to the sudden rise in eating disorders.

'I am very concerned that there seems to be no let-up in the amount of women reporting eating problems,' she told me. 'Compulsive eaters and bulimics are coming out of their closets. The anorexic experience is part of a new cultural vocabulary. Support groups and workshops are being set up to help women but this has not minimized the increase in eating problems. Far from it. Women's preoccupation with their bodies continues with greater insistence, problems are intensifying. Girls at a much younger age are affected, the eating problems now extend into old age as a proper concern for elderly women.'

She too believes that one reason for this alarming increase in eating disorders is that the Western cultural ideal is steadily decreasing. 'The standard size in the States has gone down so much that anybody of even a middle size is too big. It is a vast expensive market in which you can destabilize all women's eating habits, as opposed to a few years ago, when the decrease in size affected only those women who were already compulsive eaters and considered outsize.'

Much evidence supports the thesis that all Western women's eating patterns are destabilized, and that a large group have patterns that are clinically disordered. In a world where for most people getting enough food is the critical issue, where genuine starvation is at stake, where plumpness is considered a sign of health and prosperity, it is highly disturbing that for women in the West the issue is the calorie content of a carrot or the amount of sugar in a diet cola.

Marly admitted that if she 'let go of that ideal', if she 'let the fat take hold', she would feel she had failed. She is not alone. The problem is that women who eat compulsively, starve obsessively, or binge and vomit, are perceived by others (and by themselves) as failures as women. Yet most women do not seriously question that ideal. Instead they feel a sense of tragedy about their failure to meet it. The tragedy is that there is hardly a woman in the West between adolescence and old age who does not desire to alter something about her shape or size. These women believe their life chances would improve if they weighed ten pounds less. The tragedy is that so many women are following this cursed star to its doomed end that dangerous disorders, once an occasional, abnormal phenomenon, have now become an integral part of Western women's NORMAL experience.

For O a routine day was one in which she watched the clock and timed the expulsion of what remained of her food. For Marly, it was normal to eat out publicly then privately purge her expense-account lunch. For Kelly, a twenty-year-old student I met in Oxford, her university schedule, on which she had pinned such high hopes, is regularly blighted by uncontrollable vomiting episodes. She spends days at a time eating and purging, guilt-ridden and depressed. When I met her, the bulimia had become so injurious to her health that she was attending the local hospital for intensive but not yet successful treatment.

'I *have* to vomit. I can't give it up. Days and weeks go by when I'm locked into this awful cycle, because I have this terrible fear of food. I can't bear the idea of anyone seeing me fat. For me, coming to terms with food is synonymous with being fat. How can I come to terms with being fat?'

She threw the words at me as a challenge. Opened wide the baby blue eyes, which strikingly mismatched the severe black hair pulled back into an old-fashioned chignon like a ballerina. It is not just the childlike eyes and the austere hair that are a poor fit, nor the inconsistency of the thin little body and the perception of bulk. That is something I have grown used to. It is that nothing about Kelly quite matches up. There is a strange dissidence between the taut young form and the grave voice of a tired elderly woman. There is the contradiction between the student's sharp brain and the purpose for which it is now used. 'I spend my time here at

Oxford concentrating on my calories, counting the number of times I've already been sick, asking myself whether it's time to do it again.' Kelly now devotes more hours to reading about and analysing the nature of her 'illness' than to her studies.

More than twenty years younger than Marly, in some ways more self aware, Kelly's eating behaviour is similarly tied into the obsession with shape, the fantasy of fat, the singleminded engagement with sexuality.

Kelly, like most women, saw her body fragmented. 'When I look in the mirror, I don't see myself, I see my stomach and my hips. I see myself in segments.' The fragmentation of her vision is paralleled by the alienation in her head. 'It is like I am two people, one wanting respect, the other needing sexual approval. Getting sexual attention is hard if you have a good mind. It has a lot to do with being female, not being allowed to be a person. I want to be sexually attractive, and I relate sexual attraction with being thin. If I'm overweight I can't conceive of being sexual. Sexual acceptance is very important to me, but most men don't consider women as *whole* people. I'm a serious person, I have a good mind, I have to have the best mind, I'm a perfectionist. But lots of men don't take what you say seriously. They say 'Amuse me little girl!' When you do play the little-girl act it elicits very favourable responses. I have to stop myself playing that game. If only I could feel emotions it would me very angry, but I can't feel anything, I can only eat . . .'

She pouted like a little girl; sat crosslegged on the floor looking up at me. Her slim, almost wiry body was finely arched and very supple, her legs and arms had the interesting mixture of delicacy and strength characteristic of a dancer's. She had in fact trained as a gymnast. 'That's when it started,' she told me, folding one leg neatly across the other. 'I'm sure having been a gymnast has a lot to do with my bulimia. It stunts your physical development in terms of puberty. When my friends were worried about putting on layers of fat, I was untouched. Because I was training I could eat what I liked. At thirteen I couldn't eat if there were fat people around me. I went to America where I saw lots of huge women putting cream cakes in their mouths. It revolted me to such an extent I could not eat. That was before I was weight conscious! I had to have a perfect body like a perfect mind, I had to be the best gymnast. It isn't easy for a woman to be the best. I looked at the models in magazines and knew I had to be skinnier than they were. So once I stopped being a gymnast I could never relax with food. I can't see how I can eat what I like without getting fat and I can't see how I can live with that, so I just do these dreadful things.'

For bulimics like Marly, a considerable factor in the 'drive to do dreadful things' is repression of emotion. But for bulimics like Kelly the factor is almost a negation of emotions. She explained: 'Part of the problem is not being able to feel properly. Or if occasionally I do feel, not being able to say what it is. Any kind of emotion, positive or negative can prompt a binge-purge cycle. If anything goes wrong I turn to food for comfort. When I can't go through with a feeling I eat dozens and dozens of mini mars bars. That dissipates the feeling. Then I think, 'Oh God I'm going to get fat', so that brings new anxieties. Once I get into that kind of state any food at all will start a cycle. If I binge in a day, I will continue eating all that day. I might start with things I don't allow myself. Cream cakes, chocolate, bread, cereal. Then I'll get to the stage where I'll eat anything. I'll make white sauce and put sugar in it. I'll eat spoonfuls of this, then get frantic and throw it in my mouth. I don't chew. My stomach gets distended. I feel very ill. I might open ten tins of baked beans and eat them cold. Then I realize that the releasing or relieving of my emotions has not been for free. I am now a stone heavier so I have to make myself throw up as fast as possible, quite often aided by drinking vast amounts of water. I keep on doing it. The following day I try not to eat at all. Once you've done that cycle, the probability of doing it the next day is increased because you've broken some rule and it is very cyclical. I get in a downward spiral; I can't get out of bed, so I stay in bed and eat and eat. Then I throw myself over the toilet, to dissipate the emotions. I feel instant relief followed by more depression, then anger and guilt.'

This is a predictable pattern for bulimia, as are the consequences. 'I know about kidney damage, I know about stomach stretching, I know about the dangers. I want to avoid them, but I go on being bulimic.'

Like O, a danger area for Kelly is her parents' home. 'It is the worst place. I can't go home without bingeing.' Unlike O, Kelly has managed to talk to her parents about her problems. 'I was so ill, I decided that part of getting over it would be to be honest. But my parents can't do anything. They think I am like a crystal ball and I might break. That is what is confusing. On the one hand I am quite weak, at the same time I am very strong. I have to be strong to suppress my feelings. I can manage without people, so I do. I am not the little girl I look. I would be better off if I wasn't so strong, if I could turn to people. Then perhaps I might not have got in this state. But I operate as an island. I am very selective about seeing people. They only see me when I am feeling good and presentable and when I'm not doing it. It is all very private. During the worst of my bulimia my relationship with my boyfriend broke up. I became clinically depressed but I had no one else. There were a lot of people who liked me but no one knew me. Vomiting and bingeing are not things you can easily tell people about.'

Kelly, like Marly, looks how 'successful' Western women are expected to look: slim but not at starvation point. I use the word 'successful' as they do to mean clever at being 'feminine' rather than at exhibiting talents or skills the way 'successful' men do.

Like O, Marly and Kelly's investment is in the perpetual hell of a discreet denial of food. Like O, their method is secret. And that secret appals them. They stuff and they gorge. They expel and they vomit. And nobody knows. People know they are greedy, but they appear not to pay for it.

Bulimics' frightening fear of fatness is matched by their desperate desire to keep their grim slimming weapon, two fingers down the throat, a hardwon secret. They daily weigh their repellence and self-disgust at vomiting against the misery and self-aversion of perceiving themselves plump. In this punishing cycle, women like Kelly fill themselves up and empty themselves out. They wait for exposure. They stay fraudulently thin. They rarely express what they fear or what they feel. What is not expressed is evacuated with the leftovers.

The women who flush away their self-respect with their food, share with anorexics the constant anxiety of whether each day, or sometimes each hour, will be a 'good food time' or a 'bad food time'. But there is one substantial difference between anorexic women, and women who are bulimic or laxativiac. Anorexic women feel 'safe' or 'in control' of themselves as long as they maintain an ever-decreasing weight statistic. Their biggest fear of loss of control is represented by the act of eating. Bulimics, on the other hand, though they similarly *fear* loss of control through a weight increase, actually *experience* it when they vomit, whilst at the same time using their organized addiction to prevent expression of other more disturbing emotions; a fact that Kelly recognized.

Troy Cooper, who has been studying bulimia, found similar evidence to mine.[9] The women she talked to also led her to believe that though bulimia is popularly seen as a behaviour aimed at *controlling* weight, a syndrome overtly indicative of *loss* of control, once you look into it, you can see it is also a method used to *keep* control of the elements in women's lives they find frightening, disruptive, or destructive. The same pattern can be seen with laxative addicts.

Troy Cooper suggests that there are in fact two kinds of bulimia. The first, pragmatic bulimia, is essentially a weight-loss method, used intermittently for this specific purpose. It is none too pleasant but certainly effective, and may not be addictive. The second kind, control-oriented bulimia, is considerably more complex, pyschologically addictive and highly dangerous. Women like Marly and Kelly find themselves in an endless cycle

191

of bingeing and vomiting, which they pretend to themselves is to stabilize their weight but which fulfils certain important emotional needs; which is why like any addiction, distasteful though it is, they cannot give it up.

'The control-oriented bulimic is trying not only to control certain emotions in her life, above all she is trying to control their expression.' Troy Cooper was talking. I listened to her voice but I heard other voices.

I heard Kelly's voice: 'I'm not a little girl . . . it would make me angry . . . but I can't feel emotions . . . I can't feel anything.'

I heard Marly's voice: 'If there's a big creative meeting and I'm afraid I might be subtly put down and I know I can't express what I feel . . .'

I herd O's voice: 'I couldn't take the risk . . . I couldn't tell you . . . I couldn't tell anybody . . . there are some things I can't feel about . . . there are some things I can't say.'

Troy was talking again: 'A lot of research indicates that control-oriented bulimics try to lead successful lives.' I thought of the two-edged success which Marly and Kelly still struggle with. 'They might be business women who cannot regularly explode in anger at people they work with, or at families or boyfriends who don't understand the strain of their double role. In those cases a bulimic episode can be a good mimicking of a release of tension and anger.' I thought about Kelly and Marly, both trying, in Kelly's words, to be 'the best' in a society they acknowledge won't easily let them.

I read the research, and I thought about the women hooked on their own vomit. What kind of a mess are we all in? Who and what is responsible? Outright anger would be a reasonable response to these women's situations. To all women's situation. The bulimic 'mimicking' of anger is the twisted response women feel called upon to use. Anger turned in on themselves. Anger and debilitating depression that is at the heart of the eating patterns suffered by the other women I talked to.

Kelly and Marly are at the extreme end of a spectrum. There are many other women whose eating patterns distress them, but who fortunately have not reached that emergency state. Not *yet*. They are the women who eat compulsively. In their eating habits too we can see the same themes.

Annette, a twenty-three-year-old factory worker I met in Harlow, was typical of many who turn in upon themselves frustrated ambitions and vexed acrimony, and lead miserable lives as relentless compulsive eaters.

Annette, who lived with her parents and brothers, had been forced to subdue her own hopes of self-improvement while watching her elder brother Keith succeed and her younger brother Billy being encouraged to follow him. Like O's, Annette's brothers were made much of, and made much of themselves. She was made little of, and felt little could become of her.

'Mum and Dad never had much money or education. They were kind, wanting the best for us, but they never understood about my wanting to learn. Of course they encouraged the boys. We all went to the same comp but it was their reports that were read out. Dad always praised them, Mum spoilt them with food. My main job was to cook for Billy and Keith. I left school at sixteen, got a job in the factory to help out. Mum was putting away for Keith to go to college. She literally starved herself to get him sent there. She'd give Dad and the boys treats; puddings and sometimes a bit of cream. But she'd have bread with no jam or butter herself. She didn't give me jam either, said we couldn't afford it. Sometimes the bread she kept for herself got so stale that she'd hack and hack at it with this huge carving knife. Sometimes she'd get so hungry, she'd pull rough at the slices and stuff them in late at night when she thought we weren't watching. But it was only ever the stalest loaf.

'After Keith went to college, I got hungrier and more uptight. I knew if I'd had the chance I'd be as good as him, but I stopped talking about it. I'd lie in bed at night raging with the awful unfairness. I wanted to fill myself up. I'd creep down when they were asleep. First I'd go through a jar of sickly coffeemate because it was filling, then I'd look in the bread bin. There it was, that bloody new bread kept on one side for Dad and Billy, and those awful stale hunks for Mum and me. I'd get the carving knife she used and I'd hack till I had this load of stale slices just like she did. Some nights I'd spoon out loads of jam, some nights I honestly didn't care. Mind you I didn't dare spread it on the new bread, I had to keep it separate, like I knew I wasn't allowed. I got fatter and fatter. I hated Billy and Keith, but I hated Mum and me more.'

The tears trickled miserably down her cheeks as she said 'I knew I wasn't allowed.' I remembered Susie Orbach telling me that anorexics who subdue and express their emotions through starvation also feel not allowed.

What I think the anorexic is finally saying is: 'I am not entitled. All of a sudden I am being told I am entitled but inside of myself I feel deeply unentitled. I feel so unentitled I can't even have the body that I am. I can't even eat like other people. The only way that I dare survive in the world is that I create this perfect person who hasn't any needs, who hasn't any appetite, who is superhuman, who can defy most biological laws.' That's what I think is going on. Now I know that is an exaggeration but there is something valid there about women's experiences vis-à-vis the world. They don't really feel entitled, they feel angry.'

Kelly certainly wants to create the perfect person. She told me she did not feel entitled because she is female in a world where being a woman is not the same as being a person. Annette has not reached the same point of despair, but that does not mean that she won't.

I asked Annette if compulsive eating made her less hungry. 'No, never,' she said woefully. 'I went on stuffing in breaks at work, but I was empty inside. You want a different life but you're stuck with the one you've got so you give up and you get fatter and angrier so you go on eating.'

Although Annette's hunger and emptiness are similar to Kelly's and Marly's, to some extent their rage is being used more constructively than hers. Kelly is partially trying to direct hers into her studies, Marly is trying to direct hers into her work. They have achieved at least a small measure of independence and

self-development. Annette's anger, compounded by lack of education and poverty, is consuming her, and is aimed solely at her
eating. Instead of directing it against her family's values, which
are the values of our Western culture, she directed it only against
her body. She allowed her reasonable rage further to limit her
growth, which was already restricted by a society that still does
not easily allow sisters and mothers the creative and imaginative
choices extended to brothers and fathers.

Bunny Epstein, a counsellor for women with eating disorders,
who works at the Women's Therapy Centre, London, discovered
that compulsive eaters, feel their anger, like their eating, is out of
control. One becomes an expression for the other. They mis-
direct what may be perfectly sound outrage away from its social
and psychological causes to focus instead on food intake, because
this is seen as safer.

'Anger is one particularly disturbing feeling for women,
although many other so-called 'bad' feelings such as jealousy,
envy, competitiveness, loneliness, sexuality, or sorrow may be
avoided by the compulsive eater in much the same way she
avoids her angry feelings.'[10]

Ironically two of the few permissible feelings are loathing of
fat and disgust with greed. It was obvious in Marly's case in that
she was able to express anger when she revealed her self-loathing,
both of which emotions were usually kept well away from the
public gaze.

Marly and O, employed in the worlds of advertising and
beauty, had the additional problem of 'compulsory femininity'.
It is no accident that these women are frightened and confused
by their anger and its consequences; because the dominant media
image of feminine women (at last changing, but far too slowly)
has not been that of integrated people with power, rights and a
sense of purpose. Far from it. The damaging social myth of
femininity as receptive and passive has placed the skills of
assertion and potency firmly in masculine hands.

In *Reflecting Men*[11] we pointed out that it is not feminine for
women to be confronting, powerful, and assertive. It is not

feminine to direct anger against the appropriate person or situation. Women are taught to placate, manipulate, reflect men and male values, subdue their own talents, deny their own responses. This reflection distorts women's anger to ensure they will continue to act roles that please men and stifle or negate fundamental aspects of themselves.

Marly said if she grew fat the board would not take her ads seriously; I think if she grew angry at the misuse of her talents, or her lack of promotion, the board would not take *her* seriously.

The anorexic denies herself food openly. The bulimic or laxativiac does it covertly. But in every denial of food lurks the denial of distress, the denial of resentment. Women deny their well-merited fury because the social phenomenon of women's wrath is deeply disturbing to our culture. Overtly angry women are labelled 'aggressive' or 'balls-breaking'. The culture that condones men who rape or batter, encourages women to 'understand', not to rave or lash back.

As novelist Fay Weldon pointed out to me, in a culture where 'the oppression of women by the state and by the laws is very real, anger and outrage in women is extremely useful'. She said, 'I think you need to be angry because society has somehow drifted into a certain way of looking at things, and anger is the other side of depression. Depression is what women have to guard against because it makes us incapable of action.

'Many women find themselves in situations where they are powerless to act. Many husbands need looking after. Children need looking after. It is always up to the women. So you get trapped by totally unfair circumstances. Sometimes you cannot do anything about it, but it is better to be angry than to think that society in its expectations of you is justified. Or to sink into a miserable slumber and not know what is going on. It is better to understand what is going on, to be angry, to look at the situation, to see what you can do about it. But it is hard . . .'

It is hard because there is little room in our society for women to express discomfort with men's expectations; little room for women who have the capacity to outstrip men to forge ahead and do so. It is hard because there is little room for the proper outrage of women who demand a better deal for their sisters and equality and genuine social change for us all.

Ironically, it seems all too easy for modern women to accept that female bigness, which seemed maternal or voluptuous when confined to the home, is now viewed as threateningly devouring when it appears in an equal opportunities setting. Why do we accept, without anger, that in an era where women's political and social expectations have increased, the binge-purge cycle and the deathly laxative addiction have also increased? We cannot write it off as an 'accident'.

In this culture, women are not permitted to be threats to the male order. So women who once retired to the bathroom to powder their noses whilst the men drank port and ran the world, now retire to the bathroom to vomit up their food and expel their rage, whilst the men still run the world and label us 'disordered'.

It may be difficult, but it is essential to look at this situation, to see what is going on, to reappropriate our anger, to make it work for women not against them.

In order to see what lies beneath the labels fixed to women's eating behaviour, we need to view it in a new way. I see this label 'disorder' as women's extreme but *orderly* response to the disorderly world around them. I see women's denial as an expression of the confusion about how much space we are allowed to take up in society. Women's denial and expulsion of food can be seen not as weakness but as iron-willed control over bodies that have become painful symbols of conflict and repressed social expectations.

Beneath the labels of anorexic, laxativiac, bulimic or compulsive eater, women negate who they are, what they feel, and what they might become. If food and body image is to be viewed as the language of women's inner experience, then righteous anger is what lies beneath 'disorder'. I use the word 'righteous' because I recognize that women with self-destructive eating patterns operate them in a misogynist culture that promotes pornography, permits battering, accepts rape and condones incest. It is a

197

culture which matches men's abuse of women's bodies with women's self-abuse.

It is tempting to believe such misogyny operates only against an unlucky few. It is necessary to remember that it is in this culture that experimental work has established that 80 to 90 per cent of women are victims of what is technically called restrained eating. This means that ordinary women habitually reduce their calorie intake to a specifically low level; consistently eat less than they need. For many women the cut-off point is only just above the measuring line for detecting anorexia. Because it was obvious to researchers and doctors that Western women restrain their eating because of an overwhelming social condemnation of female fat, nobody would dream of suggesting that all women need treatment.

What I am suggesting needs treatment, what is in urgent need of repair, is the myth that female fat is bad. For it is this myth that is a part of the misogyny that keeps women powerless and battered in the home and powerless and discriminated against in the job market. It is this myth that puts *all* women under pressure to restrain their eating, and leads some to dangerous food addictions, whose consequences include tooth decay, gum disorder, heart strain, permanent stomach damage, and worse.

Kelly had read everything written on bulimia to try and cure her condition. Kelly knows that persistent vomiting can change the balance of chemicals responsible for maintaining the nervous system; that changes in electrolytes and fluid balancing can severely affect the functioning of the heart, cause kidney damage, or bring on epileptic fits. Kelly is still a bulimic. Kelly is afraid of her feelings. Kelly is afraid of getting fat.

Marly is aware that massive overeating can suddenly stretch the lining of the stomach, and that this stomach stretching can result in death. Marly continues to overeat massively. Marly is afraid of her anger. Marly is afraid of getting fat.

O already has the bloated skin characteristic of oedema. O fears the level of potassium in her blood is lowered. O told me: 'I know how the body works . . . I know I could get cancer of the bowel . . .' O is frightened of the physical consequences of her addiction, but more frightened of obtaining help, because the helpers might ask her to put on weight. O is most frightened of getting fat.

These women may appear to live in a shocking world somehow different from the worlds of those of us not condemned to the jailhouse of food rejection, not committed to the asylum of self-loathing. But women like these are not freaks. They are several of my respectable, admirable workmates. They are several of my sanest and most supportive friends. I suspect they may be several of yours. They could be our sisters, our mothers, our daughters, our aunts or ourselves.

One end of the spectrum is women feeding others while denying themselves; the other is women routinely caught in the bitter-go-round of binges and diets. If deny-diet-deprive is the sad starting point of the race to decrease pounds, then distort and disorder is the tragic finishing tape to which so many women push themselves, egged on by the constant message that fat is bad and food is dangerous. It is a race with no winners and women the only losers. It is a race we all take some part in.

The food behaviour and emotions of Annette, Kelly, Marly and O are merely the other side of the coin to the food behaviour and emotions of Mary's mum or Gwynneth, whose lives are dominated by mince and gristle, spoons of purée and slop on the floor. Their anger and anguish over food is the explicit expression of an underlying anger and anguish over a social situation they are powerless to change. The anger of Mary's mum is the same anger felt by O, repressed through a different mechanism.

All women have an engagement with food and fat. Most women have an emotional investment in over- and under-eating, not just a strange and select few. It would be patronizing and shortsighted for any of us to believe that women with food disorders are in any essential way different from ourselves. It would be fraudulent and dishonourable for me to pretend to objectivity, to write from the sidelines, to say I am different from those women I have talked to.

Until I researched this book, I did not realize the awesome significance food has had in my own life, nor did I accept the extent to which my own eating patterns had been disordered. I had avoided certain labels, attached myself fervently to others. Over the years I variously called myself a writer, a mother, a lover, a wife, a worker, a feminist. I never called myself an anorexic or a bulimic. I never saw myself as a woman with a food disorder. That is what other women were. Women I chose to write about. Looking back painfully today I accept that at particular times I have been some version of both.

Like many women I have been angry, confused, uncertain of social or sexual roles, professionally powerless, emotionally insecure. Like many women, I turned to or away from food as a solution. As for Helena the Israeli woman, for years food was my enemy as well as my friend. A brief look at just three significant passages in those food-filled years will illustrate the 'disorder'.

The first passage was the years as a Fleet Street fashion editor, the wife of a celebrity. I consistently starved to keep slim; not as anorexics do, by iron will, but by taking speed. I took amphetamines mistakenly believing they would keep my mind constantly alert amidst the pressures of a difficult job, two tempestuous marriages. I took speed to keep a flagging flabby body trimly in line with an unattainable ideal I daily promoted in my newspaper columns. I feared fatness. I hung on in for male approval. At work more than at home. I went from popping pills to injecting needles, from ten stone to seven. Yes, I lost weight. Yes, I kept awake. Sometimes for twenty hours at a time. I also lost my night vision, sense of navigation, hold on time, and my balance. I developed speech defects, and violent rages. The lines between truth and falsehood became a blur. The lines between needing to live and wanting to die but a shadow. I talked merrily about being 'high', if I talked at all. Speed in the sixties had style. I refused to recognize I was on drugs. It took until my move to Cambridge, to make a successful attempt at a healthy life, and to come off drugs. What I had lost when I shed all those pounds was my personal identity, and control over my own life.

The second passage was the year I was pregnant with Marmoset. I was frightened of losing my figure and of losing her father, the man who did not want any more children, the man I lived with, the man I loved. I was most frightened of getting fat.

I stopped eating properly. I started throwing up. I was hospitalized with hyperemesis, a disease that only affects women, making them 'uncontrollably sick' as soon as they eat. I lay in University College Hospital, London, and vomited twenty or thirty times a day for eight months. Larry brought me roses from the hospital florist; flew to Amsterdam and returned with fresh tulips. Larry did not leave me. The fat did not spread.

Today I recognized that what had started as self-induced bingeing and vomiting, trade-name bulimia, developed holistically into a full-scale medical condition that 'saved' me from fatness, that 'saved' me from abandonment. All I had controlled was my calorie intake. All I had gained was male approval. What I had denied myself were the pleasures of pregnancy, the belief in my own ability to bring up a loved child singlehanded, the right to my own point of view.

The third passage has been well documented in Chapter 2. It was the year I felt so disturbed at losing the children, and the domestic life that had given me such contentment, allowed me such confidence, I binged on jam sandwiches. When the binges were over, the additional pounds registered, all I could do was lose them by dieting. What I had denied myself were the pleasures of solitude, the fulfilment of an independent existence.

Today I am again trying to remedy these flaws. I have again gained a measure of control both over food and my life. But I could always slip back. What do those years tell me? That there is some 'progress' from the abyss of amphetamines to the stupidity of jam sandwiches? Or that at any stage in a woman's life, her eating patterns can become as violently disordered as those of her sisters? I cannot stand apart from Kelly or Marly or Annette because in some sense I have been there. Although I am quite sure I do not want to go back, I am not sure that women have made much progress in this area; any of us could still slip back.

We women are trying to show through our relationship with food what is our social and psychological situation. Food is a metaphor in which we try to tell a world that will not listen about our anger and confusion. But what goes on inside us is mediated and coloured by how the body politic treats us. We still do not have an adequate voice in the political world that hems us in. So we still use food intake, food distortion, strangulated body images, to express our deeply repressed sense of injustice, our unuttered righteous anger, our intensely felt emotions.

For most of us, a major emotion is fear of fat and fat hatred. We all believe to some extent the prevalent myths about fat people, and we continue to labour under various misapprehensions about dieting.

EIGHT
THE CALORIE-COUNTING CON

We need to examine the damaging myths about fatness which imprison overweight women within the private walls of their flesh and the public confines of contempt.

Fat women are lazy, stupid and cannot succeed. This injurious myth is learnt early in childhood, particularly by chubby girls. But as the fat girl grows up the myths proliferate and the misery extends. Fat boys certainly suffer, but research suggests that this does not seem to stop them succeeding.

Fat women overeat to make up for personality problems, or character defects, or because they are out of touch with their true feelings. This myth is frequently shortened to the statement that fat women overeat. Just as no woman is too thin to feel fat, so no fat woman can consume sufficiently little to avoid the stigma of overeating. Fat-hating forces women to accept that genuine hunger is imaginary or unjustified. Hunger pangs are looked on as an appropriate spiritual agony for an imagined sin of gluttony.

Being fat and staying fat is a personal choice. This carries with it the corollary that the fat state can be altered with effort. Given this illusion of personal control, punishment for what is then seen as lack of control appears merited.

Once a fat women loses the 'excess' weight, a slim figure can be maintained by merely eating as carefully as thin women. This is fervently believed by fat women who go to bed hungry every night in an effort to maintain a minute weight loss, wondering whether this is how their skinny sisters live!

Fat women are not sexual beings. Most men don't desire fat women, and somehow seem persuaded, as are other women, that fat women are outside the sexual pale, and don't experience desire. The myth is painfully internalized by women who told me they would rather risk a dangerous illness or an abusive operation which might decrease their fat rather than risk not being thought desirable by both male and female lovers.

Being fat is always unhealthy. When this relates to women's *physical* health, it is asserted by doctors and diet magazines alike without adequate reference to the significant *contradictory* medical literature. When women's *mental* health is at stake, the role that persecution plays in fat women's lives is rarely taken into account.

Fat women have no will-power and no self-control. Of all the malevolent myths which keep fat women oppressed and thin women in a state of fear, this is the most pernicious. It is also the most far-reaching, because it is used by the multi-billion-dollar diet industry to sustain itself and destroy the confidence of its thousands of customers.

Figure control is one of the new and few forms of control which most women are allowed to exercise. Hunger clubs, sweat salons, body reshaping programmes, slendertone adverts, women's magazines that fervently preach the think-thin gospel, all use damaging dietary diatribes to persuade women to spend their money and invest their dreams in starving themselves to a male-defined, unrealistic 'acceptable' size.

Failure for thinnish women on a diet is often thought to be bad luck. Failure for *fat* women is usually attributed to lack of willpower. This is mendacious moonshine. Most of what we are routinely told about how weight is gained or lost is either wrong, misleading or meaningless, and much of the misinformation is cunningly connected to our culture's fat hatred.

Let us start with our own experience. Have *you* been on a crash diet and lost some weight, then a few weeks, sometimes only a few days later, seen that weight inexorably creep back on? I have. Again and again and again. Did you use willpower? Of course you did. I most certainly did. Time after time. Yet despite this unerring evidence, women in the West are programmed to believe that diets work. The bitter truth is that diets do *not* ultimately work. In the long run diet failures outnumber successes by an extraordinarily wide margin. The statistic usually quoted is that 99 per cent of diets fail. Nobody talks about this because everybody is too busy talking about the latest diet!

In a controversial study *The Dieter's Dilemma: Eating Less and Weighing More*, authors William Bennett and Joel Gurin present the case that 'the amount of fat a person carries is automatically regulated and that some people are naturally fatter than others. Being fat reflects neither weakness of character nor neurotic conflict; it is a biological fact of life, an aspect of the human species inherent variability.'

The authors point out that although the reducing diet is never an effective means of weight control, it has become our modern ritual of self-improvement and self-purification. And like any ritual, dieting needs a myth to give it meaning. 'The central tenet of the diet mythology is that thin people are *better* than fat people – more beautiful, healthier, stronger of will.' Fat women as well as thin ones believe this.

In order to validate this invidious and disturbing comparison, it is argued that virtually any fat woman can, with a reasonable amount of effort, control how fat she becomes. But as Bennett and Gurin, amongst many others, now point out, 'the best evidence and common experience both contradict this rationalization. With rare exceptions, dieters lose weight temporarily and then, despite great determination gradually regain it.'[1]

Other women's treacherous experiences and our own futile attempts should convince us of this. The fact that one diet programme after another appears on the bestseller lists, illustrating that none works for very long, should convince us also. But fat phobia and weight-hatred is so powerful that if dieting is seen as a cure, then a belief in the efficacy of dieting *must* be maintained, despite the contradictory and clear evidence, firstly that dieting does not work, secondly that dieting is dangerous.

National statistics amply demonstrate the failure of dieting. Americans now eat about 10 per cent less than they did fifteen years ago so they ought to weigh less, but they do not. Since the mid sixties the typical American has grown as much as five pounds heavier. One reason is that the effects of a national drop in activity level have outweighed those of lower intake, but it is not the whole story.

The common conception of weight control is based on three assumptions, which affect how we view dieting in general and the diet attempts of fat women in particular. The first assumption is that eating (usually called 'overeating' when applied to fat women) is the significant behaviour. It is always assumed that fat women eat *more* than women of 'normal' weight. The second assumption is that the body doesn't really 'care' how much fat it has, it merely stores the energy leftovers from each meal. Therefore any woman can permanently change her weight. The third assumption is that the conscious mind is capable of balancing intake and expenditure of energy in order to achieve any desired weight; a fat woman can do it if she really tries.

There is a great deal of evidence to show that all three assumptions are false.

The first assumption: Fat people eat more than thin people. This idea is unsupported by the evidence. Food is a red herring. No one gets fat solely by satisfying a big appetite. Of course it is difficult to be sure exactly how much someone is eating in the course of their daily life. The very fact of being observed may distort some women's food behaviour, and self-reporting of eating habits is subject to self-censorship. Lying about food intake is about level with lying about sex! But even allowing for these problems the strongest indications from a plethora of studies, are that fat people, (and it is mainly fat *women* whose eating habits are studied) eat about the same amount as thin ones.

Psychologists Susan and Orland Wooley, who direct a weight-control research programme at the University of Cincinnati College of Medicine, make this point most emphatically. The

Wooleys do not, unlike some researchers, express moral judge-ments about fatness. This makes them more likely to receive honest replies to their questions about food intake. The majority of their clients, not surprisingly, are fat women. In several of their studies, they asked each fat woman to record every morsel of food she ate. The interviewees duly turned in hundreds of records of literally every bite, every snatched snackerel. The results were a revelation. Orland Wooley commented: 'Either all our patients were lying or they weren't eating very much.' A few of them may have been outrageously deceptive. A number of them may have underestimated their total intake. Nevertheless, even taking these possibilities into account, not one was glutton-ous, and the majority were far from greedy. Characteristic of the rest, two women who weighed more than 260 pounds appeared to be maintaining their weight on only 1,000 calories a day! This is probably a considerably lower calorie count than many very thin women achieve.[2]

Another researcher, psychiatrist Albert Stunkard, decided to overcome the inherent uncertainties and possible inaccuracies attached to self-reporting by devising a way to watch people eat in a natural setting. His team observed fat patrons at fast-food restaurants, icecream parlours and snack bars where portions are so standardized that it is reasonably easy to calculate the number of calories on each tray. The team stationed themselves where they could unobtrusively monitor virtually everyone and record what each individual ate. Obviously it was a public place where outright piggish behaviour might be avoided through embarrass-ment, and the researchers only studied one of people's daily meals, but any study can be criticized on methodological grounds, and as Bennett and Gurin who analysed the study commented: 'Anonymity in the surroundings should have been sufficient protection for anyone who wanted two or three ham-burgers instead of one.'[3] When the observers' sheets were tallied, the fat customers had eaten no more than the customers who were thin. Thin foodies in fast-food places often ate a great deal more.

A series of significant studies bear out those of Wooley and Stunkard to reveal that 'when food intakes of obese individuals were accurately assessed and compared with people of normal weights, the intakes were identical.' One study pointed to the well-established fact that 'there are thin people who eat excessively . . . and never put on a pound, and there are fat people who eat too much. Likewise there are thin people and fat people who have small appetites. The average fat person is euphagic' (moderate).[4]

These findings are the rule, not the exception. In addition to the data I picked out, I have read a score of studies which offer substantial evidence that fat women eat no more than thin women. The Wooleys cite an even greater number of studies in addition to their own all of which show that fat people, including fat women, eat normal quantities of food, or even slightly less. Not one study in the last thirty years shows that there is any significant difference in the amount eaten by fat and thin people, or that fat women eat more than thin women.[5]

Yet so deeply internalized in all of us is fat hatred that even fat women who live out this truth find it hard to credit. Overweight women swallow the lie that they eat more than thin women because fat oppression makes all of us believe that fat women are unworthy creatures who do not deserve to have appetites.

Linked to the myth that fat women eat more is the myth that once a fat woman loses her 'excess' her slim figure can be maintained by 'normal' eating patterns.

When the average euphagic fat woman reduces her moderate food intake, a United States Public Health Service Report found, 'One well-controlled study showed that young women who lost weight on 1000-calorie diets experienced a decrease in basal metabolism rate, and in (calorie) intake required to maintain their reduced weights. Follow-up studies indicated that a lower calorie intake than recorded initially must be maintained indefinitely in order to maintain the reduced weight.'[6]

In other words, fat women who have endured the pain of starvation to 'cure' themselves of this excess so that they can live like the slim women who in all the research are called 'normal', find that 'Those who lose, and maintain a normal weight, must accept some degree of hunger and unsatisfied appetite as a way of life.'[7]

This of course is not a way of life, but a way of death. Death by constant dieting and prolonged hunger; death by the unendurable scorn fat women still receive because they can never lose enough. The hunger forced upon and accepted by fat women who buy into this myth is a painful condition which our instincts compel us to avoid. It is not a real possibility for those of us who wish to stay healthy.

Every study so far echoes the following conclusion that a 'review of the literature since 1958 did not reveal a successful longterm study using a diet regimen by itself or in combination with drugs, psychologic treatment, or an exercise program.'[8]

The evidence shows that fat women do not eat more, and diets up to starvation level do not work. But the myths which lie beneath these assumptions about weight control are stronger than the facts which do not support them. A fat woman and a thin woman both feel constant hunger when they live on a thousand calories a day, but whereas the intake is considered 'undereating' (even near starvation) for a slim woman, it is what nutritionists label as 'overeating' for the fat woman who remains fat on it.

The second assumption: the body does not really 'care' how much fat it has, therefore any woman can permanently change her weight, and how it is distributed. The evidence from an alternative theory, posed as correct by radical scientists and doctors, by writers like Bennett and Gurin, and by women in the Fat Activist Movement, and now widely accepted, is that the body does 'care' (and therefore cannot permanently be changed), because built into every person is a control system dictating how much fat she (or he) should carry. This control system determines the setpoint for body fat.

A setpoint mechanism is like a thermostat which determines the temperature of a room by turning the furnace on and off to maintain the temperature at which it is set. Obviously the mechanism to control the setpoint for body fat is more complex, it receives more information, it has more than one way to produce results. But its function is similar. It actively seeks to maintain a given 'set' amount of fat on the body.

Some people come with a high setting, others with a low one. So some women are naturally fat, others naturally thin. The difference is not between the weak and the strong or the greedy and the iron-willed but between internal, probably innate controls that are set differently in different people.

Our natural setpoint is determined by heredity, and only two ways to change it have so far been discovered – exercise and dieting. Exercise seems to function as a handle to crank down the setting, and indeed vigorous physical activity will lower it, but not by much. Weight-loss diets actually push the set point *up*.

This is why in the long run 99 per cent of all reducing diets fail. When stringent dietary measures suddenly shove up a fat woman's setpoint, it makes her weight *increase*, because fat people on diets do not immediately start to live off their fat reserves. Fat cells are an emergency resource to be used for survival in times like famine. It takes between four and eight weeks for the body to convert itself to disgesting its fat. During this time the body makes up the extra energy it needs by digesting its own muscle, heart, brain, etc., before it gets to the fat. The first weeks of a diet are exactly the same for a fat woman and a thin woman. Both start to starve. After this initial period the body, seeing itself in a state of 'famine', starts to tap into the fat reserves, then to slow down, to conserve energy, making the dieter lethargic and exhausted. Remember that feeling of fatigue and misery?

At this point the dieter has two choices: her first choice is to continue to starve; her mind becomes so cut off from the body's messsages, that ultimately she could starve to death. This is what happens to anorexics. The frightening problem attached to this choice is that extreme and incessant dieting puts women into a state of almost constant hunger which renders internal signals useless as a guide to either mealtimes or meal size. So chronic dieters become unable to recognize true physiological feelings of hunger, which is very threatening to their health.

The dieter's second choice, the one most of us are pushed into, is to remain sane, give in to the body's compelling and furious messages to nourish it, and watch the weight inexorably creep back on. Women who have dieted long enough to lose weight only to succumb to a binge of guilty eating will recognize this experience. Most of us can recall the ceaseless hunger that a single 'wicked' indulgence in no way relieves, which is usually followed by unbearable internal pressure to continue eating until all the pounds triumphantly shed have returned.

Ordinary plump women, like all the guinea pigs in weight studies, have setpoints. What differs is the setting. It is crucial that we understand that fat women are by nature no more binge eaters than anyone else. What a fat women is, by nature, is fat!

Their weight, like everyone else's, will creep back to what has been called our natural setting, which, give or take a few pounds, is the weight we maintain when we are not dieting and preferably not thinking about it. It is true that chronic dieters, through a lifetime of eating by the calorie charts, may be out of touch with their own healthy weight, but even they can usually identify a weight to which they spontaneously return. Certainly young women (and men) who have been experimentally starved or overfed always return rapidly to their previous weight. And many women who make no real effort will maintain the same weight for twenty or thirty years. This is because the setpoint we inherit is a result of natural selection and how much it can be changed is also inherited. Some of us have the potential to weigh 520 pounds or more whereas others of us could not weigh more than 140 pounds under any conditions.

When a fat women goes on a diet, it is because fat hatred pushes her to believe that her body doesn't care how much fat it has, that she and her deathly diet can overpower the body's setpoint. What will be overpowered, with dreadful consequences, is usually the woman. For it is a battle the fat woman cannot ultimately win. For that matter, a skinny woman who goes on an overeating programme to gain weight permanently cannot ultimately win either. But the thin woman who cannot *gain* weight finds there are no penalties for failing.

Constant, extreme dieting renders fat people unable to follow their bodies' cues about hunger and food intake. People on stringent diets are *always* hungry, and have to learn to ignore the internal signals which normally control intake and weight. In one study, the Wooleys point out that these facts help explain the near inevitability of weight gain after dieting – so that the cure for obesity may also be one cause of it.[9]

What confronts the fat woman on a diet is mercilessly summed up by poet Christine Donald who, with thirty-five years of fat oppression behind her, and stuck with a setpoint of two hundred and fifty pounds, has written a wonderfully humorous book of poems called *The Fat Woman Measures Up*.[10] Here is her view of what happens when:

> *The Fat Woman Confronts a Diet*
> The fat woman went on a diet
> because that is what fat women are supposed to do.
> The diet sheet said: fat women never eat breakfast,
> so that is one meal which is not a problem;
> the fat woman stopped eating breakfast.
> Fat people, said the diet sheet, should use
> smaller plates and only eat half as much;
> the fat woman drank glasses of cold water
> to keep her stomach quiet and she used smaller plates.
> Fat people should not, said the sheet sternly,
> stuff their fat faces between meals;
> the fat woman was not a nibbler nor a drinker,
> so she considered taking up smoking.
> The fat woman now felt tired all the time
> but the diet sheet said serenely, that was psychological.
> She collapsed one day; the diet sheet
> was beside itself with joy, fine
> it said, you're doing fine.

The third assumption: weight control is simply a matter of measuring calories consumed against calories expended, and *all* women can lose their fat by doing their sums.

Innumerable diet manuals and fat haters in professional capacities present fat as the bottom line on a balance sheet that looks like this:

CREDITS: breakfast, lunch, dinner, snacks.

DEBIT: effort used in breathing, walking, jogging, hoovering, cooking, cleaning the kitchen floor, washing nappies, walking the dogs, heaving the coal, having sex, changing light bulbs, etc.

NET: one ounce of adipose tissue. Fat to you and me!

It is argued that any woman, fat or thin, can do this sum, and lose that fat.

But let us look more closely at the arithmetic. Theoretically, to gain ten pounds in one year (the fastest rate at which most adults ever gain weight except those just coming off a diet) requires no more than 100 'extra' calories a day. These are calories not considered necessary. This excess is minute. It could be one tablespoonful of butter, one apple, one pear, one cup of minestrone, or one thin biscuit of shredded wheat. And this caloric mistake is not one made at a single meal. It is spread out over a whole day in which 2000 to 3000 calories are consumed and burnt away. If a fat woman takes a few extra flakes of cereal at breakfast, or three more bites of cheese at lunch, she's probably torn it.

This error is so subtle that according to the research even trained nutritionists shadowing a fat person for twenty-four hours cannot accurately estimate to within 400 calories how much she has eaten.[11] But the ordinary fat woman is supposed to be able to.

Measuring caloric intake is only half of this arduous task. To know whether food is a necessity or a luxury, whether it constitutes that 'extra', women need to know exactly how much energy they use each day.

If we scrub a floor for fifteen minutes, or swim a fast crawl for thirteen minutes, or energetically cook dinner for fifty minutes, we probably use up the caloric equivalent of one biscuit of shredded wheat!

The kind of things we are required to know to get it right are ludicrous. For instance the mental exertion required to subtract say accordion playing from eating apples is beyond most people's capacities. Did *you* know that one apple equals about thirty minutes of playing the accordion as opposed to about fifty minutes of sitting listening to someone else play it? Did you even care? Fat women are required to care.

It is obvious that these estimates of energy output are even less accurate than women's self-assessment of their food intake. As researchers Wing and Epstein point out, for women to keep a running total of accurate intake and exertion and 'come out within 500 calories of the right count is ridiculously small'.[12] It is also an unrealistic expectation.

Should women have to indulge in these measures? Of course not. It is a ridiculous way to behave. But fat hatred leads women, fat and thin, both to be unrealistic about their abilities of caloric measurement and also to believe they ought to be able to perform this largely useless task, because shedding a few pounds will bring them praise and gaining a few pounds will subject them to downright contempt.

And that contempt, that oppressive scorn of a woman's fatness, will lead every fat woman to hate herself and her body when she fails to get the arithmetic right. She does not think, what a nonsensical series of sums this is; she thinks, oh what a failure I am for getting these serious sums wrong.

Fay Weldon, who, as a fat woman herself, sees fatness as a symbol of depression caused by the way patriarchal society still treats women as a secondary sex, believes that the fatness that comes out of that kind of arithmetic is always seen by women as a symbol of failure.

'If you are fat,' she told me, 'you feel a failure because you haven't managed to get thin. Forget everything else. I think it is ridiculous. I mean it is obviously ridiculous. I suppose I haven't made this properly clear . . . it is a ridiculous thing to want to be thin. But our lives are composed of ridiculous matters, like wanting to look nice, or wanting to steal other women's men, or other women, or whatever and do it by physical looks.'

When Fay Weldon said that to me I laughed because I had never thought quite how absurd a cultural matter it was, wanting to be thin. But absurd though it is, it has become a tragically serious problem for women in the West.

NINE

WHO SAYS FAT IS BAD?

'Please slip off your clothes, Mrs Cline,' the nurse said pleasantly. 'then we'll put you on the scales.'

'It's Ms not Mrs,' I said politely.

I have been coming to the hospital monthly for check-ups and I have said it politely every time. The staff say 'Mrs' politely too. They think it carries more respect. You need a bit of respect when you are only an out-patient fumbling with bra straps and knicker elastic.

'Of course, dear,' she said tolerantly. 'Now, Miss Cline, just put your hands through this nice white gown. Sorry it hasn't got a belt. I often think our more difficult patients take them home! You mustn't worry about the gown adding a little extra weight. Some of our ladies try to be weighed in the altogether!'

'I don't want to be weighed,' I said, trying not to sound tetchy. 'There isn't any need.'

I've said this every time too. The staff smile a lot when I say it. Some of the staff feel fat at size 12.

'There's a lot of evidence which suggests there isn't a necessary correlation between moderate amounts of fat and disease,' I continued wearily, dragging the gown around me. Lacking a belt, my ample bosom lurched through the gap. It made it hard to be taken seriously.

'Now, Miss Cline, we do have to remember you are a heart case. Let's have no more fuss.' Her voice had that edge of steel I remembered from my time as an in-patient. 'Got your clothes off? Good. You can tell the doctor all about what you've been

216

reading once we've got you settled. If you'll just follow me to the waiting area, we'll pop you on the scales.'

Undressing in a cubicle is relatively private. The weighing machine, however, is in the crowded public waiting room. The other women looked up with interest.

The nurse's well-trained gaze ran over my body, taking in the bulges inside the flapping gown. 'Difficult not to overeat in the run-up to Christmas,' she said sympathetically. 'And of course you want to look nice as well, don't you?'

Dutifully I popped myself on the scales, and she sang out the kilograms. I was not the only woman who busily translated into stones and pounds!

I stood on the scales, as I was told, despite my knowing that the idea that health automatically benefits from weight loss is dubious at best. Bennett and Gurin, who challenge that convention point out: 'Nobody has ever proved that losing weight prolongs the life of moderately fat people, much less those of average weight. On the contrary fatness itself appears not to be the major cause of disease, as we have been told it is.'[1]

As for women considered very overweight, these researchers emphasize that the medical profession treats 'excessive overweight' with drugs, hormones and dangerous surgery, when it is clear that if we did not regard fat as excessive and unhealthy in itself, such treatment would be unnecessary. Certainly in cultures without prejudice against fatness, fat people show patterns of health and nutrition more like those found in slim people in our culture, which suggests that the 'sickness' and misery of fat women depends as much on their sensitivity to persecution as on the weight itself.

There I was weighing in as usual, even though I knew just how little evidence there is connecting women's fatness to bad health. Most of the studies linking high blood pressure and coronary disease with obesity were done on *male* subjects. Studies that did use women found their subjects through diet groups, and dieting consistently and to excess has been conclusively found to be highly dangerous. Most fat women studied were striving to fit an acceptable image. Most had experienced persecution because of their bulk. Several studies revealed that repeated dieting could cause atherosclerosis (a form of hardening of the arteries with fatty degeneration), and long-term fasting can achieve dangerously elevated blood fat levels. Most recent research supports the view that chronic dieting plays a major role in many of the disorders associated with fatness. The stress of the cycle of dieting, losing weight, putting more back on, is often the cause of heart disease.

Dr Rubin Andres of the National Institute of Ageing in Baltimore, to whom Cheryl Lean and I talked at length, made some surprising relevant findings. He found that people who gain weight as they age actually live longer. He found that men and women should weigh the same and not markedly differently, as is suggested by most weight table guides based on insurance companies' 'desirable weights'. He also told us that the type of body fat typical of most women, which is fat in the lower part of the body, is quite healthy. 'The evidence is that the fat which is more characteristic of women on the lower body is really not dangerous in terms of health. It is not associated with more diabetes, nor with the development of coronary disease, nor with high mortality. It is just the kind of fat women do not like because it is not fashionable. But it is not dangerous.'

I had spent months reading the available evidence, but as a patient in a traditional Western medical system, confronted with a nurse who reminded me I *was* a heart case, and *did* want to look nice, I weighed my fat and my fears.

So powerful is the ideology connecting fat with disease (particularly with heart conditions); so powerful is our culture's hatred of female fat, that it would have taken a stronger woman than I was then, to make more than a nominal stand against the scales.

I stood crossly by the weighing machine having lost most of my poise and none of my pounds. I was still somewhere between nine and a half and nine and three-quarter stone, still unwilling to tell myself . . . or you – exactly what I did weigh, I was both unwilling to give in to the medical viewpoint that I should lose every pound above eight and a half stone, and unable to uphold my own viewpoint that it did not matter and that I should go home and forget about it.

Vacillating and grumpy, I shifted from one bare foot to another. Suddenly someone spoke.

'Could I have your autograph? You are Sally Cline, aren't you?'

A mellow melodic voice with a tantalizing transatlantic accent. Obviously a person of style and discrimination. An individual of consequence.

How amazing! How flattering! Here I was, caught lumbering off the scales, a flabby, feeble, unclothed patient. Rolling around, an anonymous cog in a terrifying medical wheel, trying to improve my life chances by subduing my recalcitrant flesh; suddenly transformed by a single sentence back into a human being, with a positive identity and a mission in the world.

I drew the gaping gown across my wan breasts (winter is not my best time), pulled myself up to my full height of under five foot four, and feeling almost like an author, looked around for the owner of the Voice.

The room was littered with bored women flicking through magazines. No candidate of consequence presented herself. Indeed no one looked up at all. Had they not heard the voice of the goddess?

Two seats away from me a sort of cloth pyramid was earnestly flapping a paperback in my direction. Near the top of the pyramid, which was entirely shrouded in unbecoming beige, like yesterday's melted toffee, an extraordinarily pretty face beamed out at me. She stood up, reaching *her* full height of five foot one, and shuffled what looked like sixteen stone over to me.

Somewhere in the back of my mind I heard Fay Weldon say: 'Most women are, in the eyes of the world, fat. If you go into the streets or the supermarkets, especially away from the city centres where women don't have so many aspirations, women are frankly shapeless, fat and not squeezing into, but falling into drapes rather than clothes.'

Drapes indeed were falling all around the pyramid, who now spoke. '*Could* I have your autograph? I did so like your last book. I work here.'

The voice was unmistakeably Canadian. The words were heart-warming, but to my horror I realized that I felt disappointed. Let down. Confused. As if the praise of a fat woman was somehow not as legitimate as the praise of a thin woman or of a man.

I asked her name. I signed her book: 'To Trudie, In Sisterhood' and felt a shit.

Fat women are everywhere but they are practically invisible. The razor-thin stereotype of femininity contradicts their very existence. That tyranny of inoffensive and compulsory slimness has bred a hatred of fat which means that women who have swallowed it, women like me, have closed their minds to the possibilities of anything positive or beautiful in the shape of women who are indisputably fat. Women like Trudie. That inoffensive thin stereotype that sat like a ghost in the empty seat between us is an urgent social issue. I looked at Trudie, we started to talk, but I knew I was not yet ready to deal with it.

We talked, of course, about food. 'I can go without food, I can be very good and go without it all day,' she said, as if she or I needed to be convinced.

'Every time my mother speaks to me she asks "Have you been good today?" She means have you been eating, have you lost any weight? She's the opposite of a proper Jewish mother, she never says "Eat, Trudie, eat." Eating is misbehaving. Mother has literally pulled food out of my mouth, physically removed it. I know she only wants the best for me. Being good is not eating and finding a husband.'

'Being good has nothing to do with not eating. Nothing at all.' I knew the right words. 'We should be able to eat what we like when we like and still feel good.' Somewhere beneath the right words, my thoughts were not right. Had she found a husband? Had he been good to her? Why was I wasting time on such irrelevancies? Maybe if I was fifteen or sixteen stone and only a speck above five foot I too would think goodness lay in food denial. Maybe I did think it, even though I was stones lighter and inches taller. Why did I need to remind myself of these comforting facts? Surely it was Trudie who was in need of reassurance? I began to feel uneasy. Trudie, however, had perked up.

'I know you're right,' she said eagerly. 'Thank you for saying that. I knew from your book you'd be an understanding person. But I do see eating as misbehaving. It's because my body looks so terrible. It always has. I was made fun of at school. We'd go to Hebrew School, stop at the delicatessen, we'd all buy food, they had more places to put it, they were thin, so they had the right to call me terrible names. They thought I was stupid and disgusting.'

Children can be very cruel, and mockery is the fat child's lot. Ten-year-old Anna, who at ten stone was kept perpetually on a diet by her mother who took her weekly to an adult slimming club, had told me: 'The girls won't let me join in games, they say I'm thick. The boys won't go near me, they say I'm smelly.'

In a study by Staffieri[2] six- to ten-year-old boys were shown silhouettes of average and thin children to whom they responded uniformly favourably. When the boys were shown silhouettes of fat children, they described them as cheats, dirty, lazy, sloppy, mean, ugly, stupid, and said that fat children tell lies, get teased and don't have best friends. When girls were tested,[3] they ascribed virtually all the same attributes to fat children, but went even further, describing the fat child as having 'worries' and 'fights' and stressing that fat children are 'naughty, sad, and lonely'. As early as six girls already recognized the social isolation which accompanies being overweight. This is hardly surprising when studies show that from the age of two, American children prefer thin rag dolls to fat ones.[4]

'It was hard to have friends as a fat child,' Trudie was saying. 'When I was eleven I had very big breasts. None of the other children did. One day my friend's little sister came up to me.

After she'd stopped staring she actually put out her hand and started to feel my breasts. I shall never forget the way she stared, as if I were a different species. She was stroking my breasts because I was so odd. I can remember how I felt to this day.'

Her eyes were filling with tears. I let my own eyes discreetly wander over her large bosom, trying hard to subdue comparison with my own. With those kind of thoughts, I certainly didn't have the words she wanted. I felt ashamed. I remembered ten-year-old Jen who could no longer get into children's clothes because of her big bust. 'I was aching for a track suit for Christmas,' she'd told me. 'But I knew I wouldn't run in it because my boobs bounce. One girl said I was truly gross because I had jumbo nipples. It's true, all the boys call me "bignips".'

'Go on about being a teenager,' I said to Trudie, trying to sound jolly.

'As a kid, eating made me feel guilty. I still can't eat in public. I remember once eating in the street. Someone I knew walked towards me, so instantly I threw the food aside. Nobody told me to do it, but being fat, being a very fat teenager . . .'

She stopped, the big warm beam left the flushed pretty face, left it looking small and secretive. Did Trudie say, 'If you're very fat, you don't need other people to tell you what to do', or did we both merely think it?

'I expect it was a popsicle I threw away,' she said. 'Something fat girls mustn't eat. I guess fat girls shouldn't eat at all.'

'Did you eat a lot of sweets as a child? Do you eat a lot of sweets now?' I tried not to sound severe. It was a question she'd heard many times. 'I eat cheesey knicknacks but not sweets. Eating candy isn't what has made me this fat,' she said quietly. 'I was fat right from three years old. There were four of us, two boys, two girls; I was the eldest, they were all thin. Mum and Dad always worried that I was so overweight. The others probably teased me, yes they did; everybody else did anyway. Once over a hamburger and french fries Father had this deep discussion about how I must lose weight because boys might like

222

a fat girl but they wouldn't ask her out. So they kept taking me to doctors. Maybe I have an over-active thyroid. They tested me for years. They put me on pills, on diets, nothing worked. Once I was an in-patient and I lost twenty pounds but I put it straight back on. I'm now forty-two. I still feel different from normal women.'

'Of course you are a normal woman,' I said sturdily. I found I was thinking she did look different. She did seem different. *Why was I thinking that?* Trudie said she knew from my book that I'd be an understanding person, but I wasn't understanding anything. I did not want to understand either Trudie's emotions or my own. Keep talking Trudie, keep me from examining my own frightening thoughts.

'My earliest memory of being different . . . I was six. I was the only child who had to have special clothes; size 6X, I knew then I was something bigger than ordinary, something other children hated. If you knew how upsetting that was . . .'

This time I looked away to give her time to recover. My eyes lit on a woman with a small child in the waiting room. They were cheerfully chewing chocolate bars to stave off boredom. The child was thin and excitable. The woman had a tired, patient look but her free hand proudly smoothed the belt round her wasplike waist.

'They don't give fat children candy. Fat children can't have what other children have,' Trudie said. 'They?' I asked. 'Mother, I mean, and the storekeepers. Plump children can't buy candy. Mother only ever wanted the best for me. She never said you must be slim to get a man, it was always, "You do the best you can because you're bright, yes you do the best you can." She used to say, "Don't settle for anything less."'

Suddenly I was afraid to ask what Trudie had settled for. Do we stop fat women reaching their full potential? I remembered I'd asked that question of Toni Laidlaw, the psychologist, a big woman, who had stopped worrying about it and worked on fat and food with women who did worry. Toni had taken the question very seriously.

223

'What you are really saying is, is there such a thing as fat oppression, and indeed there is. It has been shown empirically that women deemed fat in our culture are less likely to get jobs, less likely to get husbands and boyfriends, are considered sexually unattractive, and therefore are treated as "non-sexual beings". This is a very serious form of oppression and it's understandable that women who are fat by these standards are terrified to remain that way. In very real terms, just as if they were black or lesbian, they lose out: on jobs, on relationships, on respect, on power. And we all contribute to this fat oppression. We all hate fat women.'

Do we? More to the point, do I? It wasn't something I was prepared to think about half-dressed in the middle of a hospital appointment. I felt rattled. Obviously the hospital environment was subduing my interview technique. Anyway, this wasn't an interview. I was just chatting to a fat woman with a pretty face who had spoken appreciatively to me. I was glad Trudie was still talking.

'If you're fat, you can't get a job where you need to be seen. Mother didn't understand how I felt, so I once tried to explain about getting turned down. I said, "This is how I feel, discriminated against." I've been a bottle washer, a clerk, I've worked in hospitals, shops, libraries, jobs where you can hide. But I could never apply to be a receptionist. Maybe I got paranoid but I got turned down a lot. I even got turned down through postal applications, and I thought this is stupid, they haven't even seen you! But it's true I never got a job where it said "attractive person wanted".'

Quickly I said: 'But Trudie you are attractive.' Trudie looked at me in disbelief. 'Do I believe that?' she said softly. 'Or do I think that other people won't believe it?' She pulled her chair nearer to mine. 'I've got a split personality. Half of me thinks I'm this big fat slob, and half of me thinks I'm beautiful and wonderful.'

Was she waiting for me to say something, or was she somewhere inside remembering? Soon she spoke again. 'Other people told me I had to be pretty. I had to be slim, to get a man. I tried not to believe them but they were right. In North America you can't be a fat teenager and lead any kind of sex life. Not even romance. Girls date from age twelve but no one in the whole of North America ever dated me. Not one boy or one man ever asked me out except an older man who was fatter and shorter than me. And he was a cripple. He'd had polio. He couldn't ask a normal girl out. I guess I felt like he felt. Crippled. When girls date from twelve you can be an old maid by nineteen. I felt an old maid at sixteen.'

What was a safe subject? I settled on clothes as more neutral than sex. 'They make better, brighter clothes for larger women now, don't they?' I proffered. 'Do they?' she said flatly. We both thought about it. After a bit she roused herself to make me feel more at ease. 'Well, I guess young fat women can go into Mothercare and find something bright that fits, not too horrendous. But when I was sixteen there was just nothing. I was suicidal. Clothes counted so much.'

I remembered Isabel, twelve stone at sixteen years, who had told me, 'You can't go out if you're a fat teenager, because you can't wear cool gear. You can't even get a job selling it! I work Saturdays in this draggy chainstore because no one else would employ me to sell clothes. The trendy shops wouldn't even interview me. One bloke laughed and said I'd be a bad advert!'

A BBC TV programme called The Wannabees which interviewed image-conscious youngsters at London's Hippodrome Club found ten-year-old girls dieting to achieve 'nice figures like Madonna', to wear her kind of clothes. Reporter Helen Bone told viewers: 'Madonna's sleek new look – she's lost more than a stone this year – has intensified the deep desire of very young girls to lose weight. Image is everything and that means being skinny.'[5]

Trudie was right, the changes are not major. 'Once, in despair,' she said, 'my grandmother took me into an old-fashioned maternity shop. I just nearly died. Suppose someone I knew had seen me! After that they took me to fat wear shops where only really fat older women go. It was mortification. I took to wearing men's clothes because at least they were big enough. Clothes have always made me feel different, worse than other women. In a loose dress I'm 18 or 20, in a tight one, even bigger. I feel angry that shops don't stock higher than 14 but I never say anything to the assistants. I never say I'm angry to anyone. You don't if you're fat because people think it's your fault. They don't care about how you feel. They think you deserve it. I do as much shopping as possible by mail order. Those awful communal changing places, oh no, I just can't go in there. Like I won't go to a swimming pool. At school having to take those communal showers, with towels the size of a teatowel, it was just hell. I got off it whenever I could. Oh yes my life is a misery. I won't go on a beach either, though I love the water. My mobility is restricted by my weight, sure it is, but that's how it is. I haven't dared buy a bathing suit since I was eighteen. I can't undress in front of anyone.'

There was a study done on five- to six-year-old white urban children, which found that when the children were tested with headless photographs of chubby, average and thin children in bathing suits 86 per cent of these under-tens had assimilated the message that fat is bad, ugly, and fat children shouldn't be seen in swimsuits.[6]

Jannie, a twelve-year-old over ten stone, had recently confessed her misery of school showers. 'The others call me fatbum. It's worse on the beach. Mum's so ashamed of my size she carries this huge towel to shroud me like a corpse. She makes me hold it round me all the way to the water, then she calls out: "You can drop it now, Jannie, run and hide in the waves."'

Trudie was not alone.

'I am sure your friends don't mind how you look,' I said, hoping it was true.

'I believe good friends, good women friends, won't care what you look like, but they do. One woman said she was my best friend, but she started a rumour that I was having sex for money in the afternoons when I was supposed to be looking after someone else's child. Can you believe that?' Her voice rose in

226

indignation. 'If I could have made money off sex – what a joke – *me*! I wouldn't have had to look after other people's children. But people say things like that if you're fat, even your friends. It's hard to have a best friend if you're fat. I had a good view of women then I sort of lost it. Women have not always been very nice to me. They do care what you look like.'

Her eyes had filled with tears again, but resolutely she went on. 'I couldn't walk about with nothing on, even in front of women who say they are friends. A couple of times I've sneaked a bra off in the presence of women but it was terrible, I'm not comfortable at all.'

She paused, her rather thin hands with neatly manicured nails comforting each other as they unconsciously touched the shelf of her bosom. I remembered the story of her friend's little sister. I was not surprised when she said, 'I guess I feel angry, real angry but I can't express what I feel. I even get angry on buses when I notice everybody passes me by. Nobody wants to sit next to me. I take up too much space. I ought to be angry with public transport, but I get angry inside. I once wrote to a bus company but they didn't answer. They all think I haven't any willpower, but I've tried . . .'

She did not sound angry, she sounded as she looked, terribly distressed. I wanted to cheer her up. 'I expect jobs with uniforms are a great help,' I said. I couldn't have picked a worse target.

'Oh no, they're *not*,' she said. This time she did sound enraged. 'That's another area that needs remedying. When I worked in a Little Chef cafeteria everyone had to wear uniform. But I couldn't get into the women's uniform, so they put me in the men's one. There I was, sticking out again, knowing all the staff and customers would notice me. Here in this hospital they are talking about getting a skirt and blouse uniform. I told them I can't get into separates. If I can, I look ever worse, divided up like that, cut into two fat halves. They said, "Oh well, it won't be compulsory, don't worry. The others can wear it, but you

227

won't have to." How can they say don't worry, when I'll be the one person sticking out?'

Two neat uniformed nurses walked by. They took two bedraggled patients off to weigh them. Trudie and I exchanged wry grins. 'As soon as you enter a hospital they weigh you,' she said, 'even if the trouble is your eyes!'

I told her the hospital wanted me to lose nearly two stone, and that I often felt fat myself. Trudie stared at me incredulously as fat women do when thinnish women talk mournfully about losing a few pounds.

I remembered a poem by Christine Donald, who at 250 pounds, said she had been persecuted all her life for fatness.

> This thin woman is desperate to lose
> eight or ten pounds
> 'oh god,' she wails, 'I'm so fat.'

> 'If you call yourself fat,'
> thus the fat woman politely,
> 'what word would you use to describe me?'

> Silence ensues.

> At moments like this, the fat woman,
> hurt in her body, feels moved
> to physical violence.[7]

Silence ensued. Trudie and I sheltered separately within it. I recalled a happily married bisexual friend telling me she'd felt oppressed when she occasionally told other people she had a 'gay side'. 'Their reactions were really hurtful,' she'd said, looking for sympathy. Angrily I had wanted to say, 'You don't know what oppression feels like,' but I said, 'Poor you'. I imagine Trudie felt much the same way about me.

I told Trudie about O, Marly, and Kelly. Then I realized that the paranoid fear of fat felt by women who are seven stone and afraid of gaining two pounds contributes to but is not the same as the daily harassment and discrimination suffered by women who may be fifteen stone but cannot lose a single pound. There is a profound difference between the fear of fat these thin women experience, and the fat hatred experienced by women already indisputably fat.

'I know how they feel,' Trudie said slowly. 'But they're lucky. They can't know how I feel. I once went to my doctor and said I'd thought of smoking to try and lose weight. She looked at her charts and said, "Better you are four stone overweight than that you start to smoke", but I was lighter then.' She sounded happier.

I knew those doctors' charts well. At five foot one they would indicate Trudie's weight should be between seven stone eleven and nine stone. The charts would suggest that Trudie was seven stone overweight, not four. But she was lighter then. All of us tell stories about our lighter, thinner, happier past. Or about the future when we are going to be seven stone three.

We decide our worth on the basis of some stupid number. We say things like, 'When I am thin . . . That means, I am no good *now*. We believe if we are fat we don't matter. We look towards that male-defined slim ideal. We believe in it because we have been told that *all* fat is unhealthy.

Trudie interrupted and echoed my thoughts. 'There are heart attacks in my family. I really think I should be carrying around less weight. The doctors think much much less, they see my fatness as a disease.' A note of fear had entered her weary voice. This was where I came in.

I told her about the evidence which suggests that despite statistics showing fat people are more likely to suffer from certain diseases (including arthritis, mature-onset diabetes, high blood pressure) fatness itself does not cause them. Indeed all attempts to show that fatness itself causes high blood pressure have so far failed.[8]

I told her that though fatness is shown to be associated with certain diseases, it is only one risk factor amongst many, and although high blood pressure increases the risks of coronary heart disease, coronary heart disease is *not* associated with fatness. I told her that though in about 30 per cent of very fat people their fatness is a warning (a signal, for instance, that diabetes might be developing), if the disease does develop, *moderate* weight control can be one element in treatment, but *excessive* dieting is always dangerous, and careful scientific investigations in the last ten years have repeatedly failed to show that moderate amounts of body fat are harmful to health. Though fatness may be a risk factor for a tiny minority of the population who are termed severely obese (those who are from half to two-thirds adipose tissue), the research shows that for women who are up to 30 per cent over their 'desirable weight' fatness is not even a risk factor for disease. It certainly is not a disease in itself.

Trudie listened, then said quietly: 'It's not my health that upsets me, it's the way people treat me, it's what I know they think of me. They make me think I am one big blob.' I was beginning to realize that Trudie's problem was not being fat, but the way people like me thought about her.

Christine Donald had said: 'Most of the symptoms that fat people like me have that are supposedly unhealthy are actually stress symptoms suffered by any kind of oppressed minority.' An American study by Monello and Mayer[9] confirmed what Christine Donald had said and Trudie's experiences. By testing two groups of thirteen- to seventeen-year-old girls (a fat group attending a weight-reducing camp, and a group not considered obese attending a typical summer camp next door), the researchers revealed the dreadful psychological and emotional price paid by fat women. All the fat girls demonstrated the sad lifeless attitudes similar to those of persecuted ethnic and racial minorities. The researchers compared the fat girls' 'obsessive concern' with weight to the chronic feelings of helplessness, anxiety, and impending doom experienced by victims of racial discrimination and anti-Semitism.

One girl made the following entries in her journal: 'Over the years I have been prodded, badgered, passed judgement on by so many people . . . my self-esteem eroded to a point beyond tolerating. (Nov 15)

'The more I hated myself the better job I thought I was doing. The hate snowballed until I . . . entered a state of inertia. (Nov 16)

'A mountain of fat, great volumes of larded flab, covered with over-stretched and sagging skin. Buried deep within is a bit of joy slowly drowning . . . Hope too is suffering the death-agony . . . There is only one cure for the indignities . . . Marking time, hiding misery, extravagantly wasting my life.' (Dec 29th)

Trudie: one big blob. The girl at the fat camp: great volumes of larded flab.

These are not accounts of unhealthy women, but of persecuted women. It is not their fat which is making them unhealthy, it is the way they are treated as fat.

This persecution goes on even if a fat woman is clever or famous. I remembered that after a cover story in *Time* magazine on Boston Symphony conductor Sarah Caldwell, this letter to the editor appeared: 'I am proud to see women take their place in music. However one cannot regard Sarah Caldwell as anything but a big blob of blubber.'

Trudie called herself a big fat slob. She cannot express her anger or misery because fat women cannot. Where in all this did women like me fit in?

I was relieved when the nurse told me the doctor would see me. Trudie gave me her phone number. 'Ring me if I can help with your food book,' she said. 'I'm sorry I sounded as if I hated myself. There's a lot more I could tell you.'

I was sure there was. I was not yet sure I was up to hearing about it. I drove home slowly, thinking about Trudie's misery as a child. I wondered what had happened later to the young woman with the exceedingly pretty face and the terribly over-weight body. After the man who was disabled, had other men (or women) asked her out? Had the bright schoolgirl settled for less than her best? As I began to accelerate on the quiet country road, her voice pounded in my head: 'It's the way people treat

231

me . . . It's what I know they think of me . . . I'm one big blob
. . . I hated myself so much.' I thought of the girl in the fat camp
rolled inside that snowball of hate.

Trudie had said people told her being fat was her fault. 'They
think you deserve it.' I looked at the studies done by Orland and
Susan Wooley on the hatred of fat children. They pointed out:
'The child whose build is socially 'deviant' comes early in life to
be regarded by others as responsible for her 'condition' and
deserving of social disapproval, and sooner or later is subjected
to pressures to restrict food intake in order to 'correct' her
condition. Failure to do so is seen as weakness, 'wanting to be
fat' or even a masochistic desire for rejection.'[10]

The fat woman who insists on eating without regard to the
consequences, in our culture based on the notion of achievement,
is deemed to have failed. This concept of failure is intrinsic to
the principles of fat hating which is why neither age nor intellect
decreases women's obsession with the folds of their flesh. But to
be fat is not merely to fail, it is also to be deviant. Trudie had
told me she wasn't a 'normal woman'. I tried to forget I too had
thought she seemed 'different'.

To see just how 'abnormal' fatness is considered, I looked at
two reports on studies designed to compare children's attitudes
to various kinds of handicaps, among which they included
fatness. The researchers showed photographs and drawings of
handicapped children and fat children to eight samples of mentally and physically 'normal' children of ten to eleven years old
and asked who they would most want and who they would least
want to be friends with. The 'normal' children consistently
ranked the fat child lower than a child with crutches and a brace,
or one in a wheelchair with a blanket over both legs, or one with
the left hand missing, or a child with a bad facial disfigurement.[11]

Seven of the sample groups ranked the fat child last. Only the
group of white working-class Jewish children in New York City
rated the obese child anywhere but last. They put the fat child
third.[12]

The arrant ablebodyism and anti-handicap attitudes of such

surveys makes them in my view highly problematic but I quote them for the significant things they tell us about both the researchers' and children's attitudes towards the stigmatized state of fatness; an attitude I was beginning to recognize I had internalized.

When the drawings were shown to a ninth group, this time of seventy-two adults in the 'helping and caring' professions, every one of them (doctors, nurses, psychologists, social workers, physical and occupational therapists) rated the fat child last.

A few years later an independent team of investigators showed the 'handicap' drawings to two hundred adults 'deliberately chosen to sample populations presumed to value fatness or at least be tolerant of overweight.' These tolerant two hundred included fat people, and those of low socio-economic status. Every one of them rated the fat child last. Additional data suggested that this was because the obese are held responsible for their condition, whilst other handicapped people are not.[13]

Older children, far from shaking off fear of fat, had imbibed it to such an extent, that in one study it was reported that 144 high school students preferred to be at a greater 'social distance' from the fat child than from any handicapped child depicted. Researchers used a scale of graded statements ranging from 'would exclude this type of person from my school' to 'would be willing to marry this type of person' in order to illustrate social distance. Not one student wanted to share their personal, emotional or geographical space with a fat child.[14]

Every study was a document in fat hatred. The impact this obsessional loathing has on the individual child is probably irreversible. But it is not only the fat child who suffers; these anti-fat attitudes learnt in childhood become the basis for the self-disgust and self-loathing felt by adult women thin and fat. What I believe is even more significant than the expectable findings of our society's ingrained fat hatred (as well as dislike and fear of disablement) is the initial research decision to include fatness as a stigmatized handicap along with facial disfigurement and missing limbs. I see it as an unconscious fatophobic decision that was implemented for nearly a decade in a series of studies whose findings in one sense only mirror the oppressive research tool, and which cripple all of us in our relationship with fat people.

I felt I had reached the point where I could talk to Trudie again.

I phoned, and Trudie came round. She seemed nervous but eager to talk. I served afternoon tea. She took a toasted bun. 'I'm a secret eater. It will be hard to eat this in front of you.' But she did. 'I've been married. Some people are surprised. But I was only ten and a half stone at the time. I put on weight with each child – two boys. I've never lost it. Now I don't even aim to get lower than twelve stone, but oh how I would love to be able to see my pubic hairs, just once. I've never seen them.'

It was a hard line to follow. I poured another cup. She picked up when she talked about her boys. 'They are the best thing from my marriage. Though there's the problem of snacking their leftover chips. They never tease me. I'm just their mum. I even started saying, "Do you wish I was slimmer like other mums?" and they say, "No, you're just fine the way you are." No one else says that. If I have to jump out of the bath to answer the phone I'll even walk around almost naked in front of them. My friends are disgusted. "What if the kids see what you look like?" they say.'

Trudie's marriage had been tough. 'My husband was a drinker, English, I met him over here. Men liked me a little more in England, but only married men. Single men never asked me out. I was married ten years. I was in the kitchen a lot. When I'm alone I head for the kitchen. My marriage was such that I was at home alone every night.'

She was half crying half laughing again. 'I cry easily. I can always find something to cry about. They say there's a relation-ship between food and married life, but there isn't so much for me because I was fat before, fat afterwards and fat during. When I was just dating I wouldn't eat so much because I was with someone, but I wasn't with anyone in my marriage. I used to sometimes be positive about being fat. I used to want to think fat is strong and powerful, until my husband started beating me, then I realized I wasn't powerful at all. I was just this fat slob. He was strong. He beat me up a lot. That was so frightening it took any hope of feeling powerful away. He'd always been violent on the football pitch, it was naïve of me to think he wouldn't carry through at home. One morning he came down the stairs and tried to strangle me. After that I moved out of the bedroom, kept a bottle by my bed, put a lock on the door. But I stayed a long time. I was always scared; I wanted to get the youngest to school, then I'd get a job and try and cope alone.'

What happened when her marriage broke up? I asked. 'My so-called friends didn't want to see me any more. I wasn't even going to be a fat *wife*. So I went through this promiscuous stage. I slept with about a dozen men. I didn't really let them see me. It was always in the dark. I was quite happy to be there at the time, but it wasn't important. Afterwards I thought, if all those strange men have sort of seen my body why can't my friends see it? But I knew I'd never see the men again. Sometimes sex is like sports, you have to make a joke of it. I do, I make a joke out of myself, but I'm afraid of being ridiculed.'

She had one good memory. 'I never thought I was pretty until I saw my wedding pictures. I looked at them and thought, "Hey you were pretty", so I did once think that.'

I said: 'If a man tells you you're pretty, don't you believe him?' She began sobbing, this time with no laughter. 'They don't. They always say, "You have a pretty face." I hate that. I'd rather they didn't say anything. I'm just constantly upset. I'm sure they mean to be nice, but why don't they ever just say "Aren't you pretty?" They'll always say you have a pretty face as if the rest of you is a mess. If one man had ever said "You've got a wonderful body" it would have been memorable. One man said, "You're all girl, aren't you?" You feel sexual, but nobody thinks you are. They think you're asexual.

'Once I booked an Anne Summers sex aids in the nineties party to sell nighties and vibrators. I took the invites round at work. *Four* people said 'Oh, I didn't think you were that type of person,' so I'm obviously giving off the wrong vibes. It made me inhibited about making advances sexually. I won't ask a man out, not just because I'm fat, also because I'm a woman. I do flirt but I know I hold back, thinking, Why would you want to be with *me?*'

I asked her if she thought being thin was attractive in others. She said: 'No, not particularly. I don't think thin is attractive, but there's always been this battle wanting and not wanting the perfect body. I resent the fact it should matter. Recently I stood at a bus stop, next to me was a beautiful girl. A man literally ran off the road looking at her. I don't want a man to look at me like that. It was just animal. He didn't know her, or anything about her. He wanted to fuck her. I don't want to be animal. I want someone to know me, who I really am. But they don't want to. Not even fat men, not if, they're single. Single men don't have to have a fat woman.'

Tell me about the single men, I said encouragingly. 'I've only ever had disastrous relationships with single men. Well I've only gone out with single men twice in my whole life. I want to think it's their problem not mine. One of them later said to someone he was homosexual. The other was so strange, so attached to his mother, he might as well have been. He wanted to go to bed with his boots on because he said his feet smelt. Then one night he just didn't turn up. Later he rang and said, "Sorry, I fell asleep." I thought, well, next time you come I'll be asleep. But there wasn't a next time. He didn't come around again. I just try not to mind.'

I wondered about computer dating, but I didn't like to ask. Then suddenly she said: 'I've applied for those lonely hearts clubs. I've never heard back, not from one lonely heart. I always tell them straight away that I'm fat so they never write back.'

Had it been easier with married men? I wondered. She said: 'I go out with men who know what a mature woman's body looks like, who sees what it's gone through. I go out with men who have wives who've had children, who have stretch marks, who are not slim. I had stretch marks and my bosom sagged long before I had kids, so at least I wasn't worried about it. I know women who won't have children because they're afraid of the stretch marks. There must be some positive things about being fat!' She was laughing at herself again.

'Something inside me makes me go for married men because they're unavailable. Yes,' she stopped eating, and wiped her eyes again. 'I can't have expectations they can't meet so I can't be disappointed.'

Trudie had been seeing a married man for several years, once a week. 'That's what married men can manage. I still feel shy in bed even with married men, even with my friend. I'm still not happy walking around naked in front of him though we'll do anything in bed. For years we didn't even have a bed, we met in the back of a car. The first time we had a room available, I said, "This is the first time you're going to see me properly," and I was scared. He said, "Well there's nothing I haven't felt," so I guess he didn't mind.'

Somewhere underneath she minded the men being married. 'I don't necessarily want to get married again. It wasn't what you'd call a success. But I'm still looking for someone to be there when I want them at least more than once a week. So far no man likes me enough. I never like myself either, and I want never to diet again and to like myself.'

Recently her social life had improved, she had lots of women friends. 'Yes, some older women think I'm wonderful. *So why can't a man*? Some older married men like me, but I haven't cracked single men yet. I'm on diets every day, but none of it helps.'

We talked about why she felt men were so crucial to her life. She said. 'Sometimes I think of the women who like me. I think all the things I like in bed a woman could do and I could do with her, so why can't I go one step further and have a woman as a sexual partner? Something stops me. Maybe it's the hassle it would involve. I already have enough hassle. I wish I could deal with the anger I feel about the hassle and hatred. People assume the fat person doesn't want to be that way, they assume the fat person has got the problem. I'm angry about that.'

She leant across and asked in a low voice: 'Is it because I'm a woman? If you're a fat man, it doesn't matter. Fat men think they're wonderful. I know I need to think my body is beautiful or at least OK. I need to say that, but how? No one has ever said my body is OK. They say I look healthy. If this is healthy, then I'm too healthy! I feel oppressed but I don't know how to fight that oppression. Do you?'

I thought about it. As a feminist I'd found it deeply disturbing to be oppressed but I'd also found the fight elating. There had been anger, but there had been a warrior joy in challenging the victimization of women, of lesbians, of Jews, of those with more disabilities than others.

I had often felt miserable, put down, patronized, overlooked, discriminated against, but I had also felt righteous. I'd spent years pulling one good brave cause after another out of the shadows. I expect if I'd been a man I'd have been like Jimmy Porter. I expect if I'd been the right age I'd have been a suffragette. If I'd had the guts.

But here I was, coming on fifty, size 14, sitting opposite this sixteen-stone woman, wide as the Sargasso sea, playing the worthy feminist author, drawing her out, wondering secretly how she could bear to look like that, smirking slyly at my own slim legs, thankful the scales only registered nine and a half stone today.

How can I write this in cold blood, and with a clear conscience? How can I write this and feel unashamed or good about myself knowing that Trudie will suffer (again) as she reads it . . . because she will read it. How can I print out these words and know that Trudie, a sad, fat, betrayed woman trusted me enough as a sister, a feminist, to tell me all the things that have hurt her because she is fat? Trusted me to understand, to be on her side, to help her towards self-love when she is surrounded by other people's hatred of her flesh? Trusted me not to feel those things, trusted me to say the words that might start to improve her confidence.

She did trust me and I did say some of the words.

'Of course you haven't *only* got a pretty face,' I said.

'There's nothing wrong with being fat, there's something wrong with a society that thinks so,' I said.

'I can't imagine why you think your fat turns people off you,' I said.

I spent three hours listening and saying those words, knowing that for me they were just words. Unjust words. My brain was teeming with other lines. Lines that lie. Damaging lines. Destructive lies.

Why are you eating the toasted bun I offered you? I thought. Surely you can't afford to put jam on it?

Should I have given her the larger chair? She's spilling over, I wondered irritably.

How do you ever buy anything decent to wear? Well at some level it must be your own fault, I caught myself thinking.

Aren't you ashamed to walk about naked? Your flesh must wobble more than mine, I said to myself and poured another cup.

Was I ashamed as I thought those things? Not enough, Trudie. Not enough. My mind was suffused with dreadful notions I had not known were there. Or had not dared to know. Fear of fat? My own, yes. Hatred of fat? Yours? Other women's? No. After all my research, all the women I had talked to, I had not really known. I had not really looked deep enough inside.

I am telling the horrors of your story, Trudie, because they need telling. I am telling the horrors of my own story because they too need telling if we are ever to make any progress. I am not telling you this to hurt you, though it will. You will be less surprised than I am. You already know. Your life as a fat woman has forced you to know. Once it is aired at least I shall be one person who may just start to get to grips with her own oppressive feelings towards another human being. Another woman. I hope

I may begin to change some of these feelings as I hope that the Jew baiters, the homophobics, the misogynists, may change some of their feelings.

To understand someone else's oppression, you have to feel it as they feel it and be angry about it as they are. I expect I sounded right-on, but what was happening in my heart was right-off. I could not put myself in your shoes, Trudie. Your shoes, your fat, you yourself were far too threatening to me; and not just to me, for fat women are a threat to our patriarchal society because they don't conform to male specifications. Being fat carries a *visible* stigma, like being black or being disabled. A fat woman cannot 'pass'. But unlike racism, fat hatred is based on the frightening notion that this-could-happen-to-me. I know I shall not suffer racism, but at any time – if I do not take care – I could suffer discrimination for becoming fat.

Trudie was what I could become.

Trudie was what made me give in to the hospital's edict, that I lose six or ten pounds 'for the sake of my health' despite the contradictory evidence that six or ten pounds may *not* be bad for my health.

It is my fat hatred, not my desire for good health, that I weigh, when I stand on those scales; I sustain my hatred when I diminish my own size 14 by a few pleasing pounds, and I evidence it when I repeatedly mention that I am size 14 and not 20, and when I envy someone of size 10. It is my fat hatred I am trying for the first time to give voice to when I write you into this chapter.

Trudie, you have given me more trouble and more insomnia than any other interviewee. I have written this chapter and left you out. I have written you in, and left my own reactions out, I have told myself that confessing my unworthy thoughts will cause you to suffer and will do the readers no good. What I meant was that I would come out in a bad light.

What I now believe is desperately needed, by writers on food and fat, by women of every size, is just that bad light.

If any light, however bad, can be shed on this closeted, outrageous roomful of horrors, it must be better than keeping the door tightly closed.

Meeting you Trudie has opened that closed door, just a crack.

I drove Trudie home in my car. She had great difficulty fastening the seat belt. I masked my momentary irritation. When I got back, there was an inviting parcel outside my door. A 'friend' (a very thin friend) had bought me a 'suitable present for a food writer'. It was a lurid plastic typewriter mat with, across the centre, the word DIET in gargantuan glossy golden letters. The rest of the mat was ablaze with slogans:

Before you begin, think thin.

Don't let a fat frame of mine come between you and the great body you deserve. (They do not of course mean a *great* body.)

Only one letter separates chunky from hunky.

Fat fat go away, go and visit Doris Day.

In food, fat settles at the top, in women, fat settles at the bottom!

A moment on your lips forever on your hips.

A scale in the kitchen will ambush snack attacks.

A diet is the penalty for exceeding the feed limit.

Exercise your will-power, set your goal, then zap that fat.

If at first you don't recede, diet and diet again.

To live through a diet, you have to love yourself.

What this country needs is chocolate candy with a lettuce centre.

My machine was not big enough to cover all those instructions. The slogan that kept slipping into sight was the worst:

Overweight is often JUST DESSERTS!

It seemed a suitable place to start to examine what underlies the 'jokes' on the fat mat, and what underlies the way people treat fat women like Trudie. I now know that overweight is not a woman's just desserts. It is a matter of metabolism mixed with stress and misery. Fat women's just desserts would undoubtedly be better treatment by the rest of us; an acceptance of their fat, approval of who they are and what they look like. But most of us are locked into the fat mat's negative philosophy. I know there is no such thing as a 'fat frame of mind', there are only different-sized people, but society's aggressively anti-fat frame of mind keeps most of us from recognizing this. Me included.

It is nonsense to pretend that to live through a diet 'you have to love yourself'. All the experiences of the women I have talked to prove you have to *hate* yourself. It is this self-hatred, this loathing of fat flesh, which is what comes across in the fat-mat's threats of punishment and dreadful consequences: 'body you deserve', 'snack attacks', 'diet is the penalty'.

I knew all this but I now know that my attitude towards fat women under stress is not the same as my attitude towards thin women with food disorders. What our culture needs is not lettuce in the candy but a new vision of women's body image which will allow us to accept, as Trudie said, that candy isn't the problem, other people's attitudes are. All of us, women and men, need a new vision. We need to throw out the scales in the bathroom and tear down the scales before our eyes.

In a society where injustice and violence towards women are daily enacted, women have limited social power, and a lot of that power is exercised through food and our bodies. Food is a central part of our identity. Food has many warm and positive associations. If women can restructure this emotional relationship to food, and if women and men can alter their attitude towards food and fatness, that power can work for women and not against them. We will have taken a giant leap for womankind.

Notes

INTRODUCTION

1. *The Eating Sickness: Anorexia, Bulimia, and the Myth of Suicide by Slimming* by Jill Welbourne and Joan Purgold, Harvester Press, 1984.
   The Art of Starvation by Sheila MacLeod, Virago, 1981.
   Hunger Strike: The Anoretic's Struggle as a Metaphor for our Age by Susie Orbach, Faber and Faber, 1986.
   The Anorexic Experience by Marilyn Lawrence, Women's Press, 1984.
   The Hungry Self by Kim Chernin, Virago, 1986.
   Womansize: The Tyranny of Slenderness by Kim Chernin, Women's Press, 1983.
2. Orbach, *op. cit.*
3. *ibid.*
4. Ideas Program: 'Just Desserts', edited and researched by Sally Cline and Cheryl Lean. Canadian Broadcasting Corporation, October 1987.
5. *Reflecting Men* by Sally Cline and Dale Spender, André Deustch, 1987.

CHAPTER I

1. Denigratory slang for Gentiles.
2. Pancakes of potato flour mixed to a thin batter with eggs and water, cooked on one side, filled either with meat or sour cream cheese, folded into three-cornered pieces and fried in chicken fat.
3. Dumplings of matzoh meal and egg with chicken fat, parsley, nutmeg and ginger, cooled for one hour, then dropped into boiling soup for fifteen minutes.
4. *I Know Why the Caged Bird Sings* by Maya Angelou, Virago, 1984.

5. Concoction of either carrots and brown sugar, or stewed dried fruits and vegetables. Used metaphorically to describe a fuss.

6. *Thinking Like A Woman* by Leah Fritz, WIN Books, 1975.

7. Florence Greenberg, author of several books including the famous *Jewish Cookery*, Penguin, 1947.

8. *The World is a Wedding* by Bernard Kops, MacGibbon and Kee, 1963.

9. 'Split at the Root' by Adrienne Rich in *Nice Jewish Girls: A Lesbian Anthology* edited by Evelyn Torton Beck, Persephone Press, 1982.

10. New English Library, 1981.

11. Rich, *op. cit.*

12. Haggadah: book of prayers, psalms, readings, containing the Passover service.

13. Gefillte fish: grated, fried or boiled haddock, mixed with ground almonds and matzoh meal.

14. This joke appears in Larry Adler's book *Jokes and How to Tell Them*, Doubleday, 1963.

15. *The Belle of Amherst* by William Luce, adapted by Micheline Wandor, Thames TV, September 1987.

16. The date given in the play for the start of Dickinson's correspondence with Higginson was 1853, but Thomas H. Johnson's introduction to his edition of the complete poems suggests that it was April 15th 1862. The original letters bear this out.

17. Quoted by Thomas H. Johnson in his Introduction to *The Complete Poems of Emily Dickinson*, Faber, London, 1970.

18. Poem 67, *The Complete Poems, op. cit.*

19. Quoted in *Letters to Marina* by Dacia Maraini, Camden Press, 1987.

20. *ibid.*

21. Quoted in Introduction to *Complete Poems* by Thomas H. Johnson.

22. Quoted in the play.

23. *ibid.*

24. *ibid.*

25. *ibid.*

26. *Complete Poems, op. cit.*

27. Quoted in the play.

CHAPTER 2

1. *Eating Your Heart Out: Food, Shape and the Body Industry* by Ramona Koval, Penguin, 1986.

2. Halal meat is prepared according to Muslim custom.
3. *Movable Feasts: Changes in English Eating Habits* by Arnold Palmer, OUP, 1984.
4. *ibid.*
5. *Fat is a Feminist Issue* by Susie Orbach, Hamlyn, 1978.

CHAPTER 3

1. 'The Power Game' by Janet Watts in the *Observer Review*, April 1988.
2. US Bureau of Labor Statistics, 'Current Population Survey Data', March 1986, US Dept of Labor. This also shows that 78% of married women of working age with no children have full-time jobs and suffer similar inequalities.
3. Watts, *op. cit.*
4. Conversations with Sheila Kitzinger, plus an account of the treadmill in her article 'Voluptuous Vegetables' in *Cosmopolitan*, January 1986.
5. *Women and Love: A Cultural Revolution in Progress* by Shere Hite, Knopf, 1987.
6. Mentioned in Watts, *op. cit.*
7. 'Forty Minutes' produced by Ruth Jackson Toomey, reporter Sally Burton, BBC, May 1988. Sally Burton, who interviewed dozens of Hollywood wives, reported that the only 'unfettered laughter' was in the room occupied by the Ladies.
8. *My Own Story* by Emmeline Pankhurst, Greenwood Press, 1985.

CHAPTER 4

1. *The Fat Woman's Joke* by Fay Weldon, Hodder & Stoughton, 1967.
2. *Housewife* by Ann Oakley, Allen Lane, 1974. Similar material also gathered by Ann Oakley for *The Sociology of Housework*, Martin Robertson, 1974.
3. *ibid. To the Lighthouse* by Virginia Woolf, Grafton, 1977.

CHAPTER 5

1. 'An Apple a Day: some reflections on working class mothers' views on food and health' by Roisin Pill, in *The Sociology of Food and Eating*, ed. A. Murcott, Gower, 1983.

2. 'Cooking and the cooked: a note on the domestic preparation of meals' by Anne Murcott, in *The Sociology of Food and Eating*, *op. cit.*

3. *ibid.*

4. 'Eating Properly, The Family and State Benefit' by Nickie Charles and Marion Kerr in *Sociology*, vol 20, no. 3, 1986.

5. Murcott, *op. cit.*

6. Pill, *op. cit.*

7. 'Changing Food Habits in the UK' by Chris Wardle, 1977, quoted in *Turning the Tables: Recipes and Reflections from Women* compiled by Sue O'Sullivan, Sheba, 1987.

8. Hite *op. cit.*

9. *A Corridor of Mirrors* by Rosemary Manning, Women's Press, 1987.

10. 'Eating Virtue' by Paul Atkinson, in *The Sociology of Food and Eating*, ed. Murcott, *op. cit.*

11. 'The symbolic significance of health foods' by Paul Atkinson, in *Nutrition and Lifestyles*, ed. Michael Turner, Applied Sciences Pub. 1980.

12. Conversations with Anne Murcott; also material from her article 'You are what you eat. Anthropological factors influencing food choice' in *The Food Consumer*, ed. C. Ritson, L. Gofton, J. McKenzie, 1986.

13. 'The Fragmentation of Need' by Joan Dye Gussow in *Heresies 21: Food Is a Feminist Issue*, Heresies Collective Inc.

14. *Prevention of Health: Everybody's Business. A Reassessment of Public and Personal Health*, HMSO, 1976, 1981.

    'Inequalities of Health' The Black Report. D. Black, J. Morris, C. Smith, P. Townsend, Penguin, 1982.

15. Ministry of Agriculture, Fisheries and Food. Household Food Consumption and Expenditure, 1982, 1983, 1984.

    Annual report of the national food survey committee. London. HMSO 1984, 1985, 1986.

    'On the state of the public ill-health; premature mortality in the UK and Europe', J. Catford, S. Ford, British Medical Journal, 1984. pages 289, 1668–1670.

CHAPTER 6

1. *The Art of Eating* by M. K. V Fisher, Faber and Faber, 1949.

2. Anne Sexton, quoted in *Between Ourselves: Letters between Mothers and Daughters*, ed. Karen Payne, Picador/Pan, 1984.

3. 'The Furies' by Anne Sexton in 'The Fury of Rainstorms', from *The Death Notebooks*, Chatto and Windus, 1974.
4. Cline and Spender, *op. cit.*
5. Fran Ansley quoted in *Sociology Themes and Perspectives* by M. Haralambos, University Tutorial Press, 1980. Also quoted in *The Future of Marriage* by J. Bernard, Penguin, 1976.
6. *The Sociology of Food and Eating*, ed. Murcott, *op. cit.*
7. 'You are what you eat: food and family reconstruction' by Jacqueline Burgoyne and David Clarke, and 'The way to a man's heart: Food in the violent home' by Rhiann Ellis, both in Murcott, *op. cit.* Transcript Ideas Program, Just Desserts: Women and Food by Sally Cline and Cheryl Lean, CBC, October 1987.

CHAPTER 7

1. *Femininity* by Susan Brownmiller, Hamish Hamilton, 1984.
2. Cline and Spender, *op. cit.*
3. Brownmiller, *op. cit.*
4. *Ways of Seeing* by John Berger, Penguin, 1972.
5. In *Ms* magazine, February 1987.
6. *Bulimarexia: The Binge-Purge Cycle* by Marlene Boskind-White and W. C. White, Norton, 1983.
7. *Ms* magazine, February 1987.
8. *Hunger Strike*, Orbach, *op. cit.*
9. 'Anorexia and Bulimia: The Political and the Personal' by Troy Cooper, in *Fed up and Hungry: Women, Oppression and Food* ed. Marilyn Lawrence, Women's Press, 1987.
10. 'Women's Anger and Compulsive Eating' by Bunny Epstein, in *Fed Up and Hungry*, ed. Lawrence, *op. cit.*
11. Cline and Spender, *op. cit.*

CHAPTER 8

1. *The Dieter's Dilemma: Eating Less and Weighing More* by William Bennett and Joel Gurin, Basic Books, 1982.
2. *ibid.*
3. 'Obesity and Food Choices in Public Places' by Milton Coll, Andrew Meyer, Albert Stunkard, in *Archives of General Psychiatry* 36, 1979.

4. 'Childhood Obesity: Prelude to Adult Obesity' by A. M. Bryans, in the *Canadian Journal of Public Health*, November 1967; quoted in *Shadow on a Tightrope*, ed. L. Schoenfielder and B. Wieser, Aunt Lute Book Co, 1983.

5. 'Theoretical, Practical and Social Issues in Behavioural Treatments of Obesity' by Wooley, Wooley and Dryenforth in the *Journal of Applied Behaviour Analysis* 12, 1979; *Energy Balance and Obesity in Man* by J. S. Garrow, American Elsevier, 1974.

6. 'Obesity and Health', US Dept of Health, Education and Welfare, 1966; quoted in *Shadow on a Tightrope*, *op. cit.*

7. 'Appetite suppressants as an aid to obesity control' by W. L. Asher, in *Obesity: Causes, Consequences and Treatment*, ed. Louis Lasagna, Medcom, 1974; quoted in *Shadow on a Tightrope*, *op. cit.*

8. 'Weight Reduction: An Enigma' by Joseph A. Glennon in *Archives of Internal Medicine* vol. 118, July 1966; quoted in *Shadow on a Tightrope*, *op. cit.*

9. 'Obesity and Women: 1. A Close Look at the Facts' by Wooley and Wooley, *Women's Studies Int. Quarterly*, vol. 2, 1979.

10. *The Fat Woman Measures Up* by Christine Donald, Ragweed Press, 1986.

11. Bennett and Gurin, *op. cit.*

12. *ibid.* (using caloric estimates from *Nutrition, Weight Control and Exercise* by Frank Katch and William McArdle, Houghton Mifflin, 1977.

CHAPTER 9

1. Bennett and Gurin, *op. cit.*

2. 'A study of social stereotype of body image in children' by J. R. Staffieri, *Personality soc. Psychol. 7.* in *Obesity and Women II: A Neglected Feminist Topic* by Orland W. Wooley, Susan C. Wooley, Sue R. Dyrenforth, *Women's Studies International Quarterly*, ed. Dale Spender, vol 2, no. 1, 1979.

3. 'Body build and behavioural expectations in young females' by J. R. Staffieri in *Devel. Psychol.* 6, 1972.

4. 'The Goddess is Fat' by Kelly, in *Shadow on a Tightrope*, *op. cit.*

5. The Wannabees, BBC TV, December 1987.

6. 'Body build identification, preference, and aversion in children' by R. M. Lerner and E. Gellert, *Devel. Psychol.* 5, 1969 in Wooley, Wooley, Dyrenforth, *op. cit.*

7. 'This Thin Woman' in *The Fat Woman Measures Up* by Christine Donald, Ragweed Press, 1986.

8. *Eating Your Heart Out* by Ramona Koval, Penguin, 1986. Also 'The Fat Illusion' by Vivian F. Mayer in *Shadow on a Tightrope*, *op. cit.*

9. 'Obese Adolescent Girls: an unrecognized "minority" group?' by L. F. Monello and J. Mayer, in *Am. J. Clin. Nutr.* 13, 1963. in Wooley *op. cit.*

10. Wooley, *op. cit.*

11. 'Cultural uniformity in reaction to physical disabilities' by S. A. Richardson, N. Goodman, A. H. Hastorf, S. M. Dornbusch, *A Sociological Review* 26, 1961, in Wooley, *op. cit.* 'Variant reactions to physical disabilities' by N. Goodman, S. M. Dornbusch, S. A. Richardson, A. H. Hastorf, 1963, *Am, Sociol. Rev.* 28, in Wooley *op. cit.*

12. The researchers speculated that Jewish cultural values and practices linked with eating view well-fed stocky children as both healthy and loved, but that exposure to mainstream USA culture had biased even this group.

13. 'Overweight as social deviance and disability' by G. Maddox, K. Beck, V. Liederman, *Health Soc. Behaviour* 9, 1968, in Wooley, *op. cit.*

14. 'A preferred method for obtaining rankings: reactions to physical handicaps' by V. Mathews and C. Westie, *Am. Sociol. Review* 31, 1966, in Wooley *op. cit.*

Bibliography

Adams, Carol & Laurikietis, Rae *The Gender Trap*, Book 3: Messages and Images, Virago, London, 1976.

Aldebaran 'Fat Liberation' in *Issues in Radical Therapy*, Summer 1973.

Aldebaran, (Mayer Vivian) 'Compulsive Eating Myth' in *Off Our Backs*, New York, July 1979.

Aldebaran, 'Liberal on Fat' in *Off Our Backs*, March 1980.

Alta *Momma*, Times Change Press, New York, 1974.

Alta *The Shameless Hussy*, The Crossing Press, New York, 1980.

Angelou, Maya *I KNow Why the Caged Bird Sings*, Virago, London, 1984.

Atkinson, P 'The Symbolic Significance of Healthfoods' in Turner, M. (ed) *Nutrition and Lifestyles*, Applied Science Publishers, London, 1980.

Atwood, Margaret *The Edible Woman*, Virago, London, 1980.

Atwood, Margaret *Murder in the Dark*, Jonathan Cape, London, 1984.

Bennett, William, and Gurin, Joel *the Dieter's Dilemma*, Basic Books, New York, 1982.

Berger, John *Ways of Seeing*, Penguin, Harmondsworth, 1972.

Binney, Val. *et al. Leaving Violent Men*, Women's Aid Federation, London, 1981.

Black, D., Morris, J., Smith, C., Townsend, P. *Inequalities in Health* (The Black Report), Penguin, Harmondsworth, 1982.

Borkowski, M. *et al. Community Response to Marital Violence*, Final Report to DHSS, Tavistock, London, 1983.

Boskind-White, Marlene *Bulimarexia: the binge-purge cycle*, Norton, New York, 1983.

Burgoyne, J. and Clark, D. 'Reconstituted families in the family' in The Family Research Committee (eds) *Families in Britain*, Routledge & Kegan Paul, London, 1982.

Brownmiller, Susan *Femininity*, Hamish Hamilton, London 1984.

Bruch, H. *Eating Disorders: Obesity, Anorexia Nervosa, and The Person Within*, Routledge & Kegan Paul, London, 1974.

Bruch, H. *The Golden Cage: The Enigma of Anorexia Nervosa*, Open Books, London, 1978.

Cannon, Geoffrey *The Politics of Food*, Century, London, 1987.

Catford, J. and Ford, S. 'On the state of the public ill-health, premature mortality in the UK and Europe,' *British Medical Journal*, 1984.

Charles, Nickie and Kerr, Marion. 'Eating Properly, The Family and State Benefit' in *Sociology*, London, August 1986.

Chernin, Kim *Womansize: The Tyranny of Slenderness* The Women's Press, London, 1983.

Chernin, Kim *The Hungry Self*, Virago, London, 1986.

Chicago, Judy *The Dinner Party: A Symbol of our Heritage*, Anchor Press/ Doubleday, New York, 1979.

Clarke, Caro 'Weighing in' in *Gossip* No. 6, Onlywomen Press, London.

Cline, Sally and Lean, Cheryl. 'Just Desserts: Women and Food Transcripts.' from Ideas Program October 1987, Canadian Broadcasting Corporation, Montreal, 1987.

Cline, Sally and Spender, Dale *Reflecting Men at twice their natural size*, André Deutsch, London, 1987; Seaver Books, New York, 1987; Fontana, London, 1988.

Coward, Rosalind *Female Desire: Women's Sexuality Today*, Paladin, London, 1984.

Daly, Mary *Gyn/Ecology: The Metaethics of Radical Feminism* Beacon Press, Boston, 1978; The Women's Press, London, 1979.

Davies, Kath, Dickey, Julienne, Stratford, Teresa (eds) *Out of Focus, Writings on Women and the Media* The Women's Press, London 1987.

David, Elizabeth *Summer Cooking*, Penguin, Harmondsworth, 1965.

Delamont, Sara *The Sociology of Women*, Allen and Unwin, London, 1980.

DHSS *Prevention of Health: Everybody's Business. A Reassessment of Public and Personal Health*, HMSO London, 1976, 1981.

DHSS *Eating for Health*. HMSO, London, 1978.

Dickinson, Emily *The Complete Poems*, Faber and Faber, London, 1970.

Luce, William *The Belle of Amherst*, adapted by Micheline Wandor, based on the life of Emily Dickinson, Thames TV, London.

Dobash, R. And Dobash R. *Violence Against Wives*, Open Books, Shepton Mallet, 1980.

Donald, Christine *The Fat Woman Measures Up*, Ragweed Press, Charlottetown, PEI Canada, 1986.

Douglas, M. And Nicod, M. 'Taking the biscuit: the structure of British meals.' in *New Society* vol 30, no. 637, 1974.

Douglas, M. 'Deciphering a Meal' in *Implicit Meanings*, Routledge & Kegan Paul, London, 1975.

Eichenbaum, L. and Orbach, S. *Understanding Women*, Penguin, Harmondsworth, 1985.

Forbes, Alec *The Bristol Diet*, Century, London, 1984.

Gelles, R. *The Violent Home*, Sage, New York, 1974.

George, Susan and Paige, Nigel *Food For Beginners*, Writers and Readers Publishing Co-operative Society, London, 1982.

Good Housekeeping Institute *After Work Cook Book*, Ebury Press, London, 1980.

Goody, J. *Cooking, Cuisine and Class*, Cambridge University Press, Cambridge, 1982.

Gordon, Alexie and Bliss, Trudy *Come Into the Kitchen*, Victor Gollancz, London, 1947.

Greenberg, Florence *Jewish Cookery*, Penguin, Harmondsworth, 1967.

Grimstad, Kirsten and Rennie, Susan (eds) *The New Woman's Survival Sourcebook*, Alfred Knopf, New York. 1975.

Grosswirth, Marvin *Fat Pride – a Survival Handbook*, Jarrow Press, New York, 1971.

Guerard, Michel *Cuisine Minceur*, Macmillan, London, 1977.

Haralambos, Michael *Sociology: Themes and Perspectives*, University Tutorial Press, Slough, 1980.

Hayman, Amanda 'Fat Oppression' in *Gossip* 3, Onlywomen Press, London.

Heresies 21, 'Food is a feminist issue', Heresies Collective Inc., New York. 1987.

Herridge, Bridgid *The Food Value Counter*, The Essential Dieter's Guide, New English Library, London, 1981.

Hite, Shere *Women and Love: A Cultural Revolution in Progress*, Alfred Knopf, New York, 1987.

Innes, Jocasta *The Pauper's Cookbook*, Penguin, Harmondsworth, 1971.

Kenton, Leslie *The Biogenic Diet*, Arrow, London, 1986

Kitzinger, Sheila *The Experience of Breastfeeding*, Penguin, Harmondsworth, 1979.

Kitzinger, Sheila 'Voluptuous Vegetables' in *Cosmopolitan*, January 1986.

Koval, Ramona *Eating Your Heart Out: Food, Shape and the Body Industry*, Penguin, Australia, 1986.

Lawrence, M. 'Anorexia Nervosa: The Control Paradox' in *Women's Studies International Quarterly*, (ed) Spender, Dale, vol. 2. 1979.

Lawrence, M. 'Education and Identity. The Social Origins of Anorexia' in *Women's Studies International Quarterly*, (ed) Spender, Dale, vol. 7, no. 4, 1984.

Lawrence, M. *The Anorexic Experience*, The Women's Press Handbook Series, London, 1984.

Lawrence, M. (ed) *Fed Up and Hungry: Women, oppression and food*, The Women's Press, London, 1987.

Levi-Strauss, C. *The Raw and the Cooked*, Jonathan Cape, London, 1970.

Levi-Strauss, C. *The Origin of Table Manners*, Jonathan Cape, London, 1978.

Llewelyn Davies, M. (ed) *Maternity: Letters from working women*, Virago, London, 1978.

Luce, William *The Belle of Amherst*, adapted by Micheline Wandor, Thames TV, London, September, 1987.

MacLeod, Sheila *The Snow-White Soliloquies*, Secker and Warburg, London, 1970.

MacLeod, Sheila *The Art of Starvation*, Virago, London, 1981.

Maisner, Paulette with Turner, Rosemary *The Food Trap*, Unwin, London, 1986.

Manning, Rosemary *A Corridor of Mirrors*, The Women's Press, London, 1987.

Mansfield, Katherine *In a German Pension*, Penguin, Harmondsworth, 1911.

Mansfield, Katherine *Letters and Journals*, Penguin, Harmondsworth, 1977.

Maraini, Dacia *Letters to Marina*, Camden Press, London, 1987.

Matrix *Making Space, Women and the Man Made Environment*, Pluto Press, London, 1984.

Mayes, Kathleen *The Salt Watcher's Guide*, Thorson Pub. Group, New York, 1986.

Melville, Joy *The ABC of Eating*, Sheldon Press, London, 1983.

Millar, Ruth 'Shadow on a Tightrope: Writings by women on fat oppression, a review' in *Gossip*, 4 Onlywomen Press, London.

Millman, Marcia *Such a Pretty Face*, W. W. Norton, New York, 1980.

Millum, Trevor *Images of Woman: Advertising in women's magazines*, Chatto and Windus, London, 1975.

Ministry of Agriculture, Fisheries and Food, 'Household Food Consumption and Expenditure 1982, 1983, 1984', Annual report of the national food survey committee, HMSO, London, 1984, 1985, 1986.

Mitchell, Lynette. 'Skinny Lizzie strikes back: an apologia for thin women's liberation,' in *Gossip* 3, Onlywomen Press, London.

Montagne, Prosper *Larousse Gastronomique*, (eds) Froud, Mina and Turgeon, Charlotte. Hamlyn, London, 1901.

Murcott, Anne 'On the social significance of the cooked dinner in South Wales' in *Social Science Information*, vol. 21, nos. 4, 5.

Murcott, Anne 'It's a pleasure to cook for him! Food, mealtimes and gender in some South Wales Households' in Garmarnikov, E. *et al.* (eds) *The Public and the Private*, Collected Papers 1982, Conference British Soc. Assoc., 1982.

Murcott, Anne 'Cookbook's images of technique and technology in the British Kitchen' in *Women's Studies International Forum*, vol. 6, no. 2, 1983.

Murcott, Anne (ed) *The Sociology of Food and Eating*, Gower, Aldershot, 1983.

Murcott, Anne 'You are what you eat: Anthropological factors influencing food choice', *The Food Consumer* (eds) Ritson, C., Gofton, L., McKenzie, J., London, 1986.

Munter, Carol 'Fat and the fantasy of perfection' in (ed) Vance, Carole S. *Pleasure and Danger: Exploring Female Sexuality*, Routledge & Kegan Paul, Boston, 1984.

Oakley, Anne *The Sociology of Housework*, Martin Robertson, London, 1974.

Oakley, Anne *Housewife*, Allen Lane, London, 1974.

Orbach, Susie *Fat is a Feminist Issue*, Hamlyn, London, 1978.

Orbach, Susie *Hunger Strike*, Faber and Faber, London 1986.

O'Sullivan, Sue *Turning the Tables: Recipes and Reflections from Women*, Sheba, London, 1987.

Pahl, J. *A Refuge for Battered Women*, DHSS, London, 1978.

Palmer, R. L. *Anorexia Nervosa: a guide for sufferers and their families*, Penguin, Harmondsworth, 1980.

Palmer, Arnold *Movable Feasts*, OUP, Oxford, 1984.

Payne, Karen (ed) *Between Ourselves*, Picador, London, 1984.

Piercy, Marge *Stone, Paper, Knife*, Pandora Press, London, 1983.

Pizzey, E. *Scream Quietly or the Neighbours will Hear*, Penguin, Harmondsworth, 1974.

Reichl, Ruth *MMMMM: A Feastiary*, Holt, Rinehart & Winston, New York, 1972.

Root, Waverly *Food*, Simon and Schuster, New York, 1980.

Root, Jane *Pictures of Women: Sexuality*, Pandora, London, 1984.

Roth, Geneen *Feeding the Hungry Heart*, Grafton Books, London, 1986.

Schoenfielder, Lisa and Wieser, Barbara (eds) *Shadow on a Tightrope: Writings by women on fat oppression*, Aunt Lute Book Co., Iowa, 1983.

Sexton, Anne *The Death Notebooks*, Chatto and Windus. London, 1974.

Slimmer Magazine Editors *Let's Start to Slim*, Ward Lock, London, 1977.

Spare Rib, No. 190. London, May 1988.

Spare Tyre Theatre Company *The Spare Tyre Songbook*, Virago, London, 1987.

Spender, Dale (ed) *Women's Studies International Quarterly*, vol. 2. no. 1, Pergamon Press, Oxford, 1979.

Spender, Dale *Man Made Language*, Routledge & Kegan Paul, London, 1980.

Spender, Dale *Women of Ideas*, Ark, London, 1982.

Spender, Dale *Invisible Women*, Writers and Readers Co-op, London, 1982.

Spender, Dale *For the Record*, The Women's Press, London, 1985.

Stewart Katie *The Pooh Cook Cook*, Methuen, London, 1971.

United States Dept. of Labor, 'Current Population Survey Data', US Bureau of Labor Statistics, March 1986.

Van Gelder, Lindsy, 'Patterns of Addiction' in *MS* magazine, February 1987.

Watts, Janet 'The Power Game' in *The Observer*, Review, April 24, 1988.

Welbourne, Jill and Purgold, Joan *The Eating Sickness: Anorexia, bulimia and the myth of suicide by slimming*, The Harvester Press, Brighton, 1984.

Weldon, Fay *The Fat Woman's Joke*, Hodder & Stoughton, London, 1982

Weldon, Fay *The Heart of the Country*, Arrow, London, 1987.

Women's Monitoring Network 'Sexism in the Media: Report No. 6: Women and Food.' London, 1984.

Wood, Victoria *Up to You, Porky, the Victoria Wood Sketchbook*, Methuen, London, 1985.

Woolf, Virginia *To the Lighthouse*, Grafton Books, London, 1977.

Wooley, Orland, Wooley, Susan, Dyrenforth, Sue 'Obesity and Women ii A neglected feminist topic' in Spender, Dale, (ed) *Women's Studies International Quarterly*, vol. 2, no. 1, Pergamon, Oxford, 1979.

Index

access
  to food, power 1, 3
Adler, Carol 23–4
Adler, Larry 13, 23, 32–3, 65–6,
    80–81, 201
Adler, Marmoset 13–14, 19–20,
    23–4, 26, 56, 58, 87, 114, 132,
    135–7, 163, 201
Adler, Peter 23–4
Adler, Wendy 23–4
adolescence 106, 221–2, 225–6, 230–2
advertising see propaganda
Albee, Edward 44
alienation 99, 195
  see also fragmentation
amphetamines 25–26, 200–1
Andres, Dr Rubin 218
Angelou, Maya 15
anger
  and bulimia 192
  and fat oppression 227, 231, 238
  repression and food 1, 7, 25–6, 146,
    184, 188, 192–5, 196–7, 231, 238
  and powerlessness 26
  usefulness of 196–7
anorexia 3–5, 161–2, 168, 185–7, 191,
    194, 196, 210
Anselmino, Mary 118–9
Ansley, Fran 146
'anxiety hours' 73, 75, 93–4, 100
anxiety 157, 166, 182, 191
appetite 31, 153
approval (male) 5, 16–17, 21, 24,
    35–8, 60–1, 64–6, 79, 88, 93,
    101–3, 113–14, 129, 167, 200–1
  see also eater approbation

army (and food) 52, 134
Atkinson, P. 117–8
Axelrod, Rebecca 181–2

bacon 11–12, 13–15, 30, 106
beauty see femininity
Bennett, W. and Gurin, J. 205, 207,
    209, 217
Berger, John 165
bingeing, irrational 7, 25
  see also bulimia; compulsive eating
black women (and food) 6, 47–8, 78
  see also cross cultural food practices;
    Muslim food behaviour
bodies as objects 5
body image and food intake 2, 5, 17,
    60–1, 78–9, 151, 164–202
  see also fat oppression; femininity;
    self-loathing; sexuality
borscht 30–33, 123
breakfast
  cooked 14–15, 105
  Sunday 14–15, 72
breastfeeding 3–4, 114–15, 127,
    174–5
Brodie, I. 13
Brownmiller, Susan 164
bulimia 3–4, 7, 170–202
  see also bingeing; compulsive eating

cake
  in crisis 34–5, 52
  for men 65–6, 86

Caldwell, Sarah 231
caloric intake, measuring 213–14
Campbell, Bebe Moore 83
capitalist system 146
   and consumerism 3, 5, 165
case studies 58–61, 62–4, 65, 68,
   69–70, 73–5, 76–7, 78–9, 80, 82,
   89–90, 92–3, 100–1, 106–8, 112,
   139–44, 145, 150–1, 152,
   154–63, 169–82, 182–7,187–91,
   193–5, 217–41
catering as women's responsibility 3,
   67–8, 70, 71–85, 93–100, 105,
   112, 116, 120–1
celibacy and food 79, 123
Chapman, Clare 115–16
Charles N. and Kerr, M. 118, 130
childbirth 77
childrearing 21, 135–8, 139–47
children and food tyranny 132–63
chocolate, general 60, 120–3, 126,
   170, 182, 184
   spread/sauce 122–4
   and romance 122–4
Christmas 51–2
class differences and food habits 50–1,
   105, 120, 128, 140, 167
clothes and fat women 225–8
cold/hot food 73, 104–5, 109–10
comfort 14, 21, 35, 95
compulsive eating 25–6, 96–7, 192–5,
   198
   see also bingeing; bulimia
conflicts/contradictions, women's 2,
   72–8, 87
control
   male 5, 7, 60–61, 110–14, 120, 135,
   139–41, 143–4, 147–51, 155–63,
   167
   use of food as a weapon 1, 54–5, 98,
   132–63
convenience foods 116–22, 128–9,
   142–3
'cooked, a' 105–108
cooking 11, 14, 16, 19, 23, 33, 35, 39,
   42, 49, 56–8, 68–9, 71–2, 77, 81,
   89, 92, 94, 99–100, 104–131,
   133–4, 138–40, 143–5, 147–8,
   150, 153, 156, 158, 171–2

Cooper, Troy ix, 191–2
counselling groups *see* groups
cultural restraint 8
customs *see* rituals and customs

David, Elizabeth 68
death 34–5, 104, 145
denial (and food) l, 4, 87, 190, 196–7
depression 97–8, 105, 145, 161–2, 214
desertion (and food) 60–1
DHSS statistics 120
Dickinson, Emily 35–8
diet industry 9, 204
dieting 96
   dangers of 217–18, 230
   does not work 202, 204–15, 225
dinner parties 3, 39–41, 43, 46,
   101–3, 156
disablement 225, 231–3
discretionary cooking by men 15, 67,
   71–5, 79, 85
discrimination 4, 224
'doing it right' 45, 87, 90, 93
domestic inequality 76–9, 83–5
   see also patriarchy
Donald, Christine: *The Fat Woman
   Measures Up* 212–13, 228, 230

earnings, comparative women/men 75
eater approbation 55–60, 64–6, 93
   see also approval
eating 1–3, 7–10, 12, 112, 114, 116,
   121–3, 126, 129, 132–4, 136–8,
   144–5, 147–9, 161, 168, 170–1,
   177, 188, 198, 220–1
   see also compulsive eating
eating as a shared activity 56–60, 128
eating disorders 3–4, 55, 161–2,
   168–202
   see also anorexia; bingeing; bulimia
emotional investment in food 1–2, 8,
   21–4, 35, 48–50, 67, 86, 113,
   121–2, 127, 129, 133, 182, 199
employment, women's 16–17, 107,
   139
   see also workforce, women
energy output, measuring 213–14

Epstein, Bunny 195
equality/egalitarianism 66–7, 73, 76–7, 197
exercise 210
expectations, women's 1, 26, 45, 196–7

family meals 3, 5, 13–14, 16, 21, 67, 106–9, 111, 114–16, 121, 128–31, 138, 140
fat activist movement 209
fatness 160, 166–9, 172–4, 179, 184, 198, 202, 217
    fat oppression 4, 25–6, 49, 60–1, 66, 151, 160, 166–9, 198–9, 204, 208, 212, 216–42
    fear of 25–6, 66, 165, 190, 198, 229
    and social control 8–9, 26
    and disease 217–18, 229–30
    feminists and 4–5, 168, 238–42
    hatred of 169–91, 195, 198–9, 202–5, 208, 211, 214, 216–42
    myths about 203–15
    obesity, severe 230
    and pride 8–9
    as stigma 4, 61, 209, 233, 240
    see also body image; dieting; femininity
femininity, male stereotypes of 4, 164–6, 169, 185–6, 195–6, 204, 229, 240
feminism, feminist 3–7, 25, 54, 83, 138
    and fatness 4–5, 168, 238–42
festivals 51
Fisher, M. K. 138
Fleet Street 17, 31, 200
food, general 4, 17–18, 21–3, 30, 32–5, 46–9, 52, 61, 66, 74–5, 89–91, 104–31, 134–53, 155–6, 168, 171, 174–5, 186
food coercion 8, 9, 110, 112, 132–42, 144, 156–62
food, cross cultural 12, 46–50, 78, 81
    see also black women and food; Muslim food behaviour
food disorders see eating disorders
food fear 2, 79, 133, 169–200

food forbidden 1
food and gender 21, 105, 112, 115, 131, 134, 147, 150
food industry 3, 116–18, 120
food love/pleasure 1–2, 14, 106–7, 113
food management 4, 67, 72–85, 111–13, 119, 121–7, 129–31, 141–2, 145, 147, 152
food meanings/significance 2, 39–66, 128, 199–200
food politics 3, 8, 138
food preparation 3–4, 16, 77, 106–8, 112–13, 116–19, 162
food and social order 39–46, 50–1, 131, 145
food taboos 47–8
forbidden pleasures 14
fragmentation 99
Fritz, Leah 18–19
frozen packaged meals 121–2
    see also convenience foods; processed/tinned foods

Gaffin, Neville 13, 31–2
Greenberg, Florence 20
groups, self help 53, 180, 195
    see also Women's Therapy Centre
guilt 114, 116–17, 176, 178–9, 222
Gussow, Joan Dye 118–19

health
    and food, women's perceptions 104–5, 109–12, 118
    and weight 217, 229–30
heart disease 112, 216, 218
Herridge, Brigid 25
heterosexuality
    sex/relations 5, 11, 62–3, 121–4
    compulsory 5, 12, 63
Higginson, Thomas Wentworth 35–7
Hite, Shere 79
hospitals, treatment 187, 216–20
    see also medical profession
hospitality, Jewish 17–20
hot/cold food 104–5, 110, 150
    see also 'proper' meals
hyperemesis 201

inequalities 76–7, 107–8
isolation of Western women
78–99–100

jam 1, 53–66, 201
Jewish culture/practices and food
11–35, 249n
job discrimination 75–6, 198, 224
jokes, food 32–3
journalism 13, 16, 23, 31–2
broadcast 6–7
'Just Desserts' (CBC radio) 6–7

kitchens 2, 12, 14–20, 30, 45, 67, 76,
98, 111, 114, 119–20, 136–7,
142–3, 145–7, 234
Kitzinger, Sheila 77–8, 114–15
Kops, Bernard 22
Koval, Ramona 46

labels 166, 197, 200
Ladies, the (Life After Divorce Is
Eventually Sane) 83–4
Laidlaw, Toni 25, 55, 166, 223–4
laxative addiction 176–85, 196–7
see also bulimia; compulsive eating
Lean, Cheryl 6–9, 51, 71, 218
lesbianism 6, 11, 62–3
lesbian relationships and food
13–15, 62–4, 121–2, 124–7,
130–1, 138
lesbian feminist 64
lesbians and male approval 65–6
Lewis, Patti 83–4
literary food images 4, 15, 96–8,
101–3, 145
low income, welfare, social security
84, 91, 108–9, 149, 233
see also money

magazines, popular 3, 219
women's 60, 87, 189
Magezis, Joy 70–1
Manning, Rosemary 114
marriage 11–13, 16–17, 61, 67–71,
73–4, 76–7, 82–5, 93–6. 104–5,
107–13, 120, 128–30, 141,
143–4, 146–7, 154–6, 174,
234–5, 237
meal provision as women's obligation
67–85, 115, 147–8
see also catering; planning; shopping
meat for men, not for women 88,
94–5, 106–9, 148–50
media
and convenience foods 119–21
and body image 4–5, 185, 195
medical profession 217–18
see also hospitals, treatment
mental health 141
see also depression
Metson, Graham 71
misogyny 197–8
Monello, L. F. and Mayer J. 230
money 21, 66, 104, 106, 120, 130,
148, 150
see also low income, welfare, social
security
monotony 99–100
mothers 12, 18–22, 26–9, 52, 69–71,
79, 92, 107, 111–16, 122, 124,
132–3, 135, 137–43, 145–9, 153,
155–62, 169–172, 174, 193–4,
220, 222–4
mothering 13–16, 23–4, 26, 106–7,
111, 113–18, 120, 128–31, 220
motherhood 26
Mulford, Wendy 15, 56
Murcott, Anne 105–6, 108–9, 118,
148
Muslims, food behaviour 47–8
see also black women; food, cross
cultural

'natural' foods 116–18
Noble, Katina 115
nourishment/nourishing 23, 49, 78–9,
106, 120
nurturance/nurturing 67, 87, 111, 122

Oakley, Ann 99–100
obesity see fatness

obsessions, food/fat 2, 169, 186, 188, 232–3, 241
oppression, women 6, 144, 146, 165, 196, 240
Orbach, Susie 4, 53–6, 78–9, 186, 194

Palmer, Arnold 50, 52
Pankhurst, Emmeline 85
parenting 23, 91, 94
    see also mothering; single parents
patriarchy and food patterns 4–5, 17, 26–9, 33, 67–85, 94–6, 106–9, 112–13, 137–8, 146–63, 214
Pill, Roisin 105, 109
planning meals as women's obligtion 68, 70, 72–85, 88–9, 111
political demands 2
    see also power
power
    access to 1, 17, 26–7, 134, 137, 139, 144–5, 147, 166, 196
    lack of 1, 3, 5, 17, 54–5, 132–63
    relationship 3, 45, 112, 114, 132, 134–5, 137, 139–40, 145–7, 169
    see also political demands
processed/tinned foods 72, 104, 106, 116–21
    see also convenience foods; frozen meals
propaganda and body image 4–5, 182, 185, 195
'proper' meals 57, 65, 69, 104–9, 112, 116, 118, 129–31, 150, 171
psychotherapy 53
    see also groups, self-help; Women's Therapy Centre
radio programmes 6–7, 207

reflecting male values 5
    see also Reflecting Men
Reflecting Men 7, 146, 195–6
Reibstein, Janet Dr 76
rejection 2, 113–16, 127
restaurants 61–2, 71, 81, 173, 177
Rich, Adrienne 23, 26–7

rituals and customs 20, 39–52, 66, 129–31
    see also Jewish culture; taboos
romance and food 13, 19, 105, 121–7
    see also sexuality and food

scales 1, 216–18, 240, 242
school dinners 132–4
security and food 4, 21–2, 49–50, 53, 57, 66, 86, 93, 98, 127
self-esteem
    and cooking 100–3
    and catering 93
self-loathing and body image 2, 166–202, 203–15, 231–3, 242
self-reporting of eating habits 206–8, 214
setpoint mechanism 209–12
Sexton, Anne 144–5
sexuality
    and body image 166–8, 184–5, 188, 203–4, 224–5, 235–8
    and food 11, 61–4, 121–8
    see also lesbianism; heterosexuality, compulsory; heterosexual sex
shame 89, 178–9
Sheppard, Ba 13–15, 23–5, 34, 43–5, 65, 114, 117, 131
Sheppard, Elsie 51–2
shopping/stocking up 3, 86–90, 93–4, 107
single parents 19–20, 91, 109–10, 123, 130, 142–4
    see also parenting
slimming 4, 17, 166, 208
    compulsory 167, 290, 224, 229
    see also thinness
Smith, Bec 13–14, 23–4, 26, 46, 56
Smith, Cas 13–14, 23–4, 26, 46, 56, 114
Smith, Vic 13–14, 23–4, 26, 56, 58, 114, 117
social role *see* women's social role
soup 44, 81
    rules 29–30
'space-age victuals' 128–9
Spare Tyre 115–16
Spender, Dale 25, 68–9, 104, 168–9

Staffieri, J. R. 221
stocking up 86–90, 93–4
Stunkard, Albert 207–8
Sunday Dinner 129–31
supermarkets 24–5, 57, 86, 90–4
surgery, cosmetic 174–217

table manners 42–5, 132, 135–6, 139,
    150–4, 159–61
taboos 12–15, 47–8, 152
'Tampopo' 81–2
thinness 2, 165–6, 168, 178, 185–6.
    203, 206, 208–9, 214, 220, 226,
    228
    see also slimness; dieting
tinned/processed foods 104, 106,
    116–21
tyranny and food provision 132–63

USA diet statistics 206
USA work patterns 76

vegetables, fresh 104–8, 116
vegetarian 108–10, 114–17, 130–1
visibility, women's 165–6

vomiting 183–92, 197–8, 201
    see also bulimia
vulnerability 2

war (and food) 52–3
Wardle, Chris 111
weight, standard/normative 4, 181,
    204–15, 218, 229
Weldon, Fay 97–8, 196, 214–15, 219
    The Fat Woman's Joke 95–7
widowhood 55–6, 58–60, 69, 80,
    82–3
women's liberation movement 67, 138,
    165
women's social role/duties 1, 16, 29,
    67, 69, 74–6, 78–9, 85, 99–100,
    104, 121–2, 128–31, 134, 141–7,
    200
women's therapy centre 53, 195
    see also groups, self-help
Wooley, Susan and Orland 206–8,
    232
Woolf, Virginia: To the Lighthouse
    101–3
workforce, women 75–6
    see also employment, women's
working classes 105, 120